W9-DCJ-190

From Combines To Computers

SUNY Series, The New Inequalities

A. Gary Dworkin, Editor

From Combines To Computers

Rural Services and Development in the Age of Information Technology

Amy K. Glasmeier
and Marie Howland

State University of New York Press

Published by
State University of New York Press, Albany

Printed in the United States of America

For information, address State University of New York Press,
State University Plaza, Albany, N.Y. 12246

Production by M.R. Mulholland
Marketing by Fran Keneston

Library of Congress Cataloging-in-Publication Data
Glasmeier, Amy.
From combines to computers : rural services and development in the age of information technology / Amy K. Glasmeier and Marie Howland.
p. cm. — (SUNY series, the new inequalities)
Includes bibliographical references (p.) and index.
ISBN 0-7914-2199-6 (acid-free paper). — ISBN 0-7914-2200-3 (pbk. : acid-free paper)
1. Service industries—United States. 2. Rural industries—United States. 3. Rural development—United States. I. Howland, Marie.
1950- . II. Title. III. Series.
HD9981.5.G52 1995
338.4—dc20 93-49760
CIP

10 9 8 7 6 5 4 3 2 1

Contents

Figures

Tables

ACKNOWLEDGMENTS

We have extensive collective and individual acknowledgments to make. Our collective thanks go to a number of people and organizations that facilitated the execution of the original research project and the subsequent completion of this book.

Perhaps our greatest debt is to Amy Jo Kays. Amy provided research and editorial assistance throughout the project. She reviewed every paragraph of the text and ensured that our arguments made sense and effectively related to the literature. Her own research in the field of rural development greatly enhanced the book's central thesis. In countless ways she was a true collaborator on this project.

Jeff Thompson was the primary author of Chapter 6, with the assistance of Amy Kays. A former banker, Jeff brought considerable expertise to the writing of the chapter. His understanding of financial institutions greatly enhanced the arguments about financial services made in the book.

Gayle Borchard was an original coauthor of the literature review section of the project grant proposal. Her literature compilation is interspersed throughout Chapter 2. We thank her for her assistance.

We are also indebted to Ms. Judith Sartore and her assistant, Barbara Apaliski, of the Research Publications Center of The Smeal College of Business Administration, for the final manuscript preparation. Judy and her staff tirelessly combed the manuscript for hackney-eyed phrases, badly formatted tables, and other hazards of writing, and cheerfully provided us with a polished, copyedited manuscript. The services of the Research Publications Center were generously subsidized by Dr. Rodney Erickson of the Department of Geography and The

State University. Jessica Hanson created the index and we are grateful to her and the financial support of the Urban Studies and Planning Program at Maryland.

Each of us benefited from the opportunity to spend time at the Economic Research Service of the U.S. Department of Agriculture in Washington, D.C. We thank David McGranahan, Sara Mazie, Ken Deavers, and the wonderful colleagues at ERS.

Staff of the University of Texas at Austin's Graduate Program of Community and Regional Planning and the Urban Studies and Planning Program at Maryland provided important assistance throughout the grant. We also thank Bill Beyers and Thierre Noyelle for their helpful early conversations on the subject of services and regional development.

The project was funded by the Ford Foundation through the Aspen Institute's Rural Economic Policy Program and the Kellogg Foundation through the National Rural Studies Committee. At Aspen, Susan Sechler and Maureen Kennedy were particularly supportive. At the National Rural Studies Committee, Emery Castle and Bruce Weber were exceedingly helpful.

Individually, Amy Glasmeier thanks the following contributors to the research project. Special thanks go to (Lily) Jie Wo, probably the most clever, insightful, computer scientist I will ever know. Lily outfoxed the main frame, Internet, and just about every software package available to analyze large data sets. She cheerfully repeated work when I insufficiently communicated tasks to her. She kept impeccable records of data manipulations; hence, we could always retrace our steps.

Bill Beyers is owed special thanks for generously providing the original data from his enhanced County Business Patterns Data file. Bill was always supportive in discussions about services and regional development, and is one of the most generous academic colleagues in the field of Economic Geography.

Amy also thanks the staff at the University of Texas at Austin, in particular Terry Kahn, who gave generously of the Graduate Program's resources and who ensures that students learn statistics, making them employable on large data-intensive projects.

Finally, her husband, Tom Bell, and her dear, sweet son, Andrew, deserve special thanks for their patience and enthusiasm during the completion of this project.

Marie Howland thanks Bruce Phillips of the U.S. Small Business Administration for the use of the USEEM data. Mei Zhou skillfully handled the computer work, and Darrell Smith and Theodore Wimberly conducted the telephone interviews with rural computer programming firms. Calvin Beale, Edward Blakely, Melvin Levin, David McGranahan, Shirley Porterfield, and Wim Wiewel read and made constructive comments and criticism on various chapters. In addition, David McGranahan provided the 1990 Current Population Survey data on part-time, full-time employment in rural service firms. Reba Immergut, Tish Crawford, and Daniel Rosen all provided valuable editing. Jim Wattleworth helped with the Olney Case Study and his insights and experiences as a rural retailer are reflected in Chapter 8. At home, my husband Michael Wattleworth provided continuing support and encouragement, and Matthew and Colin sacrificed hours of basketball with Mom. To all of the above, she's grateful.

1

Introduction

What will the transition to a service economy mean for America's communities? A quick review of academic and popular press accounts points out widespread speculation about who will be the winners and losers in our rapidly evolving information economy.

> Tomorrow's big city is no longer going to be the office center. The exodus is already underway. Insurance companies are rapidly shifting their labor-intensive work to the outskirts of metropolitan areas. Equally important, clerical work increasingly will become "uncoupled" the way much physical office work—cleaning, maintaining equipment, running the cafeteria—already had been. Big companies of tomorrow are almost certain to keep their management people—at least their senior ones—where other senior management people are: in the city. This means that big cities will be the purveyors of specialized skills and knowledge. But even those people will have their office work done outside the city. (Paraphrased from Drucker 1989)

> "Data processing facilities of large business (notably banking and insurance) may increasingly be attracted to nonmetropolitan locations because advances in communications allow them to operate at a distance from the central office, and advances in data processing permit the employment of relatively low-skilled clerical labor, which is found almost everywhere." (Stanback and Noyelle 1982)

> Philanthropy is saving a community. The president of Philadelphia-based Rosenbluth Travel saw an opportunity to help a devastated region and simultaneously meet his firm's back-office data entry needs. A Rosenbluth team picked Linton, North Dakota, a town of 1,430 population located in the south central area of the state to open a facility to handle data processing activities. Within a matter of months, the company had hired 40 part-time workers and opened a telecommunications office for data processing in an empty farm implement dealership. (Paraphrased from *The Dallas Morning News*, April 28, 1991)

> While telecommunications improvements increase a rural community's access to information and make it possible for rural business to more easily serve non-local markets, they can also make it easier for firms located in urban areas to serve rural markets via branch offices or through the telecommunications systems. (Kirn, Conway, and Beyers 1990)

> "Despite the revolution in communications and information technology, rural officials should not yet conclude that traditional urban services are on the verge of loosening their ties to population centers and moving to rural areas." (Miller and Bluestone 1988)

Are service industries next in line, like their predecessor manufacturing, to decentralize to America's peripheral areas? Peter Drucker's view emphasizes the role of telecommunications in freeing services to locate down the urban hierarchy. Similarly, Thierry Noyelle, a noted expert on services, focuses on the relentless march of industry toward maturation. He predicts that services will follow the path of manufacturing, moving into rural areas to minimize costs. As the example notes, rural community's experience suggests that some decentralization is occurring, bringing desperately needed jobs to economically vulnerable small towns. In contrast, another interpretation suggests that urban service firms are likely to displace local rural establishments as telecommunications reduces distance costs and allows urban firms to penetrate isolated markets. Finally, from the U.S. Department of Agriculture's Economic Research Service, inadequate infrastructure, a declining skill base, and the growing cost competitiveness of less developed countries for routine service operations may all diminish rural areas' ability to attract export service activities.

Predictions about services and peripheral regions' economic development are numerous, yet we know surprisingly little about the structure and function of services outside of urban and suburban places. The purpose of this book is to fill in this gap in our understanding of contemporary services industries and the circumstances governing rural services development. Through an analysis of national-level data and detailed case studies, we assess the importance of services in the economies of rural areas. Focusing on a subset of states, we examine the organizational structure of service firms and clarify the extent to which service industries may be filtering operations into rural communities as manufacturing did in previous decades. Case studies of exporting service industries identify whether rural areas are in competition for more sophisticated service sector growth.

In this book we provide a glimpse into the spatial behavior of service industries. Models of services decentralization drawn from the experience of manufacturing ignore existing service functions and the powerful role of new technologies and new institutional arrangements that decouple services from prior modes of industrialization. Caught between old and new paradigms, peripheral regions of developed countries are being cut loose from established patterns of industrialization to traverse uncharted territory. We focus on "rural" because in an important sense peripheral locations are the first to feel any breaks between old and new trends in economic development. Peripheral regions have largely been seen as recipients of larger industrial processes or extensions of the urban economy. Thus, our assessment seeks to verify the magnitude of these changes. The trends we will describe seem a harbinger of what is yet to come in an era of globalization.

Why a Concern about Services Now?

The service sector is claiming center stage in rural development for three reasons. First, services have grown rapidly over the post-WWII period, and until very recently seemed immune to economic recession. Second, with the decline of traditional industries, rural and peripheral areas are grappling with uncertain futures. Services are seen as both a potential source of export activity and a component of modern infrastructure critical to future development. Finally, a reexamination of the development path of rural areas of the 1970s and 1980s suggests that places outside the influence of metropolitan areas have made little progress toward measures of economic opportunity and human well-being. Like the nation's central cities, a decade of neglect is beginning to show on the face of rural America. What role services can play in this period of uncertainty rests in large part with the underlying basis for services growth.

For some readers, renewed concern about rural development problems may come as a surprise. In the mid 1970s, headlines boasted regularly of a rural turnaround based on renewed growth of small communities (Beale 1975). Factors that contributed to the rural renaissance of the late 1960s and 1970s are by now well known. Rural manufacturing, which had been decentralizing since the 1950s, drew population to rural counties for the first time in decades. High energy prices stimulated demand for new petroleum reserves and petroleum substitutes, stimulating growth in rural mainstay industries. Nonmetropolitan fertility rates were higher compared with those of cities. Growth in government—federal, state, and local—contributed to renewed population levels and employment growth. This growth provided funds for education, highway construction, and new government installations—both military and civilian. The first large cohort of social-security-supported and wealthier retirees began to leave urban areas in search of a more relaxed, lower-cost lifestyle.

By the end of the 1980s, many formerly declining urban manufacturing centers were experiencing economic recovery based on the growth of services. The same was not true for rural communities. While the nation's cities moved toward an information economy, rural America remained wedded to a manufacturing growth strategy—a tactic that had made sense while manufacturing decentralized. Nevertheless, despite serious local economic development efforts, rural communities' old sources of export-led development—manufacturing, natural resources, and agriculture—stagnated. Combined with macroeconomic policies, the twin recessions of the decade wreaked havoc on rural communities' economies. Job growth in many nonmetropolitan areas came to a halt; many communities actually lost ground during the 1980s.

For agriculture, the bedrock of rural America, falling interest rates, increasing self-sufficiency of former grain importing countries, and the continuing consolidation and mechanization of farms precipitated a renewed exodus of people out of rural areas, particularly in the corn belt of the Northern Great Plains states. The mining sector—another rural mainstay—suffered a triple insult. Failing mineral and energy commodity prices were due to the 1982 recession. This was matched with an absolute reduction in the volume of commodities used to produce goods such as automobiles. Combined with the deteriorating control of world energy prices by OPEC countries, the results were devastating.

Manufacturing, once considered the savior of rural America, fell on hard times as urban firms slowed the filtration of branch plants to nonmetropolitan areas, and an overvalued U.S. dollar accelerated the simultaneous shift of manufacturing to foreign locations. Manufacturing employment growth was effectively capped. To counter the effects of intensified foreign competition, firms raised productivity by increasing capital investments, further reducing employment. Although manufacturing re-established its trend toward decentralizing to rural areas in the late 1980s, rural communities are now painfully aware of manufacturing employment's cyclical sensitivity.

Yet, rural manufacturing's decline has proved to be more than just a periodic response to the 1982 national recession. Rural America's traditional comparative advantage—cheap labor, a lax regulatory environment, and probusiness culture—

was no longer competitive. By the late 1980s, even though rural manufacturing had begun to grow again, job levels had fallen far below those of the 1960s (Majchrowicz 1990).

The 1970s may well have been an anomaly due to a unique confluence of events favorable to rural areas. However, contemporary research is beginning to question the significance of the turnaround associated with the perceived rural renaissance of the 1970s (Fuguitt 1991). Measurement of this change depends heavily upon the geographic unit of analysis studied. Just what constituted rural America in the 1950s–1980s decades is open for dispute. A pre-1970s definition of rural places using a constant area approach that specified metropolitan and nonmetropolitan county designations at the beginning of each decade shows that rural communities had indeed experienced a turnaround. Using a definition of rural that allows counties to shift from nonmetropolitan to metropolitan status as population changes, however, the 1970s decade represented more of the past—with population outmigration reaching levels of 10 percent over the decade. The greatest share of rural population growth in the decade was concentrated in the counties redefined in the 1980 Census as urban.

Definitional issues aside, the most critical effect of the perceived rural turnaround was the precipitation of a sharp reduction in the concern about rural communities. Rural advocates were so effective at proclaiming rural America's recovery that policy makers turned their attention toward more intractable concerns—the nation's inner cities.

Had the lens of analysis been more discerning, and had rural enthusiasts observed the growing importance of suburbanization, then comparisons between urban and rural might have been jettisoned in favor of comparisons of rural and suburban growth rates. Had rural been compared with suburban instead of an urban amalgamation that included deeply troubled urban centers, then rural concerns might not have evaporated from federal and state policy debate.

A more precise characterization of the changing American urban landscape would have uncovered the startling fact that the majority of Americans no longer lived in densely settled urban areas. Since the 1950s, Americans and their employers have been moving to the suburbs (Noyelle 1987). The evolution of the American spatial economy importantly depended upon the growth of services. With the failure of policy makers to recognize this broader trend, concerns about rural areas faded into the background.

By misidentifying the progressive movement toward a service-based economy, and assuming that services could play no more than a passive role in economic growth, rural areas remained wedded to manufacturing. Rural development policy still hinges on the attraction of manufacturing, a sector in which employment levels (not to be confused with output) have been declining nationally. Rural areas must now broaden their model of development. The future for rural manufacturing is not assured. The trends toward increasing capital intensity of production, recentralizing pulls associated with new inventory practices stressing rapid delivery, and increasing competition from third world countries call into question the prospect for further manufacturing decentralization.

The Transformation of the Structure of the U.S. Economy

By the early 1950s, the services sector had emerged as the largest source of jobs in the U.S. economy. Manufacturing continued to contribute the lion's share of total national output. But, due to the increasing complexity of the nation's economy, rising consumer incomes, the growing service component in manufactured goods, and the creation of unique service products, the service sector became the nation's major employer.

The 1980s proved to be a watershed decade for services. Over the ten years, services were the only effective job generator in the national economy. More than 17 million service jobs were created. Ronald Reagan's tremendous popularity owed much to the persistent growth of services which helped offset declines in other sectors. The longest economic expansion since World War II was based on the growth of services. As we entered the decade of the 1990s, most Americans were employed, the unemployment rate was at 6 percent, and 71 percent of Americans held jobs in the services sector.

The pattern was the same for rural economies. The fastest growing rural industries since 1969 have been in services and construction. In the 1980s, services accounted for *all* net new jobs created (Reid and Frederick 1990).

The structure of the national economy has fundamentally changed. The nation's employment base is no longer comprised primarily of goods-producing industries, and instead has become dependent upon information and services.

A closer examination of the restructuring to a service-based economy suggests that the experience is not all roses. Unlike previous decades, when growth in employment virtually guaranteed greater opportunity, the transition to a service economy did not produce an increasing standard of living for everyone. Although a large share of the nation's work force is currently employed, it now takes two wage earners to maintain a middle-class lifestyle (Bluestone and Harrison 1988; Gorham 1991; Levy 1988). This new labor market reality reflects the unfortunate fact that personal income levels have been stagnant since 1973. Whereas services industries did create millions of new jobs, many were part time, and a large portion of these jobs provided few fringe benefits. Low wages and part-time work characterize about 20 percent of total services employment (Christopherson 1989). Americans are now working longer hours for less pay (Schorr 1991). Hence the quality, not just the quantity, of jobs must be questioned. This dilemma has received relatively sparse attention.

Far more emphasis has been placed on the fast-growing producer services sector, activities that are intermediate goods to other business (see, for example, Noyelle and Stanback 1983; Daniels 1985; Marshall, Damesick, and Wood 1987). Producer services industries exhibit high growth rates, they pay relatively high incomes, and they employ highly skilled workers. In important instances these sectors also demonstrate significant export potential. It is no wonder that wooing producer services has become a major goal of local economic development policy. Whereas high-tech industries were the coveted prize of economic development circles a decade ago, today's targets are increasingly producer services, and the service sector more generally.

The growth of services has not been the result of a single or a profound shift in national economic circumstances. Rather, services growth is attributable to many factors, both overlapping and distinct. The early stages of internationalization forced American firms to massively restructure. Old patterns of intensive vertical integration gave way to externalization of non-core corporate functions. As firms' market niches became more competitive and more narrowly defined, demand for producer service inputs such as consulting, marketing, and sales became critical. Reorganization was made possible by the diffusion of computers and information technology that precipitated the formation of new firms providing producer services. The advent of new technology allowed the unbundling of functions previously performed by firms in-house. In addition, new service products were created to assist American firms' participation in a global economy.

Residential consumption patterns were also changing, largely in response to the growing number of dual income households and rising female participation in the labor force. This new labor market reality fostered an increase in service activities such as eating and drinking establishments as more families bought services in the private economy that had previously been performed as unpaid work in the home.

The social compact forged between labor, capital, and government in the post-World War II period accelerated the expansion of another major service employment sector—health care. The existence of private health care benefits, an aging population covered by medicare, advances made in medicine, and the increasing fragmentation of health service activities (previously performed in a doctor's office or at the local hospital) contributed to an expanded medical sector.

Education also emerged as a major services employer. Demographic trends, in particular the move of "baby boomers" through the school system, liberal student loan policies, and the growing need for new technical training to satisfy the nation's insatiable appetite for electronically literate workers, boosted employment in both public and private education. Chapters 3, 4, and 7 in this book detail the expansion of services sectors over the 1974–1985 decade.

Without a doubt, the economic changes that came to a head in the 1980s elevated the services sector out of its former dependency status (a strict dependence on consumption) to that of wealth-creating, and along with this came the potential to facilitate regional development.

The Role of Services in Rural America: An Outline of the Book

As the introductory citations illustrate, there is a diversity of opinions about the locational behavior, and therefore the regional development potential, of services. Early academic research likened services location to that of manufacturing, in which competition is intense, products are standardized, and market share depends on being the lowest-cost producer. In these instances low-skilled labor is sufficient to carry out production, and wage differences across space become a critical determinant of industry location. The cycle of decentralization is by now well known: initial urban concentration during the early life of a product when access to skilled labor dictates a central location; a first phase of relocation to suburbs as firms search for markets and large pools of both white- and blue-collar workers; and, finally, decentralization to rural areas where wage rates, unionization levels, and taxes are lower. The extent that services mirror this pattern is a major concern of this book. By way of preview, we sketch out our own model of service industry location.

In this book we emphasize the relationship between industry locational tendencies and economic development potential. Economic development based on services depends upon the functional relationship between services and income growth. Economic base theory separates industries into two categories: basic and nonbasic. According to this theory, workers in basic sectors receive income based on the sales of goods produced in the local community and sold to the outside world. Nonbasic sectors grow as this externally derived income is spent locally. The theory posits that growth of total income is a function of the export base.

This model implies two modes of services-led growth for a rural economy—either through expansion of export-oriented services or by means of import substitution. Import substitution is the local purchase of previously imported services. In the vernacular of economists, import substitution increases the local multiplier, thereby raising local incomes as dollars circulate in the local economy. In framing the issue of rural services, it is worth distinguishing between import substitution in the goods-producing and the consumer sectors—because we believe a different set of dynamics are at play for each. Our justification for each of these three categories is discussed briefly here.

Traditionally, services were considered strictly dependent upon local demand generated by the spending of export-based earned income. Exports, according to this view, were products of the agricultural, mining, and manufacturing sectors. The growing importance and changing nature of the services sector has necessitated a reconsideration of the role services play in growth, however. We now recognize that services can be a source of growth in their own right. Some export-oriented service firms create tangible and tradable goods that can be shipped (e.g., software); other services are those that can be exported by moving production to the point of consumption (e.g., consulting), and services that can be exported by moving consumers to the point of production (e.g., tourism, health care). How has the growth of exportable services played itself out in rural America, and what potential do export services hold for rural development strategies?

Over time, an increasingly diversified local economy is expected to include growing numbers of establishments providing a complex array of goods and services previously traded in from the outside. This model of development equips us with a basis to explore the pull between the goods-producing sectors and their service providers. On a more concrete level, is the decentralization of manufacturing to rural areas pulling services in tandem? Are changes in the structure of farm ownership patterns making farmers more or less likely to purchase their inputs from local sources? The rural future may hold less promise if traditional rural exporters rely on urban centers as the source of producer service inputs.

The development literature has virtually ignored consumer and retail services' role in economic growth. Whereas their function has been assumed to be passive, these traditional services may fortify or frustrate efforts at local economic revitalization. The more vital a local retail and consumer services sector, the greater the share of local consumer dollars spent in the rural economy, and the greater the level of local income. Conversely, when a community loses its retail base, the spiral of decline accelerates.

Whereas economic growth theory provides a valuable framework for the analysis of rural services, data sources and the complexities of real life are not so accommodating. Therefore, it is not always possible to exercise this model through analysis. Data are not neatly divided into export or residentiary services, and although researchers have used SIC-based industrial categories to denote residentiary and producer services, not all firms (much less industries) fall neatly into one or the other category. Moreover, a service industry may behave as an export activity in an urban economy, but in fact be a residentiary or a consumer service in a rural economy. For example, as we show in Chapters 4 and 6, although banking and insurance tend to be exportable services for the nation as a whole and for urban America, employment trends in rural banking reflect import penetration on the part of urban banks rather than growth in rural export services.

Within our three-way categorization, the issue of external versus local control is an underlying theme. Even in instances where aggregate employment is stable or growing, a rural economy can be adversely affected by the displacement of locally owned services by externally controlled firms.

Issues surrounding external control are complex. Aggregate growth statistics may hide changes in who controls rural services firms. When services formerly provided by locally owned establishments are replaced with services provided by firms distantly headquartered, rural incomes are affected. No better example exists than that of the Walmart Corporation, a full-service retailer, which has formulated its growth strategy around locating stores at the crossroads of many small communities. Walmart sells into geographic locations with highly dispersed population bases. By spreading sales across many small population concentrations, the firm ensures the necessary market size and sales volume to provide a variety of consumer nondurable goods at a low price.

This successful strategy comes at a price. Rural merchants who once enjoyed a spatial monopoly that allowed them to offset the costs associated with distance from suppliers and lower sales volumes can no longer compete. Rural residents exchange lower individual costs of goods for reduced levels of local profit circulation. This intensification of retail trade is illustrated in Chapter 7, where we show that the commonly cited Walmart example is more than an anecdote. Retail employment in rural communities is stable, but the share of employment in independently owned enterprises is declining dramatically.

In chapter 2 we set up the rest of the book. We begin by reviewing the growing literature on service industry development and location. This analysis exposes considerable disagreement about the very definition of services—let alone their measurement. A detailed review of the literature suggests that the 1980s concern about producer services growth overshadowed the influence of services as a form of derivative development.

In Chapter 3 we evaluate the extent to which rural services mirror national trends. Whereas export services may suggest promising new development potential, the vast base of rural services are dependent on existing sources of income. This reveals the pervasive dependence of services on other forms of development. In this chapter we also clarify the importance of the underlying economic base and the existence of producer services. Most urban-based services research suggests economic base differentiation is coupled with a varied service base. On the contrary, the composition of services in peripheral areas are remarkably similar regardless of the local economic base.

In Chapter 4 we take up this issue through an examination of existing research on producer services. While highlighting the considerable debate about what constitutes tradable services, we also add our assessment of the spatial location of tradable services. On this account, we focus specifically on producer services—those sectors considered intermediate products to other industries.

Producer services industries are heavily dependent upon telecommunications technology. The expansion of this component of the services sector is tied to the increasing information content of modern industry. By some estimates, 50 percent of the American work force is involved in the creation and dissemination of information (Dillman and Beck 1987). Information technology is a key to the nation's transformation from a goods- to a service-producing economy. Access to telecommunications technology and skilled labor govern the location of producer service firms.

A growing body of literature documents the spatial tendencies of producer service firms. These sectors are predominantly found in large metropolitan areas where markets, skilled labor, and advanced technologies are found. Producer services are therefore fundamentally metropolitan in character. Unlike manufacturing firms, which decentralized branch plants to rural areas, service firms exhibit a tendency to sell into remote markets as demand develops. Service branch plants rarely leave the confines of suburban America.

Although there is some evidence that producer services are decentralizing to rural communities, it is necessary to clarify the importance of establishment ownership in this context.

As suggested in the case of import substitution services, the penetration of nonlocally owned establishments into markets with stagnating population and income growth brings a loss of local profits. The development consequences of service branches also differ from those that are associated with locally owned firms.

In Chapter 4 we examine producer services using both aggregate statistics of producer services among the nation's counties, followed by a more in-depth assessment of producer services in six states. In Chapter 5 we present a case study which examines branch plant filtering in data processing industries. Although we, too, find modest evidence of filtering, these establishments are very much tied to urban areas for markets and are vulnerable to foreign competition. The data processing industry also appears to be in a state of significant transition. Most rural data processing firms start out like urban firms—small. While some grow larger and fill momentary niches in labor-intensive computer processing, most have little more to offer than low wages. This cost-based market niche is eroding as lower-cost and international centers emerge as competitors. Rural areas appear as little more than momentary stopping off points as firms search for lower-cost alternatives.

For rural areas, service branch plants present similar challenges to those associated with manufacturing branch plants. Although jobs are created initially, service branch plants rarely bring with them the requirements for a full complement of skills. Instead, branches buy complex administrative functions from the parent. Moreover, expansion of the firm does not necessarily translate into increased numbers of jobs in existing branch locations. Service firms are market-oriented, and expansion usually results in growth near sources of new demand. Yet, our research also shows that rural communities are particularly disadvantaged even in those instances when upturns in demand require labor force expansion. Rural labor markets are often quickly exhausted. Consequently, service firms are forced to set up additional branches rather than expand in place.

In Chapter 6 we continue the analysis of producer services' role in rural development by examining the changing structure of the banking sector. This analysis shows that banks are consolidating and altering the labor process at the same time. In the future rural communities can be expected to have more difficulty accessing funds for business development. Jobs in banking are also being consolidated as regional banks shift certain tasks to regional centers in an effort to achieve economies of scale in service delivery.

An important contribution of our study is the analysis of service firms headquartered in rural communities. This type of establishment tends to create a full complement of skills, and thus is likely to encourage the expansion of rural communities' competencies. Profits circulate locally, and demand from these establishments forms the basis for import substitutes which may stimulate growth in other industries. Nevertheless, comparisons of rural and urban firms in the data processing industry point out significant limitations in the technical sophistication of rural service firms.

In Chapter 7 we look carefully at services traditionally dependent on other sources of income. We note two important findings. First, traditional sectors such as retail, once thought to be dependent on population concentrations, are changing spatial distribution patterns. As income-dependent sectors become regionalized due to technological innovations in the distribution sector, once sacrosanct services such as retailing are moving up the spatial hierarchy. Regional centers of consumption are accumulating demand and unlocking former spatial monopolies. For consumers the benefits in terms of lower costs and greater variety are real, but this trend may spell doom for small town Main Streets and necessitate longer journeys to purchase.

Throughout this book we highlight the distinctions between the formation of rural services establishments that are income-dependent, import substitutes, and export-oriented. On the basis of these distinctions, we offer evidence about the extent that rural and urban services differ.

The Current Rural Situation

This book is written at a time when rural fortunes have taken a decided turn for the worse. Despite major advances in population and employment growth in the 1970s, rural America still lags behind the nation's cities on a number of important measures. Almost half of rural counties lost population in the 1980s. Although by the end of the decade rural unemployment rates had fallen to within a half of a percentage point of urban rates, this did not translate into tangible growth in income. Per capita income levels in rural areas remain at 72 percent of those in urban areas, and although poverty rates have fallen from the post-recession high of the early 1980s, more than 16 percent of rural families still live in poverty. More disturbing, poverty levels are much worse for rural black and female-headed families, hovering at 40 percent. Thus, the dramatic growth of jobs nationally—primarily service jobs—did not translate into better quality of life for many rural Americans.

Researchers are now beginning to suggest that conditions in rural America are turning back toward those of the 1950s, when a great divergence existed between life in urban and rural areas. Calvin Beale (1991), the nation's undisputed expert on rural America, is quick to point out, however, that conditions in rural communities today are a far cry from those found in the 1950s. At the end of the 1940s, almost 50 percent of the rural housing stock had no running water or indoor toilets. Most lacked electricity. Two-thirds of rural adults had never been beyond grade school, and about three-fifths of rural roads were unpaved.

Yes, conditions are markedly improved from three decades ago, but we cannot ignore the fact that rural America is in danger of losing the progress gained in the 1960s and 1970s. Perhaps more crucial, evidence is mounting that serious problems are forming dark clouds on the horizon of rural America. The following statistics from the U.S. Department of Agriculture capture the basis for future problems in rural America:

Rural America now has about 50 percent of the nation's low-skilled, low-wage manufacturing jobs. (Bloomquist 1987)

Only 59 percent of rural workers have finished high school, compared with 69 percent in urban areas. More worrisome, only 11.5 percent of today's rural workers have completed college, compared with 18 percent in urban areas. And disparities in levels of educational attainment between urban and rural areas, once converging, now appear to be widening, according to some measures. (Teixeria 1991)

The 1982 recession accelerated rural communities' loss of college educated people. Net outmigration of college graduates averaged two percent per year between 1986 and 1989. (McGranahan and Ghelfi 1991)

The skill levels of new rural manufacturing jobs have declined by 50 percent in key areas such as data handling, verbal aptitude, and GED requirements. (Teixeria 1991)

Studies have shown that for rural areas, the historic link between education and employment and earnings growth has considerably eroded. (Killian and Parker 1991)

Forty-two percent of rural workers receive earnings at or below the nation's poverty level for a family of four. (Lichter 1991)

Rural workers between the ages of 16 and 24 are particularly disadvantaged. Fewer than 50 percent receive more than poverty-level wages. (Gorham 1991)

Twenty-four percent of rural workers work part-time involuntarily, compared with 7 percent of urban workers. (Lichter 1991)

Rural workers experienced a 30 percent difference in returns to education. (McGranahan and Ghelfi 1991)

Rural workers are more likely to experience a longer duration of unemployment after job loss than urban workers. (Swaim 1990)

These solemn statistics add up to one undeniable fact. Rural workers are working harder, for less pay, in less stable and often unfulfilling jobs than are urban workers. If the American economy is truly becoming one that produces information rather than goods, then it is critical that rural communities are able to compete effectively in this new environment. If America is to benefit fully from the emerging global economy, then every citizen must have the opportunity to participate in our better future.

National attention has been riveted on the plight of urban America, in which pockets of poverty persist and whole communities are at risk of being left behind, but the same can be said of many rural communities where hard work no longer guarantees a living wage. It is vital that we know the extent that services can augment traditional sectors which are now in a state of decline.

As we enter the decade of the 1990s, it is important and necessary that we understand the potential of services to create jobs and wealth in rural communities. The evidence in this book is one attempt to fill existing gaps in our understanding of this prospect. The results presented here clearly show that there is considerable room for constructive, carefully tailored policies to help rural America achieve its potential.

2

Rural Services in an Age of Information Technology: Definitions, Theories, and Empirical Evidence

For more than two decades the service sector has employed the majority of rural workers, yet the lion's share of rural research has centered on the agriculture, mining, and manufacturing sectors. Amidst the growing recognition that some service employers are more than passive players in the national economy, a number of researchers have begun to explore what the growth in service jobs means for rural areas.

There are two opposing views of service-led development. One perspective contends that services can be a propulsive force in rural economic development. Another view suggests that services are neither independent of, nor a replacement for, older forms of rural industrialization such as agriculture, mining, and manufacturing. Our work suggests the existence of a middle ground between these two opposing perspectives. Both views fail to account for the dualistic nature of rural services growth. The service sector in rural America does not mirror the developmental experience commonly associated with services in the nation's cities. Few rural services have export potential, and the level of employment in export-oriented services is low relative to urban areas. Too narrow a focus on the export potential overlooks other changes that influence service sector growth. These are, specifically, the growth of indirectly exported services, the loss or addition of residentiary services, the capacity of local services to attract manufacturing jobs, and issues surrounding enterprise ownership.

Intertwined with the limitations found in development models, with few exceptions, spatial models applied to services borrow erroneously from the experience of manufacturing. There is an expectation that services start as innovative products produced by small firms in urban areas and then decentralize as labor-intensive standardized service operations, "service branch plants," to rural areas (Glasmeier and Borchard 1989; Glasmeier and Howland 1989; Dickstein 1991; Reich 1988a and b).[1] As work presented later in this book suggests, anecdotes aside, service sector branch plants are not proliferating in rural areas. Rural establishments, even the unsophisticated, export-oriented backoffice service activities such as data entry, are generally sole proprietorships. These rural firms not only compete with low-wage workers in other communities around the world, but now face the prospect of displacement as computer technology entirely obviates the need for human keystroke entry.

In this chapter we review the accumulating literature on services and economic development. We begin by summarizing the various definitions that frame the service sector. From definitions, we turn to a more general discussion of the growth of services nationally. We then proceed to review recent trends in rural service growth over the past two decades. We also examine models of the spatial distribution of services and the implications of these models for future rural service growth. We conclude with a summary of the major gaps in existing knowledge.

Defining Services

Current debate regarding the growth and distribution of services is hampered by the lack of a common definition of services and the absence of appropriately disaggregated data (O'Farrell and Hitchens 1990; Marshall et al. 1988). The obvious limitations are due in part to the traditional view of services as residual. In spite of their majority share of all jobs in most developed countries, services received little attention until the late 1970s, when manufacturing began to falter. In general, service industries have been seen as nonproductive and derivative of other sources of growth. Until recently, more precise definitions and disaggregated service industry data were not in great demand by scholars.

Although questions of definition and classification remain problematic, the need to differentiate between services and other sectors necessitates the identification of meaningful boundaries. Traditionally, sectors were defined by the physical characteristics of an activity or output of that activity: primary (extractive), secondary (manufacturing), and tertiary (service) functions (Quinn Baruch, and Paquette 1987; Quinn 1988; Quinn and Doorley 1988; Quinn and Gagnon 1986; Quinn Baruch, Paquette 1988). In the earliest studies, the service sector was a convenient grouping for all activities that defied definition as either extractive or manufacturing. The problem with this scheme is that it does not reveal what services are, only what they are not.

As a way of defining services more precisely, some scholars have emphasized their qualitative nature. In the past, services were considered intangible or impermanent—consumed at the moment or near moment of production (Enderwick 1987). With this distinction in mind, it was relatively easy to identify service activities. However, with the advent of new technologies, the basis of this scheme has eroded because some outputs of the service sector are tangible, permanent, storable products. New service "products," such as the magnetic storage of information, belie the impermanent or unstockable concept (Marshall et al. 1988). More importantly, services increasingly take on a quality of permanence when linked with tangible products in package deals such as hardware and software.

As a practical matter, service definitions are largely captive to industry classification schemes that may no longer precisely delineate distinctions among industries (Duncan 1988). As attempts are made to be more precise about which activities constitute services, the debate revolves around the inclusion or exclusion of activities that take on the characteristics of a tangible product (i.e., software). At least one author argues that services are really misclassified forms of manufacturing rather than distinct, and therefore separable, activities (Walker 1985). From a slightly different perspective, using occupational data, Beyers (1991) notes that occupations important to producer services are in fact found throughout the economy. This only adds to the debate about what should be included in a definition of services. Finance, insurance, real estate, and business and personal services are most commonly considered core services. But what of construction, utilities, transportation, communications, and government (Daniels 1982)? Construction and utilities are the most frequently excluded industries. The argument for their not being considered services is that their product, production-technology, and physical plant are more akin to the goods-producing, manufacturing sector. However, no hard-and-fast rules have been established.

Because the physical quality of a service provides no conclusive basis for definition, some scholars have looked toward the embedded composition of labor to distinguish among sectors. Services have been defined as activities that create or transform information and require cognitive skill, knowledge, and experience. This is in contrast to manufacturing, which involves the chemical or physical transformation of materials and relies much more directly on physical labor. According to this definition, white-collar workers within manufacturing, such as clerical workers or engineers, are identified as service workers. Again, operationalizing such a definition is difficult. For example, a high proportion of the value-added of some tangible or manufactured products is created by knowledge-intensive service inputs. The pharmaceutical industry is classified under manufacturing although production costs represent a tiny fraction of value. Most of the costs of pharmaceutical products are derived from research and development, clinical trials, patent applications, regulatory clearances, drug marketing, and distribution (Reich 1991).

An advantage of the occupational approach is that it resolves some of the confusion surrounding the growth of the service sector. The decade of the 1980s witnessed an unprecedented movement of tasks out of the firm and into the market. Activities previously performed within agriculture, mining, and manufacturing firms are increasingly executed outside these sectors. Because of this job shifting, a standard industrial classification (SIC) code-based definition of services overstates the growth of jobs since many activities previously belonging to the traditional basic sectors are now counted as services. This is despite the fact that no new employment is created for the national economy, and the same jobs are performed.

The potential for overestimating job growth in services using an industry-based definition argues for measuring services in terms of occupation. Whereas occupational data circumvent the problem of embedded service activities, there is unfortunately no adequate source of occupational data that allows analysis on a highly spatially disaggregated basis. The *Census of Population* and *Current Population Survey* are sources of occupational data, with managerial, professional, technical, sales, and administrative occupations generally defined as service jobs. One advantage of the industry-based approach is it best corresponds to SIC codes, and a wide range of geographically disaggregated employment data are classified by SIC categories. However, both data sets are based on self-selection rather than job task content, thus leaving substantial room for error.

Service Classification Schemes

Definitional problems arise not only in making the distinction between services and nonservices, but in identifying internally coherent groupings of services. Currently used classification schemes are based on market, tradability across international boundaries, occupation, and various combinations.

Market-based schemes categorize services according to whether their clients are business and government or households (Marshall et al. 1988). Attempts to define services by the nature of the purchaser are problematic in practice, if not concept, since individual establishments can serve all three sectors. Once establishments are aggregated to the industry level, the potential for error is even greater. For example, Greenfield (1966) found that the industries most considered to be producer services sold large portions of their output to households. Even research attempting to link services and manufacturing has shown that an end user definition lacks precision. Services firms are found to sell more to each other than to other industries.[2] Therefore, accurate identification of markets cannot be extracted from published data, and the only method of classifying markets is through the painstaking process of individual firm interviews (see for example, Beyers and Alvine 1985; Coffey and Polese 1987; and Kirn, Conway, and Beyers 1990).

Tradability across geographic and political borders is a second classification scheme relevant to the study of rural services. Tradable services, according to this breakdown, are those with the capacity to be consumed at a site distinct from where they are produced.[3] This framework is valuable for analyzing the location decisions of multinational service firms (Enderwick 1987) and international trade in services (Sauvant 1986), but it overlooks instances in which the production site moves to the consumption site, as is the case for consulting. Moreover, existing data sources make such a scheme difficult to implement in practice. The conceptualization of tradable services is particularly germane for the study of rural economies in which tourism is an important export service, and the degree to which rural services are exported is critical to the potential of services for development.

Within services, an *occupation-based* classification scheme inventories occupations by their degree of information processing. Hepworth (1990) uses this approach in his study of the information economy, for which labor's role in the manipulation of symbols and information is critical. Based on earlier work by Porat (1977), Hepworth groups service occupations as either information producers (e.g., chemists, economists, accountants, lawyers); processors (e.g., production workers, office supervisors); distributors (e.g., teachers, librarians); or infrastructure workers (e.g., computer operators, printers). Although this scheme includes most service workers across industries, it completely excludes some occupations traditionally considered service-oriented, such as bus drivers and shop assistants.[4] Recent research by Beyers (1991) further calls into question the reliability of occupational classification schemes to distinctly identify producer services from other forms of economic activity.

One of the most widely used service classification schemes relies on a *combination* of more than one principle (Singlemann 1979; Noyelle and Stanback 1983; Fuguitt, Brown, and Beale 1989). The Singlemann (1979) categories differentiate services by markets, final versus intermediate consumers, and by the nature of the provider: private, nonprofit, or public. Services are arranged into distributive, corporate, nonprofit, retail, mainly consumer, and government services. Employees performing tasks in the central administrative offices (CAO) and in auxiliary establishments of agriculture, mining, and manufacturing are included as a subset of the producer services category. Aside from the capture of a sizable portion of service occupations in other sectors through the reallocation of CAO employment to the service sector, the Singlemann breakdown is subject to all of the shortcomings of any scheme based on the SIC code classification.

None of the above classification schemes was developed with rural areas in mind. Extremely disaggregated and detailed data would be needed to make any of these definitions relevant to rural communities. Small counts, mainly a problem in low population areas, are not reported in census industry publications, and consequently studies of rural areas cannot be performed with the same precision as studies of urban areas.[5]

A second concern is that even when industry data is available for a rural region and disaggregated to the four-digit level, urban and rural comparisons can be misleading. The nature of urban versus rural activities within SIC codes are varied. Service firms located in Boston are likely to be centers for research and development, while a plant in rural Texas in the same SIC code is more likely to be engaged in routine, low-value-added activities. For example, the New York financial sector in no way resembles banking in rural America.

Some of the service definitions are less relevant to the study of rural economies. For example, the Porat-Hepworth groupings break out the information-intensive, high-skilled, or producer services, which are notably underrepresented in rural areas, and aggregate the more commonplace residentiary services, which are overrepresented in rural economies.

Although the most appropriate scheme varies by the intent of study, variants of the Singlemann classification scheme have several advantages for the study of rural areas. A market-based taxonomy is valuable. Regardless of the current enthusiasm about the potential of service exports, the major share of services in general, and rural services in particular, is market-driven. Additional advantages are the Singlemann classification's SIC code foundation, since the best rural data are SIC code-based. The classification gives equal weight to the less knowledge-intensive industries, apropos for the study of rural economies where workers are generally less educated, and it gives equal weight to residentiary services, traditionally considered the dominant rural service activities. The Singlemann classification is at the core of this book (Glasmeier and Howland 1989).

In the next section we review the accumulated literature on the growth of services. Each of the factors identified as contributing to services growth has spatial implications. As we illustrate in the following section, the discussion of services growth has primarily occurred within the context of the urban and suburban environments. Few authors have made an attempt to include sparsely settled and remote locations in a model of service sector location.

Social Change and the Growth of Services

Whereas there is wide agreement that services are the major source of employment growth, there is less consensus about why they are currently growing so rapidly (Eckstein and

Heien 1985). The literature includes a number of potential explanations (Tschetter 1987; Moore 1987; Kirk 1987). Part of services growth reflects general economic expansion. Gross National Product growth accounts for 40 percent of the expansion of producer services between 1972 and 1985.

Growth of the world economy, increasing complexity of corporations, and expansion of foreign trade also explain some of services' growth (Dunning and Norman 1987). Financial services are particularly sensitive to world-wide economic trends—deregulation, world markets, and volatility of currency. Their growth is both a reflection of the increasingly complex system of trade and a response, for example, to nation-based policies that regulate international trade (van Dinteren 1987).

Another factor contributing to the growth of service employment is the lack of potential for productivity increases to be realized in service employment. Services are considered by some to be less susceptible to productivity increases than manufacturing (Gershuny and Miles 1983; Kahan 1990). If service sectors have lower per capita productivity levels, all else being equal, they will employ more (less productive) workers to meet market demand. The view on this issue is not unanimous. Some researchers speculate that in the future, services are likely to create fewer jobs as pressures to raise productivity result in capital-intensification of service production processes. Marshall, Damesick, and Wood (1987) note that relatively low-productivity services are becoming more capital-intensive, resulting in lower employment multipliers. A recent article about the American Express Corporation in the *New York Times* (1988) indicates the possibilities for productivity increases. Production of American Express' monthly credit card billing once required hundreds of data entry processors, but new electronic scanning technologies have cut the size of American Express' data entry staff by as much as 90 percent in some cases.

Additional factors related to changing modes of production also account for some service employment growth. Manufacturing firms now "sub out" many service requirements previously supplied in-house (Buck 1988). Firms are using more temporary employees for a wide variety of tasks. Certain kinds of activities such as janitorial, food service, and landscaping are increasingly being acquired from firms classified in the service sector. Many of these functions were formerly done in-house by manufacturing firms, thus they are not additions to the economy. Their employment was just previously defined as manufacturing.

Another example of increased demand for services arises from growing specialization among manufacturers. As incomes rise, consumers are demanding higher quality and more specialized products. Manufacturers are responding by making products for narrower market niches. This results in more extensive demand for business services such as market analysis, advertising, and distribution services (Stanback and Noyelle 1982). Rapid rates of technological innovation in information and goods processing are also exerting a positive impact on the growth of producer services (Gillespie and Green 1987; Hepworth 1990). As the cost of obtaining information declines, demand increases, stimulating this industry.

The introduction of information-based technologies in industry generally creates additional demand for workers in such industries as software and computer equipment consulting. This technological innovation contributes to the growth of service sector jobs. Finally, there are also important developments in the nature of consumer demand that are influencing the growth of services (Moore 1987).

In spite of the attention paid to producer services, expansion in consumer services contributed the lion's share of new jobs in services over the 1980s decade. There are several explanations for this development. The income elasticity of demand for services exceeds that for manufactured goods. As consumers gain personal wealth, they spend proportionally more of their income on consumer services. Dual wage-earning families have resulted in increased disposable consumer income and account for some growth in trade (the trend toward convenience over price), recreation, and restaurants (Mawson 1987; Miller and Bluestone 1988). Other authors argue that the dual-income household has become a necessity due to wage stagnation. Thus expansion of consumer services is due to the gradual incorporation of household functions into the formal economy (Illeris 1989).

Still others suggest that a major source of services growth in the 1980s was expansion in retail operations. This type of employment is notorious for its part-time status and lack of benefits. As incomes fell and retail profits were squeezed, firms eliminated full-time employees and hired part-time workers (Christopherson 1989).

Medical services were also a major component of services growth. The administration of medical services, encompassing highly sophisticated testing and care-giving procedures, has become increasingly complex. Simultaneously, trends toward extreme specialization of service delivery through outpatient clinics and the fixing of renumeration rates for procedures covered under federally-sponsored health care assistance have contributed to increased numbers of both medical service establishments and auxiliary administrative personnel.

Other major sources of consumer services growth are tourism and retirement-related development. These two sources of growth have been important stimuli to the expansion of services (Reid and Frederick 1990). Selected locations with high amenity resources have experienced dramatic growth over the study decade. Tourism brings in export dollars as visitors occupy hotel rooms, buy gasoline, and eat in restaurants. Our results highlight this emerging trend with most services growth concentrated in consumer-based sectors.

An additional source of services growth is the expansion of the population of mobile seniors. Although detailed consumer surveys are lacking, secondary evidence suggests that retirees have relatively high and stable incomes, a portion of which is spent on local services. In addition to the expansion of the medical services sector, the mobile elderly also contribute to the expansion of other sectors including eating and drinking establishments, convenience stores, and membership organizations. Tempering the benefits of this type of development is the fact that services consumed by the elderly are largely tied to consumer spending and pay relatively low wages to workers.

The explanations for services growth have all been made on an aggregate basis. There has been a tendency to gloss over issues of spatially uneven development of services (see Marshall et al. 1988; Marshall and Jaeger 1990 for an exception). Moreover, there has been a tendency to treat services expansion outside the context of very real changes occurring in the economic base of peripheral areas.

The Growth Experience of Services in Peripheral Areas

Although services have been a major source of employment for decades, most geographic research has been biased toward manufacturing (Redwood 1988; Bender et al. 1985). Hence, our conceptual models of both service location and development are primarily derived from the experience of the goods-producing sectors. It comes as no surprise then that much of the language and discourse about services in rural areas reflects the expectation that rural service growth is a response to urban development forces and not an organically derived process. For example, the assumption that services will decentralize out of urban areas and into rural communities draws upon a model of manufacturing decentralization. We question the efficacy of this formalization and suggest instead that rural services' location and development must be seen in light of trends that are both distinctly rural (that is, associated with the underlying rural economic base and demographic trends) and global in nature. Thus we begin by reviewing research that sheds some light on the growth experience of the service sector in rural areas. One cut at this question focuses on the degree to which rural services growth mirrors that of the nation's cities.

There is broad evidence of services growth and possible decentralization over the last four decades (Garnick 1983). National data for the 1958 to 1979 period show service sector employment growing almost as rapidly in rural as in urban counties. Between 1969 and 1979, the service sector[6] grew at an annual average rate of 2.9 percent per year in metropolitan counties and 2.7 percent per year in nonmetropolitan counties (Majchrowicz 1989; Majchrowicz and Alexander 1991). Further verifying the tendency toward decentralization, Kirn (1987) studied the periods from 1958 to 1967 and from 1967 to 1977, and found that producer services such as banking, finance, real estate, advertising, management consulting, membership organizations, miscellaneous services, and accounting had all become less urbanized in 1977 than they had been in 1958.[7]

European and Asian examples further confirm the tendency for services decentralization over the last two decades (Gillespie and Green 1987; Green 1987). Howells and Green, writing about Great Britain, demonstrate that location quotients for producer services decreased in London from 1971 to 1981, while the location quotient for southern rural areas increased over the same period.[8] There is also some suggestion that growth of the Third Italy provides evidence that producer services can assist in job expansions in provincial areas (Aydalot 1984; Coffey and Bailly 1990; Bailly 1986; Bailly and Maillat 1986; Planque 1982). Martinelli, on the other hand, argues that there has been only limited filtering of service employment toward the Mezzogorno, Italy's traditionally underdeveloped region (1989, 1986). Finally, Sabina Detrick's (1991) study of the electronics industry in Singapore illustrates that services accompanied the development of manufacturing within this small island country.

A reconsideration of the motivations for services expansion has involved calls for greater precision in defining the basis for service sector growth and its geographic expression. For example, Marshall and Jaeger (1990) cite the tendency toward vertical disintegration and corporate organizational decentralization as major factors facilitating the loosening of former ties between services location and hierarchical corporate organizations. The fragmentation of corporations has led managers to recognize the benefits of subcontracting out for specialized services rather than maintaining an in-house staff. Whereas there is no denial that this process has been and is still occurring, there is little theoretical argumentation or empirical evidence suggesting that the effect of disintegration will be manifested in rural areas (Miller 1987; Barkely 1978; see Pulver 1987 and Porterfield and Pulver 1991, for an important exception).

The suggestion that these new developments might lead to services' spatial decentralization would be more precise if the authors specified that the emerging service opportunities are in suburban and adjacent hinterland locations rather than remote rural locations (Drucker 1989; Drennan 1989; Kellerman 1985; Wheeler 1986). Here the use of the term "peripheral" to describe hinterlands is particularly problematic. There is little concrete evidence to define "peripheral" in the context of services decentralization. In most literature the term appears to be interchangeable with suburban, non-urban, ex-urban, deindustrialized regions, and, in isolated cases, rural areas. The lack of precision in specifying what peripheral means reduces the applicability of this discussion to the case of sparsely populated and isolated locations.

The recession of the early 1980s slowed the process of services expansion (Richter 1985). Rural economies were especially hard hit by the confluence of weakening manufacturing, mining, and agricultural sectors. An overvalued dollar and a worldwide economic slowdown hurt rural manufacturing. Agriculture suffered from low prices and high debt-to-land value ratios, and mining was depressed by falling energy prices. Employment growth in the services sector also slowed although it continued to outpace that of the goods-producing sectors.

The slowdown in rural services expansion highlights the dependence of rural services on the goods producing sectors. Over the decade of the 1980s, traditional rural sectors such as mining and agriculture declined. Industry-based demand for services consequently diminished. Service declines further reflected lost incomes paid to workers in traditional rural sectors.

Deregulation of key sectors such as transportation and telecommunications has made rural locations more isolated and therefore less profitable for business—further contributing to a decline of services in rural areas. Prior to deregulation, rural areas' access to trucking and air services was cross-subsidized by urban areas (Abler and Falk 1981). The same held true for telecommunications services for which low-traffic rural connections were cross-subsidized by high-volume interurban connections. With the end of regulation, rural communities lost important access to affordable transportation and telephone services (Parker et al. 1989, 1992). These developments further isolated rural areas from the nation's growth centers.

Overall nonmetropolitan job growth improved during the recovery that began in 1983, but did not keep pace with metropolitan job growth. Nor did rural areas recapture the dynamic expansion of the 1970s. Rural manufacturing and construction employment exhibited strong growth, but the other goods-producing sectors languished. The rural service sector grew more rapidly than the goods-producing sector, but continued to lag behind services growth in metropolitan counties (Majchrowicz 1989). For the years 1986 to 1990, manufacturing continued to grow faster in rural than urban counties.

What the Service Sector Means for Development in Rural Areas

Although the rural services sector grew rapidly during at least part of the last 20 years, the rural share of overall employment in service industries remains lower than that of metropolitan areas (Bluestone and Hession 1986; Beale and Fuguitt 1986). Furthermore, the proportion of producer, personal, and social service workers as a share of all occupational classes is lower in rural than in urban areas (Horan and Tolbert II 1984; Fuguitt, Brown, and Beale 1989).[9]

From a developmental standpoint, the composition of services growth is more problematic. Producer services and management and technical occupations are conspicuously underrepresented in nonmetropolitan areas (McGranahan et al. 1988; Kirn, Conway, and Beyers 1990).[10] Other researchers have demonstrated persuasively that advanced producer services such as advertising, banking, insurance, and computer services are particularly concentrated in the largest cities, a pattern consistent in the United States and across the developed world (Daniels 1985; Marshall, Damesick, and Wood 1987; Coffey and Polese 1987). By default, we can conclude from this research that advanced producer services are woefully under-represented in the rural regions of the same countries. Although these findings underscore the importance of services to rural economic growth, they nevertheless highlight one striking difference between rural and urban areas: urban centers are more likely than rural areas to accommodate advanced services.

The locational experience of services in rural areas points up an important distinction between the experience of urban and rural areas over the last three decades. By and large rural areas have not received producer service shares comparable to population. The majority of service sector growth has occurred in income-dependent sectors. Consequently, the development implications of services in rural areas should differ from those of the nation's cities. Or should they? To answer this question, we now examine more directly the extent that services are tradable commodities transferable among different places based on population size. This necessarily means we must also examine the development theory literature to ascertain the role of service economic development.

Export Services

The emphasis in the literature on producer services derives from the proposition that these activities can initiate export-led development (Harrington 1992). The extent to which service industries are capable of initiating economic growth is hotly debated in the current literature on U.S. international competitiveness and regional development (Cohen and Zysman 1987; Guile and Quinn 1988; Guile 1988; Reich 1991). Most scholars would now agree that selected service industries are capable of generating export revenues for a country or a region.

The most widely traded services include consulting, banking, insurance, and data processing facilities (Riddle 1986) and accounting, design and engineering, and legal services (Sauvant 1986; van Dinteren 1987). However, just what proportions of these service activities are exported is unclear (Beyers, Alvine, and Johnson 1985).

Whether services act as an export base is a matter of some controversy. According to conventional theory, service sector growth depends on growth in the basic or export sectors of the local economy, and the export sectors are assumed to include agriculture, manufacturing, and natural resource extraction (North 1955; Tiebout 1956). Based on empirical evidence, some scholars maintain that the major share of service activities remains market-oriented; thus, services are likely to respond to, but not initiate, regional and national growth (Falk and Broner 1980).[11] Another group of scholars argues that services can be an engine for regional and national growth, and the notion of a merely passive service sector is out of date. Much scholarship postulates that advanced services are increasingly exported either directly as final services or, more often, indirectly as intermediate services to national and international markets (Noyelle and Stanback 1983; Beyers and Alvine 1985). Other studies (Daniels 1985; Marshall et al. 1988; Harrington and Lombard 1989) consistently report that corporate services, especially advertising, management, and computer services, are the most commonly traded services, and they are exported more often than previously assumed. In all these cases, findings highlight the potential of service exports from major U.S. cities, but suggest little about the potential for rural economies.

There is some indirect evidence that identifies the potential for service exports from smaller cities and towns. Using quantitative measures of export behavior, scholars show that sectors such as retail demonstrate little variation in share of jobs to total population. Other sectors such as colleges and universities show large variations in employment relative to total local population (Keil and Mack 1986). Commercial research, management services, and data processing also exhibited large variations in location quotients, suggesting these services are often traded between different cities and across rural counties. In an exhaustive review of location quotient-based studies designed to identify export services, Harrington, Macpherson, and Lombard (1991) concluded that "the broad category of finance, insurance and real estate [all] exhibited high variation, along with its specific constituent sectors of insurance underwriters and trust companies. Outside this sector, advertising, R&D, and miscellaneous professional services had large variations in location quotients across regions" (p. 88). Nonetheless, due to empirical limitations it is impossible to determine whether these findings support the possibility of service exports from rural areas.

More geographically focused research in the United States also notes the tradability of services across regions. Porterfield and Pulver (1991) surveyed service firms in the upper Midwest region of the United States and found that rural service producers exported 16.7 percent of sales out of state.[12] Smith and Pulver (1981) also found that rural Wisconsin service firms export a portion of their output. In this instance, export orientation is dependent upon size and ownership of firms. Larger, nonlocally owned firms are more likely to export.[13] Smith (1984) notes that distance from metropolitan areas is an important explanation of rural export service growth. At a certain threshold distance, nonadjacent rural areas appear capable of supporting exportable services.

International evidence supports the view that services are traded across regions. Using a survey of firm sales patterns, Polese (1982) identified substantial interregional trade in services in a rural area of Quebec. Stabler (1987) and Stabler and Howe (1988) examined exports from the four western provinces of Canada and found that in 1974, service exports accounted for between 22 and 44 percent of total direct-plus-indirect exports, and by 1979, services accounted for between 38 and 53 percent of total exports from the western Canadian provinces. They conclude that there can be no doubt that service exports made a substantial contribution to the economic growth of the four western Canadian provinces during the 1970s. In a study comparing nine firm surveys, including eight from Europe, Illeris (1989) found that in general firms purchased marketing services long distance, and accounting and personnel services locally. The above results are important because they indicate that service exports can be significant in regions which contain only small or intermediate-sized metropolitan centers. These studies suggest that remote rural areas have some chance of developing an export base that includes services. The results, however, should not be overstated. Other researchers have found only a limited capacity of rural service firms to export across spatial boundaries (Kirn, Conway, and Beyers 1990).

Although this recent literature generally finds evidence of a growth-inducing role for services, the extent to which exportable services will decentralize and diversify rural economies is less clear. Such a prospect assumes that export-oriented services will follow the path of manufacturing and decentralize to rural areas in search of low wages and cheap land.[14] Anecdotes aside, there is no conclusive evidence that this is indeed happening. Decentralization is often associated with nonlocal ownership. It is not known whether producer service firms presently found in rural areas are locally or nonlocally owned. It is also the case that existing empirical research does not accurately measure the extent that services are indirectly exported. Thus, local sales to exporters, the value-added of service inputs to exported products, or, less importantly for small rural regions, the extent that exported services are immediately reimported are not captured in existing survey studies.

Interindustry Dependence

Although it is difficult to ascertain the extent that services are exported and hence capable of increasing local incomes in rural communities, there is substantial evidence of the productivity-enhancing role played by services as inputs to other industries. Thus, even if services are not exported, their presence in a local economy presumably adds to the quality and competitiveness of local business activities. The service content of manufactured goods, for example, is significant. Service occupations provide the research, development, engineering, and design essential for creating products and processes. Consulting services identify markets and production problems. Service firms are also responsible for the storage, delivery, marketing, and sales of commodities, and financial and management services broker the above transactions.[15] The productivity of the goods-producing sectors has been substantially enhanced by improvements and increasing specialization in transportation, wholesaling, financial markets, and business services experienced over recent decades (Kuznets 1977; Gillis 1987; Marshall et al. 1988).

There is also limited evidence that producer services play a strategic role in altering the organization of firms by expanding the division of labor (Hansen 1990). As labor becomes more specialized, economies to scale are achieved, and the work force becomes more productive. Manufacturing success, for example, requires feedback from the marketplace, more specialized products in tune with consumer demands, and more reliable delivery and service. When these activities are provided by specialized producer services firms instead of in-house employees spread over numerous tasks, output per worker increases.[16]

No one doubts the critical contribution of services to the productivity of the goods-producing sectors. The significant issue, from our perspective, is whether proximity between service inputs and the rural goods producing sectors is required, and if so, under what circumstances it occurs. Although few other authors address this question directly, several presuppose spatial propinquity between services and other industries. The relationship between producer services and regional productivity differences assumes tight geographical linkages between producer services and the goods-producing sectors (Hansen 1990). However, the spatial relationship between services and other income-producing activities still remains at the level of assertion. Few scholars have tested whether the patterns thought to accompany urbanization and service development spill over into rural areas.

There is considerable evidence suggesting that services remain tightly linked to urban population concentrations. Italian studies suggest that services are strongly market-oriented but will not decentralize to rural areas (Cappellin 1988). Based on survey studies, Cappellin shows that intra-industry transactions among service sector firms are more complex than among manufacturing firms. In fact, the largest market for service firms is other service firms. Estimates are that only 11 percent of the output of the service sector goes to manufacturing, compared with nearly 35 percent of service sector output that is sold to other services firms (Marshall et al. 1988, p. 47). These results suggest that services are less footloose and in many instances are tied to other service firms, not manufacturing firms. Since services are still concentrated in metropolitan areas, dispersal is unlikely. Consequently, the urban to rural shift of manufacturing may not be a precursor to the behavior of service firms.

The high concentration of manufacturing branch plants and subsidiaries in rural economies further weakens the producer services/manufacturing locational bond. Branch plants purchase few of their legal, insurance, or banking services on location (Howland and Miller 1990). The major share of services are purchased by urban-centered head offices.[17]

Other researchers reverse the causal relationship and hypothesize that a complex service sector enhances the prospects for attracting and promoting manufacturing (Goode 1990; Hansen 1990). Goode tests the hypothesis in the rural context and finds statistical support for the hypothesis that rural communities with more complex constellations of services are more likely to attract new manufacturing plants. Services may also perform a role in local economic development through the enhancement of productivity in existing export-oriented firms. A local and well-developed service sector may reduce a client's production costs and widen and deepen markets for more traditional rural exports.[18]

The era in which locally-owned producer services establishments substantially reduced the costs of business may be over. As Beyers (1991) note, telecommunications and transportation advances provide urban firms with relatively easy access to rural markets. Urban-based producer service firms are now able to reach into rural areas and provide efficient and cost competitive services.

Residentiary Services

Although research on services and economic development focuses on the relationship between income growth and service exports, the vast majority of service employment in urban and rural areas remains tied to exogenously derived income. There is a well-established history relating the level of community development to size of place. Central place theory, formulated by Christaller (1966), is the preeminent model of service location in an agrarian economy. In the context of an industrialized urban economy, central place theory is most relevant for residentiary services, particularly retailing and consumer services. Density of demand (determined by income, population, and frequency of purchase), transportation costs, and economies of scale are determinants of the settlement pattern.

The dynamics outlined in this model are still at work in the spatial pattern of retail and consumer services within selected U.S. regions. Anding et al. (1990) found that the geographic structure of trade center systems showed remarkable stability over the 1963 to 1989 period. Morrill (1982) and Stone (1987) show that during the years that population decentralized, retailing revenues followed suit. This dependence has sustained the argument that service industries cannot stimulate labor demand in rural labor markets, but rather merely follow population (Miller and Bluestone 1988; Summers, Horton, and Gringer 1990).

This argument overlooks the fact that residentiary services can play a role in economic growth when locally produced services substitute for imported services. For example, where a new medical center provides medical services not previously available in the region, local dollars flow to local factors of production—reducing the outflow of dollars (Gillis 1987).

Unfortunately, in the case of rural areas, the trend may be in the wrong direction as a larger and larger share of rural dollars are spent in metropolitan economies. Anding et al. (1990) found a disproportionate share of service growth occurring as one moves up the trade center hierarchy.[19] Other evidence suggests that the growth of corporate retailing and reduced transportation costs have contributed to slow retail and consumer service growth in the smallest rural towns (Stone 1989). Deller and Holden (1991) found that between 1978 and 1988, 38 states witnessed shifts in retail employment out of rural areas. This problem is especially significant in rural areas adjacent to larger cities.

Thus, whereas the residentiary sector has some ability to expand the local income multiplier, this growth stimulus is lacking in the smallest rural towns and those towns adjacent to metropolitan centers.

Models of Service Industry Development and Location

Up to this point we have viewed services outside the context of sectoral and global change. There is at least some suggestion in the literature that services decentralization is part of an evolutionary process of industrialization. According to this view, whereas the bulk of service employment in rural areas is primarily residentiary in nature, nonetheless, areas will eventually receive employment as it is sloughed off from urban areas.

We now turn to discussing general issues surrounding service industry growth and location. Here we attempt to understand the global context and trends of service growth, and in particular the role of nonmetropolitan regions in an integrated international economy.

Researchers examining the service sector in the context of regional development implicitly use one of four models to conceptualize the spatial realignment of services. The product cycle, spatial division of labor, neoclassical, and producer services models frame the relationship between the rural service sector and the national and international economies.

Product Cycle

Perhaps the most widely cited model of industrial evolution and spatial decentralization is the product cycle. The hypothesized decentralization of tradable services can best be understood in the context of the product cycle theory applied to manufacturing in the post-World War II period. Nilles et al. (1976) propose a four-stage locational model for the service sector which is derived from the product cycle model for manufacturing (Thompson 1965; Vernon 1966). In the first stage, employment centralizes in urban areas. Currently this is the phase for most services, especially for most information-using industries. In the second stage, decentralization will begin to occur, primarily through the outward movement of subunits such as back office functions. For example, fragmentation of this sort may affect branch banks or accounting departments that use mail and telecommunication technology to maintain contact with head offices. Further dispersion may occur in a third stage when previously central functions are shifted to peripheral sites. A fourth phase occurs when employees work at home, connected to their offices by computers and modems (Nilles 1985). During this last phase only a small core of senior personnel will concentrate at a single central location. Nilles' (1985) model closely follows the innovation diffusion model for manufacturing in which firms spin off branch plants to rural communities while headquarters stay close to the capital markets and high-skilled labor forces of urban areas. Other researchers have also speculated on a filtering down process for services similar to the pattern experienced by manufacturing (Smith 1984; Dunning and Norman 1987; Price and Blair 1989; Summers, Horton, and Gringeri 1990).

Whereas Nilles et al.'s (1976) model hypothesizes employment dispersion, another equally compelling argument is that services will not behave like manufacturing in the foreseeable future. One reason is that services are much more dependent on sophisticated telecommunications technologies than is manufacturing, and investments in this technology are spatially uneven. Rural areas lag behind cities in the investments required to link them into the information economy—a necessity for attracting service firms.

As a consequence, service employment, which is increasingly dependent on telecommunications technology, is unlikely to decentralize to nonmetropolitan areas. In fact, it should centralize. Headquarters officials making location choices for their branches and subsidiaries are deterred from locations where data transmission technologies are inferior. According to this scenario, service sector jobs will not compensate for the loss of jobs in the goods-producing sectors of peripheral regions.

Gottman (1983) makes another argument for the continued concentration of service employment. Telecommunications are not a substitute for face-to-face contacts, but are a complement or contributor to face-to-face interactions. For example, a telephone call leads to face-to-face meetings. Thus, according to this argument, the new telecommunications revolution generates face-to-face contacts and promotes concentration, not dispersal.

Telecommuting—once thought an ideal basis for rural economic development—has failed so far to have the expected dramatic impact (Miles 1988; Forester 1988; Metzger and Glinow 1988; Kraut 1989; Lohr 1989). Serious personnel, productivity, and technological problems caution those who would propose telecommuting as the future model of rural development (Kirkland 1985). For example, studies verify telecommuting workers' needs for access to head office personnel in order to secure job advancement and job security. Thus, although some facets of the global factory no-doubt exist and others are developing (Hamilton 1990), at this point the consensus is that telecommuting will not displace people's needs to congregate in one location to work, pass on information, and maintain social creativity.

Cycle theories tend to overgeneralize industry and firm behavior. Product cycle theory applied to services ignores and overgeneralizes differences in industry and firm behavior. For example, there are major and neglected distinctions between the manufacturing and service sectors. In general service firms are more likely to be small, owner-managed, and noncorporate in organizational form, compared with manufacturing firms. Moreover, unlike in the manufacturing sector, service firms are more likely to hire women, the elderly and non-union workers, and provide primarily part-time employment (Fuchs 1968; Falk and Lyson 1988).[20] Cycle theories also ignore the role of new technology which can alter the cost structure of the firm and truncate the process of spatial decentralization. Finally, such models overlook noneconomic factors that influence the spatial distribution of industry.

Spatial Division of Labor

The spatial division of labor model provides a more qualitative basis for service industry location by allocating the functions of the modern corporation according to the characteristics of the labor force. Knowledge-intensive industries tend to concentrate in metropolitan centers with more highly educated labor forces, while routine tasks are implemented in regions of the nation and the world where low-skilled, low-wage labor predominate. Again, the model for the service sector is derived from our experience in manufacturing. In its application to service industries, it is most relevant for large service companies which will largely be firms selling to markets beyond their local jurisdiction.

Neoclassical Model of Services Location

In the absence of a definitive theory of services industry development and location, scholars have focused on place-based factors associated with the cost of doing business. Most studies indicate that factors associated with services' location do not substantially deviate from those which motivate manufacturing location decisions (Nilles et al. 1976; Daniels and Lapping 1988; Gillespie and Robbins 1989; Price and Blair 1989; Howells and Green 1986). Although some authors highlight the differences which largely relate to the knowledge-intensive nature of many services (Noyelle 1987), the literature is repetitive of what we know about manufacturing. Five factors are usually cited as relevant: market size, agglomeration economies, labor costs and quality, infrastructure, and nonconventional factors such as quality of life considerations. A review of service sector location studies indicates variations in the importance of these elements.

Markets. In traditional models of service location, proximity to market is the driving force. It is important here to differentiate among type of services. Consumer, business, and nonprofit services, particularly those with an ephemeral product, complex output, and small economies to scale, are especially driven by markets in their location decision. Given the highly linked character of services—both intrasectorally and with other activities such as manufacturing—there is general agreement that proximity to markets is a major determinant of location for most services (Noyelle 1986).

Since service firms are the most important market for other services and services are concentrated in metropolitan areas, cities will continue to function as the major draw for market-oriented services (Goe 1990; Marshall et al. 1988; Cappellin 1988; Harrington 1992).

Most research identifying the importance of markets in service location is based on the workings of the private economy. Less studied is the extent to which government installations and retirement communities draw market-oriented services (Coffey and Polese 1987; Mawson 1987; Bailly, Maillat, and Coffey 1987).

Agglomeration Effects. Industrial agglomeration—the synergy arising from the clustering of industries at one location—contributes to the spatial concentration of services (Beyers, Alvine, and Johnson 1985; Coffey and Polese 1987; Dunning and Norman 1987; Hepworth, Green, and Gillespie 1987; Harrington and Lombard 1989). In contrast to views that services are likely candidates for decentralization, most researchers argue that urban and localization economies are critical to the majority of services—particularly producer services—and that decentralization is unlikely. Specific subsectors of services such as trade, banking, finance, and other knowledge-intensive services are increasingly seen as urban industries (Noyelle and Stanback 1983; Stanback 1979; O'Connor 1987). For the major share of services, there appears to be a point where increased operating costs inside metropolitan areas—rent, wages, commuting time, etc.—are offset by reductions in communications costs that occur when activities are spatially concentrated (Mawson 1987). Given the importance of specialization in the provision of producer services, Harrington notes a tendency for services firms to reflect or complement regional economic specializations.

Labor. Labor costs are the most important expense for the average service firm; thus, labor availability and cost become critical factors in the location decision. Skill requirements for workers in the service sector differ markedly from manufacturing in that for the service sector as a whole, there is greater demand for two extremes: very low-skilled workers and labor at the highest end of the education continuum. A service firm frequently requires both types, and unless the firm is large enough to separate functions and relocate back-office tasks elsewhere, location is constrained to large, diverse labor markets. Harrington (1992) suggests that labor skill specialization is the more powerful factor in determining the location of producer service firms. Whether tested with large data sets or small samples of firms, researchers find labor availability and cost to be critical to the service firm's location decision (Enderwick 1987; Coffey and Polese 1987).

Infrastructure. Tightly coupled with the importance of labor, infrastructure levels are considered influential in service firm location. Unfortunately, the discussion of this factor in the literature tends to be vague. For example, O'Connor (1987) refers to an unspecified "well-developed local services infrastructure" as an important locational asset—particularly for trade-related service activities. Enderwick (1987) and Daniels (1987) find that services are pulled toward educational facilities and academic/industrial collaboration. However, the causal relation may be reversed, with service sector growth the result of income-derived demand and institution-based need for clerical and other support services.

Telecommunications infrastructure appears particularly important. Dillman and Beck (1986) note that rural areas have antiquated and inadequate telecommunications systems—party lines and mechanical versus digital switches—which hamper their ability to support new service industries. The potential for on-site satellite links may diminish the importance of inadequacies in rural telecommunications capacity. However, these options are not feasible for any but the largest firms. For example, it currently costs a quarter of a million dollars for corporations to buy a channel on an existing satellite that would circumvent the need for publicly provided telecommunications infrastructure.

On-site telecommunications technology may dramatically alter the importance of infrastructure levels as a location factor. For example, in Bangalore, India, Texas Instruments Corporation has established a software design center linked by satellite to headquarters in Dallas. If Texas Instruments was dependent upon local infrastructure (such as telephone and roads), the operation could not exist in this location. A former resident of Bangalore noted that the city's telephone system is severely deficient, making even cross-town communication next to impossible. Given advanced technology, however, local telecommunications infrastructure is less of an impediment to business.

Transportation infrastructure is also deemed important to service firm location decisions by some researchers. High quality air transport is referenced by Dunning and Norman (1987) and Howells (1984). Others discount air transport quality in light of technological advances in IT (information technology) (Thurow and Billard 1989). The importance to all services of a "movement" network—either physical or electronic—is obvious.

Amenities. Speculation exists that nontraditional location factors, especially quality of life considerations, may influence future rural service growth (Bradshaw and Blakely 1979). The importance of amenities is well supported, especially for services requiring a highly skilled labor force. For example, Howells (1984) interviewed pharmaceutical firms in Great Britain to assess factors important in locating their research and development facilities. Aside from proximity to other organizational units, residential attractiveness, good schools, adequate services, and good cultural amenities ranked highest on the list.

For the most part, literature on the location of service firms focuses on the location decisions of private firms. However, public services also play an important, if less studied, role in service growth. A recent Government Accounting Office study (U.S. Congress Government Accounting Office 1990) found that although federal agencies are required to give first priority to rural areas, this has not been an important factor in location decision. The preference for urban locations was explained by the demands of agency missions and their need for proximity to the population they serve, political inertia, and short-term budget pressures.

An Emerging Theory of Producer Services?

Recent attempts at theorizing the spatial location of producer services identify the critical role played by markets and key personnel in the spatial distribution of producer services. Arguing that markets exert a

> distance-measured pull common in classic location analysis: the opportunity cost of serving the market and the danger of losing clients to competitors increase with distance. The importance of personnel increases with the entrepreneurial nature of the firm, the rarity of key personnel for the particular activity, and the relative immobility of professional workers. The personnel factor exerts a more absolute pull than the distance-dependent cost of market distance, in that it is critical to be within commuting range of founding or key associates. (Harrington 1992)

With these two dominating factors, service firms tend to agglomerate in places where producer service firms complement the underlying industrial specialization of a region. Thus, in rural areas producer services would be associated with the dominant industrial base such as agriculture or mining. Given transaction costs, producer services in remote locations are at a decided disadvantage. Harrington notes four solutions for firms to overcome the absence or underserved demand for producer services: (1) provide services within the firm at great inefficiency given economies of scale and scope; (2) provide services within a branch plant; (3) seek the service from a multilocational service firm; and (4) acquire the services from a local firm. Harrington's model would suggest that rural areas' producer service needs would be served in an inferior fashion unless services were either provided by the parent of a large corporation or purchased from firms located outside the region.

Much of what rural communities can hope to attract in the nature of producer services are the routinized, labor-intensive back-office operations. Rural areas compete best with urban economies on the basis of low-wage labor (Hepworth, Green, and Gillespie 1987), but the experience of manufacturing may not be repeated with services. Several critical differences exist. In contrast to low-skilled manufacturing, services require that low-wage labor be coupled with a degree of literacy and numeracy which exists in some but not all rural counties (Fuguitt, Brown, and Beale 1989). Therefore, service industries may not decentralize in the same way as manufacturing.

Moreover, advanced telecommunications make possible more far-reaching locational alternatives than was the case with manufacturing. Back-office services may decentralize to sites directly off-shore, bypassing nonmetropolitan regions entirely. The nature of many service sector products lends itself to relatively low-cost movement across space because activities can be transmitted into appropriate markets via satellite and fiber optic technology. Thus, service companies looking to locate their back-office functions may face greater opportunities for combining appropriate skill levels with low-wage labor in regions outside the United States (Howland 1993).

Recent articles in both the *Washington Post* (1989) and the *New York Times* (Lohr 1989) verify that low-skilled service production jobs are not alone in taking advantage of the spatial division of labor. A major U.S. insurance firm shifted its software division from the United States to Ireland where they hired highly skilled software engineers at two-thirds the cost of comparably trained U.S. workers. The company is taking advantage of satellite communications linking the two countries. By using advanced IT, this company reduced its labor costs while maintaining—or even improving—quality. If this indicates a trend, then the simple manufacturing spatial division of labor model may operate even more rapidly for services than for manufacturing, and service employment may bypass rural America completely.

Conclusion

Despite a decade of research, it is still difficult to precisely describe the distinguishing characteristics of a service industry. This problem is compounded by the fact that the composition of a service, even as it is identified by the SIC code system, varies across different locations. The development implications of services growth are therefore difficult to discern without close examination of actual organizations engaged in service businesses.

Although there is considerable empirical evidence concerning the function of certain types of services such as producer or business services in a local economy, there is still much to be learned about how the operations of such industries vary across space. It is also necessary to view this type of industrialization dynamically. Past justification for the existence of services in rural communities may be obviated by developments in new technologies.

Whereas much of the attention over the 1980s decade focused on exportable or producer services, it is still the case that the service sector employment base is largely tied to other sources of income generation. Thus, the magnitude of service employment in local communities is very much affected by local, national, and, increasingly, global economic events. The State of Massachusetts' economic downturn of the late 1980s is a striking illustration of the extent of services' dependence on other sources of economic growth (Browne 1992). As this example illustrates, even producer services are tied to more fundamental elements of a local economy. When the computer manufacturers close shop, the demand for software designers declines.

Models applied to service industry location behavior largely draw from manufacturing's experience. One as yet untested hypothesis is that services will "mature" and result in branch plant proliferation and decentralization. The alternative is that the majority of service jobs are tightly tied to labor markets—hence the nation's suburbs. Rural services are largely locally-owned and, in some sectors, operate with mature technologies, and therefore are unlikely to be the next propulsive industry in rural areas.

Theorizing service industry location requires recognizing the dualistic nature of the sector. Face-to-face contact remains important for the more advanced services. Labor intensivity also necessitates access to large, inexpensive, educated labor markets—hence suburbs. Given advances in technology, many service activities that might have decentralized domestically enjoy even more far-flung locational options. Assisted by new technology, transportation, and communications, labor-intensive services can find low-cost labor halfway around the world. Thus, decentralization can entirely skip a domestic stop and go international.

In the remaining chapters we attempt to provide a basis for understanding services in a rural context. Our findings explicitly try to link the experience of rural communities to larger global economic processes. As the book chapters suggest, services are not a panacea for rural communities (or urban communities for that matter); thus, the last chapter focuses on the policy implications of the growth of the service sector in an age of information technology.

3

Rural Services: A New Source of Export-Led Development or a Continuing Dependence on Traditional Sectors?

Over the last two decades the expansion of services has brought about dramatic shifts in the structure of urban economies. There is some evidence that a transformation is also occurring in rural communities. On the basis of the literature reviewed in Chapter 2, the role of services in rural areas is likely to follow one of two trajectories. One path would rely on growing interconnectivity between urban and rural areas. As technology progresses and telecommuting gains greater acceptance, barriers associated with distance would decline. Rural areas would be increasingly incorporated into a global system of information generation and transfer. As services mature, advancements in rural area connectivity would enhance opportunities for services to reside in these more remote areas. The alternative path is more pessimistic and, unfortunately, perhaps more realistic. Given needs for skilled labor and the expansion of labor-saving technologies, firms have the option of remaining in urban centers or shuttling labor-intensive activities to countries where wages are low and language barriers are minimal. Thus communities in rural America may be little more than waystations for more advanced services development.

In this chapter we examine these as well as other hypotheses about the relationship between services and rural development. We begin by exploring the extent to which rural services mirror the structure of services nationally. This analysis shows that rural service economies are far more concentrated in income-dependent sectors than are the service sector profiles of urban areas. By examining the relationship between the underlying economic base of rural areas and the composition of services, we detect even further divergence between rural and urban areas. Thus, expectations of sectoral interdependence between services and other economic base activities reported in the urban literature (and reviewed in Chapter 2) do not characterize rural communities. On the basis of this first perspective it appears that services may have only limited potential as the foundation for a new export-oriented economic base for rural areas.

We begin this chapter by briefly examining the experience of manufacturing industry in the nation and in rural communities. We are aware that scholars debate the proper and precise definitions of rural and nonmetropolitan. We side step this controversy and use the two terms interchangeably. We have adopted the census definition and defined as rural or nonmetropolitan, all counties outside of Metropolitan Statistical Areas. See Appendix 1 for a detailed description of data analyzed in subsequent chapters. It is in large part the decline of manufacturing that has caused such great concern about the viability of services as an export base for rural areas. We then proceed to observe the role of services in the nation's communities at increasingly fine levels of spatial disaggregation. We then change lenses and review the structure of services in rural communities on the basis of their underlying economic base such as agriculture, manufacturing, or mining. Using these results we are able to make some observations about the extent to which theory is correct in predicting services coupling with other types of economic activities.

Manufacturing's Experience

The decade under study was a time of great turmoil in rural areas. Basic industries faced serious competition. Exchange rate fluctuations wreaked havoc in rural America's communities that are dominated by agriculture and manufacturing. Service growth was an important offset to job loss in manufacturing. During a period of significant import penetration due to the high value of the dollar and the undervalued currency of newly industrializing countries, U.S. manufacturing industries lost almost one million jobs. Manufacturing sectors that continued to add jobs were a handful of industries including printing and publishing, non-electrical machinery, electronics, instruments, transportation equipment, and rubber and miscellaneous plastics (Table 3-1). During the study period, America remained competitive in high-tech sectors. The expansion of the transportation equipment sector reflects both the renewed growth of automobile production (in part fueled by Japanese investment in the United States) and the rise in defense spending over the 1980–1985 period. The dramatic increase in the printing and publishing industry (302,977 jobs) reflects the growth of services and the increasing importance of information technology in the national economy.

Like the nation as a whole, rural communities lost manufacturing jobs over the decade studied. By 1985, rural America had lost two percent of its 1974 manufacturing base. Although this was a serious decline, nonetheless, rural regions retained a larger share of their original manufacturing base compared with the rest of the nation.

Traditional rural sectors such as textiles, apparel, shoes, and timber were the hardest hit—losing more than 312,000 jobs over the decade (Table 3-2). This job loss was partly offset by expansion in eight manufacturing sectors such as non-electrical machinery, printing and publishing, and transportation equipment. These three sectors were responsible for 66 percent of manufacturing job gains in rural areas. Three of the eight manufacturing growth sectors can be classified as high tech. Thus, manufacturing job growth in rural areas followed national manufacturing trends. As previous research points out, more detailed industrial analysis suggests that job gains occurred in the most labor-intensive and mature sectors within high-

TABLE 3-1

National Manufacturing Change in Employment, 1974–1985
(absolute and percentage change)

Industry Name	*SIC*	*Absolute Change*	*Percentage Change*
Printing & Publishing	2700	302,977	27.22
Electric & Electronic Equipment	3600	218,863	11.73
Instruments & Related Products	3800	83,897	15.81
Non-electrical Machinery	3500	67,560	3.09
Rubber & Misc. Plastics Products	3000	66,886	9.57
Transportation Equipment	3700	45,752	2.66
Furniture & Fixtures	2500	1,400	.28
Petroleum & Coal Products	2900	−11,516	−8.05
Tobacco Manufactures	2100	−17,204	−24.73
Paper & Allied Products	2600	−28,872	−4.46
Chemical & Allied Products	2800	−33,315	−3.73
Lumber & Wood Products	2400	−53,025	−7.47
Miscellaneous Manufacturing	3900	−91,872	−19.55
Fabricated Metal Products	3400	−93,759	−5.89
Leather & Leather Products	3100	−112,438	−42.22

Food & Kindred Products	2000	−119,894	−7.78
Stone, Clay, & Glass	3200	−126,331	−18.79
Apparel & Other Textile Products	2300	−255,693	−18.52
Textile Mill Products	2200	−295,641	−30.32
Primary Metal Industries	3300	−481,694	−38.23
Total		−933,919	

Source: County Business Patterns 1974 and 1985 enhanced data, University of Washington, Seattle, Geography Department.

TABLE 3-2

Rural Manufacturing Change in Employment, 1974–1985
(absolute and percentage change)

Industry Name	*SIC*	*Absolute Change*	*Percentage Change*
Non-electrical Machinery	3500	58,791	5.39
Printing & Publishing	2700	56,418	42.50
Transportation Equipment	3700	39,707	24.78
Rubber & Misc. Plastics Products	3000	32,415	20.52
Food & Kindred Products	2000	21,928	5.56
Fabricated Metal Products	3400	18,061	7.72
Paper & Allied Products	2600	4,134	2.48
Instruments & Related Products	3800	3,091	5.48
Petroleum & Coal Products	2900	−73	−.36
Tobacco Manufactures	2100	−1,914	−23.62
Chemical & Allied Products	2800	−3,568	−2.45
Electric & Electronic Equipment	3600	−4,906	−1.63
Furniture & Fixtures	2500	−7,319	−4.68
Miscellaneous Manufacturing	3900	−16,424	−21.84
Primary Metal Industries	3300	−23,032	−13.03

Stone, Clay, & Glass	3200	−30,930	−16.95
Lumber & Wood Products	2400	−41,099	−10.12
Leather &Leather Products	3100	−43,252	−44.54
Apparel & Other Textile Products	2300	−59,818	−13.30
Textile Mill Products	2200	−80,531	−20.29
Total		−78,321	

Source: County Business Patterns 1974 and 1985 enhanced data, University of Washington, Seattle, Geography Department.

technology industries (Glasmeier 1991). In rural areas, electronics—the boom sector of the 1970–1980s decade—actually lost jobs over the 1974–1985 study period.

Job gains in services helped offset declines in manufacturing. Traditional rural manufacturing sectors continued to lose jobs, reflecting the worsening competitive position of trade-sensitive sectors. Rural services job growth, while healthy, remained below the national average. Additionally, although producer services grew rapidly, their growth was insufficient to offset rural areas' continued dependency on service sectors associated with resident population.

An Overview of Services Growth in America

As stated in the introduction, over the 1974–1985 decade, service industries were the major job generators in the nation. Between 1974 and 1985 the national economy added almost 18 million jobs (Table 3-3). The service sector increased by 45 percent and was responsible for 93 percent of the nation's job growth. Producer services grew at an impressive rate (68 percent) while accounting for approximately 37 percent of all new job growth and 40 percent of all new service job growth (Tables 3-4 and 3-5). Of the 97 sectors studied (58 of which are services), the top 27 job generators were service industries.

Like the nation, the services sector contributed the majority of new jobs in rural communities. Yet, while the rural service sector expanded at a healthy rate (41 percent), this was still at least three percentage points below the national rate. Comparing service job growth as a share of all employment change indicates that rural areas' experience was slightly below the nation's (92 vs. 93 percent of all job growth). In contrast, rural producer services growth was somewhat above the national average (70 vs. 68 percent). Despite a higher-than-average growth rate in producer services, rural counties' share of producer services in proportion to total employment and to service job growth still lagged the nation's (Table 3-6).

TABLE 3-3

Growth in National Employment, Services and Producer Services Industries, 1974–1985 (absolute and percentage change)

	Absolute Change	*Percentage Change*
All Industries	17,748,976	28
Services	16,459,161	45
Producer Services	6,222,080	68

Source: County Business Patterns 1974 and 1985 enhanced data, University of Washington, Seattle, Geography Department.

TABLE 3-4

Share of all Job Gains, Services and Producer Services for the Nation and Rural Counties, 1974–1985

	Services Share Of Job Gains	*Producer Services Share of Job Gains*
The Nation	93%	37%
Rural Counties	92%	28%

Source: County Business Patterns 1974 and 1985 enhanced data, University of Washington, Seattle, Geography Department.

The Top Ten Job-Generating Industries: A Comparison of the National and Rural Experiences

Whereas much of recent writing on services emphasizes the spectacular growth experience of producer services industries (see Chapter 2), sectors adding the lion's share of new jobs are overwhelmingly associated with the consumer or residentiary sector. Table 3-7 lists the top ten service industries and their shares of national employment growth. Of the 97 sectors studied, these ten accounted for 55 percent of total job growth

TABLE 3-5

Share of Service Job Gains in Producer Services, 1974–1985

The Nation	40%
Rural Counties	31%

Source: County Business Patterns 1974 and 1985 enhanced data, University of Washington, Seattle, Geography Department.

TABLE 3-6

Distribution of Service Employment by Types of Service, 1985

	Percentage Share of Services		*Percentage Share of Employment*	
Activity	*Metropolitan*	*Rural*	*Metropolitan*	*Rural*
Distributive	17	16	13	10
Producer	32	20	24	13
Nonprofit	19	22	14	14
Retail	26	36	19	22
Consumer	6	6	4	4
All	100	100	74	63

Source: County Business Patterns, 1985.

in the nation. Health care and eating and drinking establishments accounted for 27 percent of the total.[1] The composition of the top ten service sectors clearly reflects major demographic and institutional changes occurring in the national economy over the period studied.

The Structure of the Service Sector in Rural Counties

Although the structure of service job growth in rural counties appears to be similar to that of the nation, the share of total job change attributable to the top 10 sectors is much larger (66 vs. 53 percent) (Table 3-8). Four sectors—health services, eating and drinking establishments, food stores, and social ser-

TABLE 3-7

National Employment, Top Ten Service Industries, 1974–1985 (absolute and percentage change)

Industry Name	*SIC*	*Absolute Change*	*Percentage Change*
Health Services	8000	2,646,476	71.72
Eating and Drinking Places	5800	2,203,830	71.15
Food Stores	5400	765,782	41.86
Social Services	8300	708,627	121.72
Wholesale Trade-Durable	5000	702,840	28.54
Educational Services	8200	574,239	60.90
Miscellaneous Retail	5900	557,880	35.41
Membership Organizations	8600	546,544	54.36
Special Trade Contractors	1700	534,729	25.83
Personnel Supply Services	7360	506,188	141.10

Source: County Business Patterns 1974 and 1985 enhanced data, University of Washington, Seattle, Geography Department.

vices—account for a startling 44 percent of all rural job gains during the study period.

Deviations from the national pattern include larger rural gains in banking, unclassified employment, and electrical, gas, and sanitary services. For example, the sector Employment, not elsewhere classified (n.e.c.), often encompasses job growth in a panoply of industries, some of which are too new and unstable to classify accurately. Whereas growth of banking over the study period may reflect the twin impacts of limited branch

TABLE 3-8

Rural Employment, Top Ten Service Industries, 1974–1985 (absolute and percentage change)

Industry Name	*SIC*	*Absolute Change*	*Percentage Change*
Health Services	8000	417,461	68.00
Eating and Drinking Places	5800	372,201	70.63
Food Stores	5400	184,579	48.13
Social Services	8300	121,604	105.91
Miscellaneous Retail	5900	99,507	36.31
Employment n.e.c.	9900	97,697	66.67
Membership Organizations	8600	96,571	66.75
Banking	6000	79,432	39.50
Educational Services	8200	75,805	74.92
Electric, Gas, & Sanitary	4900	74,204	68.53

Source: County Business Patterns 1974 and 1985 enhanced data, University of Washington, Seattle, Geography Department.

banking and deregulation, more recent analysis outlined in Chapter 6 points out that these structural trends have impacts on rural communities that go beyond numbers of jobs provided.

Finally, the growth in electrical, gas, and sanitary services no-doubt reflects the maturation of rural communities that experienced population growth during the 1970s–1980s decades. The expansion of this sector is partly due to growth in private development and the creation of single purpose public service districts—a trend arising as population growth exceed capacity limits of existing community infrastructure. Rather than taking on new debt, communities created special service districts to provide a growing array of services. It may also be the case that the expansion of utilities reflects the continuing catch-up played by rural areas that remain underserved by public infrastructure.

With the exception of banking and educational services, the large national and rural services sector job gains occurred in industries tied to consumer spending and the residentiary sector. The accentuated concentration of job growth in just four sectors reflects the limited diversity of services growth in rural areas. That 26 percent of total job gains occurred in medical services reflects the fact that the elderly are the fastest growing age group in both metropolitan and nonmetropolitan areas. Between 1970 and 1980, the population aged 65 and older grew by 27 percent (Fuguitt, Brown, and Beale 1989, p. 123). From 1980 to 1990, the elderly population aged 65 and older grew by 19 percent. The elderly metropolitan and nonmetropolitan populations grew at roughly the same rate during both decades.[2] With more than 15 percent of the rural population of retirement age (55 and over), the growth of medical services probably mirrors changing demographics and the aging of rural America's population. The economically turbulent 1974–1985 decade saw rural areas lose population and jobs. The younger, more mobile, and educated members of rural communities moved in search of better opportunity.

Rural Service Specialization

A detailed review of more highly disaggregated data for six states further substantiates the claim that the structure of services in rural areas is truncated. To explore this possibility, we briefly examine the more detailed United States Enterprise and Employees Microdata file.

When the data are disaggregated to the 3-digit level of detail, it becomes clearer that rural counties specialize in relatively few service activities, and even fewer of these activities have export potential, either as an input to a basic sector or as a direct export.[3] Services overrepresented in rural counties relative to population are local-income and population-dependent

TABLE 3-9

Services with High Employment Concentrations Relative to Population in Rural Areas

Industry Name	*SIC*	*Industry Name*	*SIC*
Electric Services	491	Recreational Vehicle Parks	703
Irrigation Systems	497	Funeral Services	726
Petroleum Bulk Products and Terminus	517	Miscellaneous Repair Services	769
Hardware Stores	525	Bowling Centers	793
Mobile Home	527	Osteopathic Physicians	803
Mobile Home Dealers		Personal Nursing Care	805
Used Car Dealers	552	Elementary and Secondary Schools	821
Auto and Home Supply Stores	553	Colleges	822
Motorcycle Dealers	557	Vocational Schools	824
Household Appliance Stores	572	Job Training Services	833
Agricultural Credit Institutions	613	Social Services not elsewhere classified	839
Hotels and Motels	701		
Rooming and Boarding Houses	702		

Source: University of Maryland analysis of USEEM data, 1986.

(Table 3-9). There are, in addition, a number of services which are related to agricultural inputs, processing, and sales, including irrigation systems, agricultural credit institutions, water transport, railroad operations, and fruit stores and agricultural markets.

The type of services in which rural counties exhibit strength relative to urban counties can be characterized as activities dealing with agriculture or raw material extraction (such as agricultural credit and petroleum bulk products); the elderly (such as nursing care and funeral homes); the unemployed or underemployed population (such as vocational education and social services); and low income populations (such as mobile home sales and repair services). None of these activities falls into the category of high-growth advanced services or corporate services.

Employment in most three-digit service SIC codes is more concentrated in metropolitan counties than is population. In addition, the activities with an urban concentration are most likely to be advanced producer services (such as insurance and banking activities), high income retailing (furriers and fur shops), and entrepot activities (freight and transport functions).

Looked at from the perspective of industry representation across city size, more disaggregated data confirms the pattern of services specialization in rural areas and vividly points up the underrepresentation of producer services in the nation's smallest cities and rural areas (Table 3-10). Based on USEEM data for six states we found that services were woefully underrepresented in cities of less than 100,000 population and smaller rural towns. Only large cities above 100,000 in population enjoyed a ratio of producer service jobs to total population that would indicate they are serving more than a residentiary function. In contrast, rural towns sized 2,500 to 4,999 population have 2 percent of the nation's population, but virtually no producer services employment.

The next section presents a different perspective on services growth—percentage change in employment. Examination of employment growth trends reveals the extent that service sector job growth is accelerating relative to national trends. Tempering the significance of this measure are the twin problems associated with a measure of percentage. First, change on a vastly different sized employment base accentuates alterations in the original economic base of rural communities. Second, the measure fails to differentiate between cyclical and structural trends.

TABLE 3-10

Share of Employment by City Size, In all Six Study States, 1986

Total		*Distributive*	*Producer*	*Nonprofit*	*Retail*	*Consumer*	*Population*
above 1,000,000	MSA	0.22	0.29	0.17	0.13	0.20	0.20
500,000–999,999	MSA	0.11	0.15	0.12	0.09	0.12	0.03
250,000–499,999	MSA	0.07	0.05	0.07	0.06	0.04	0.09
100,000–249,999	MSA	0.13	0.13	0.16	0.14	0.14	0.13
50,000–99,999	MSA	0.14	0.12	0.14	0.15	0.14	0.14
25,000–49,999	MSA	0.11	0.12	0.12	0.14	0.13	0.14
10,000–24,999	MSA	0.11	0.08	0.09	0.12	0.10	0.11
5,000–9,999	MSA	0.03	0.03	0.03	0.05	0.03	0.05
2,500–4,999	MSA	0.03	0.01	0.01	0.02	0.01	0.03

25,000–49,999	Rural	0.01	0.01	0.02	0.01	0.01	0.01
10,000–24,999	Rural	0.03	0.01	0.03	0.04	0.02	0.03
5,000–9,999	Rural	0.01	0.01	0.02	0.02	0.01	0.02
2,500–4,999	Rural	0.01	0.00	0.01	0.02	0.01	0.02
Total		100.00	100.00	100.00	100.00	100.00	100.00

Metropolitan Statistical Area (MSA) are defined as a population nucleus, together with adjacent and economically integrated counties. Each MSA must include at least one city with 50,000 or more inhabitants and a total MSA population of at least 100,000.

Source: University of Maryland analysis of USEEM data, 1980 and 1986 and the County Business Patterns, 1988. The categories are based on 1983 metropolitan/nonmetropolitan definitions and population categories. However, population is the 1986 population.

Percentage Change in Services at the National Level

In the previous section we examined the structure of the service base, noting that the majority of jobs were associated with sectors providing services to the population. Over the study period, sectors that experienced the largest percentage change[4] reflected the general national transition toward services and the growth of intermediate services to business.

The ten largest service sectors growing rapidly at the national level experienced dramatic gains over the decade both in terms of absolute and percentage change. The composition of sectors in this group fall into three largely unrelated categories. The first group of sectors can be classified as a subset of producer services. The growth of these sectors constitutes the expansion of existing sectors and the development of entirely new activities catering to the needs of an increasingly global business environment. This includes the proliferation of financial services associated with the creation of new debt instruments and other financing schemes. The explosive growth of Wall Street during the 1980s reflected a new wave of financial restructuring as buy-outs (through junk bonds) and the break-up of conglomerates (many formed in the late 1970s to boost corporate profit levels largely through paper transactions) became common events.

Services growth clearly reflects the search by firms for greater flexibility in the deployment of assets, liabilities, and the commitment to employment relationships. For example, the expansion of other sectors such as equipment leasing more appropriately reflects changes in the federal tax structure (favorable tax treatment) and gains in flexibility from the use of leased versus owned capital equipment.

As noted earlier, expansion of personnel services reflects firms' goals to reduce short-term costs while maintaining long-term flexibility. Traditionally, firms have used "temps" to fill-in for sick or vacationing employees and whenever an upsurge in demand temporarily created bottlenecks in business operations. In the 1980s the use of temporary personnel became a common strategy to momentarily expand the capacity of firms while limiting long-term expansion of the work force. Firms were replacing full-time workers (and the associated costs of pensions and benefits) with uncovered temporary personnel. This strategy reduces short-term labor costs because firms do not pay benefits, and it provides longer-term flexibility in instances when a firm wishes to quickly reduce work force size in response to changes in the economy. A portion of this growth is also attributable to new skills needed to manage information technology.[5]

Whereas there is some evidence suggesting that firms in the services sectors may be reducing their expansion in the use of temporary personnel, there is growing evidence that temporary employment is being used on the factory floor. Corporate interviews with some of the nation's premier technology corporations suggest that companies are getting around the twin concerns of unions and the costs of health care and retirement benefits by subcontracting with temp agencies for new manufacturing employees. An employee may work as long as two years without full benefits or wages comparable to the shop rate. Although there is less academic reporting on this subject, nonetheless it may be an important new form of temporarization of the labor force.

At the national level two distinct sectors, social services and agricultural services, also experienced large changes in employment. The growth of social services reflects decreasing participation on the part of the federal government in social services provision and the expansion of services to provide for the needs of the nation's working population. Starting with the Nixon presidency, the federal government began shifting social service responsibilities such as community development and consumer protection programs on to state and local governments (Ginsberg and Sheftler 1990). The private sector has also absorbed some of the responsibility for social services provisions, and in some cases community-based organizations have grown to fill the gap. The growth of social services also reflects the increase in new services and the rise in demand for child care. Together these developments have contributed to the dramatic growth of social services employment.

The growth of agricultural services is attributable to many factors. It is the case that agricultural services employment is concentrated in metropolitan areas. Businesses in this relatively aggregate category include crop preparation and livestock services, but they also encompass veterinarians, farm management services, and landscape, lawn and garden, and nursery services. Growth of this sector is stimulated by both traditional rural industry growth such as agriculture and more urban services such as horticulture.

Percentage Growth of Services in Rural Areas

The composition of rapidly growing service sectors in rural areas exhibits modest similarities to national trends. The top ten percentage gainers are part of a diverse group that includes producer services such as computers and data processing, commodity brokers, management services, more general industrial services (such as industrial labs) and consumer/recreation services (such as museums) (Table 3-11).

In contrast with national trends, the ten fastest-growing sectors contributed only 4 percent to total rural services job growth, whereas the comparable group of ten industries was responsible for 17 percent of all national employment growth (Table 3-12). Fast growth rates did not translate into large real job gains. For example, rural banking added almost 75,000 jobs while increasing by 39 percent. This expansion was singularly greater than the change in the top ten fastest growing service sectors (by more than 30 percent).

Taken as a whole, rapid growth sectors (those experiencing a 100 percent change in base employment) are tied to the slow incorporation of rural areas into the information economy, and secondarily to structural changes occurring in traditional rural sectors such as agriculture and mining. Rural areas' attractiveness to an aging and more mobile, leisure-seeking population also contributed to fast-growing service sectors.

TABLE 3-11

Top Ten Service Sectors
Experiencing the Largest Percentage Job Gains
in Rural Areas, 1974–1985

Industry Name	*SIC*	*Absolute Change*	*Percentage Change*
Services, n.e.c.	8990	15,370	1,349
News Syndicates	7350	262	1,248
Computer & Data Processing	7370	11,163	271
Equipment Rental & Leasing	7394	17,333	267
Management & Public Relations	7392	18,403	252
Detective & Protection	7393	13,069	242
Security Commodity Brokers	6200	5,945	199
Commercial Testing Labs	7397	3,072	183
Museums, Botanical Gdns., & Zoos	8400	1,950	170
Research & Development Labs	7391	6,254	149

Source: County Business Patterns 1974 and 1985 enhanced data, University of Washington, Seattle, Geography Department.

A critical question in association with these findings is the extent that percentage change matters. From the evidence just reported, do rapid gains in services such as data-processing, management and public relations, accounting, and commodity brokers signify a pending transformation of rural economies to producer service centers? The results reported here suggest that this possibility is doubtful. Over the period studied, the

TABLE 3-12

Share of All Employment Change
Attributable to the Top Ten Service Sectors
Experiencing the Largest Percentage Change:
The Nation and Rural Areas, 1974–1985

The Nation	17%
Rural Counties	4%

Source: County Business Patterns 1974 and 1985 enhanced data, University of Washington, Seattle, Geography Department.

greatest job gains occurred in income-dependent sectors. Although the growth of business services no doubt portends some potential for decentralization of industrial activity, the outcome is not conclusive.

The Impact of Metropolitan Adjacency on the Structure and Growth of Services

America's rural communities are a varied lot, and their growth experience is intimately tied to their geographic location relative to urban areas. Calvin Beale's urban-rural continuum takes into account this important distinction (Butler 1990). The next section builds upon the Beale classification scheme and highlights important differences among rural areas based upon their geographic proximity to metropolitan areas. For the sake of exposition, we collapse the Beale code system into two categories: adjacent and nonadjacent rural counties.

The Geographic Connection between Urban and Rural Areas

Adjacency to a metropolitan county exerts a number of countervailing influences on rural economies. Rural counties adjacent to metropolitan areas have the highest potential for spillover effects as industry and business shift employment to rural areas, where labor and land are cheaper. Dampening this potential benefit is the possibility that rural areas' residentiary sector will be underdeveloped because residents can easily travel to a nearby city to purchase goods and services. This issue is taken up in later chapters.

Dual development possibilities also exist for rural counties that are not adjacent to metropolitan areas. On one hand, a remote location may simply be too small and isolated to support a diverse set of economic activities (many of which may require a threshold population). On the other hand, remote locations present business opportunities due to a lack of geographic competition. Firms do not have to worry about demand leakage to more prosperous communities and can charge higher than average prices for goods and services. Admittedly these distinctions are quite subtle, and they may tend to cancel each other out in the long run. To evaluate differences associated with geographic proximity, we now turn to an examination of the service structure of metropolitan-adjacent and nonadjacent rural counties.

Metropolitan-Adjacent Counties

Over the study decade, employment in metropolitan-adjacent rural counties increased by 22 percent. This is slightly below the nonmetropolitan average (23 percent). The service sector posted healthier gains with job growth of 44 percent (Table 3-13). This was slightly below the national average (45 percent), yet slightly above the average for all rural counties. In line with national services growth trends, services accounted for 93 percent of all job gains in counties adjacent to metropolitan areas. In the same counties, producer services grew more rapidly than either overall national or rural job growth rates.

The ten service sectors that gained large numbers of new jobs in adjacent rural counties complement the national experience (Table 3-14). Together these industries accounted for 68 percent of all jobs and 74 percent of all services job gains in adjacent rural counties. Like the nation, health services topped the list, adding more than 200,000 jobs. In composition, the list of sectors is quite similar to that for all rural areas. Most of

TABLE 3-13

Employment Growth in Adjacent Rural Counties, Services and Producer Services Industries, 1974–1985 (absolute and percentage change)

	Absolute Change	*Percentage Change*
Employment	1,200,401	22
Services	1,112,337	44
Producer Services	308,481	72

Source: County Business Patterns 1974 and 1985 enhanced data, University of Washington, Seattle, Geography Department.

TABLE 3-14

Top Ten Service Sectors Experiencing the Largest Absolute Job Gains in Rural Adjacent Counties, 1974–1985

Industry Name	*SIC*	*Absolute Change*	*Percentage Change*
Health Services	8000	201,867	69
Eating & Drinking Places	5800	178,471	71
Food Stores	5400	92,087	49
Social Services	8300	65,072	124
Membership Organizations	8600	50,818	72
Educational Services	8200	50,353	88
Employment n.e.c.	9900	48,262	72
Miscellaneous Retail	5900	47,211	36
Electric, Gas, & Sanitary	4900	43,405	87
Special Trade Contractors	1700	35,457	29

Source: County Business Patterns 1974 and 1985 enhanced data, University of Washington, Seattle, Geography Department.

these sectors are dependent upon consumer spending, with only educational services constituting a viable export sector.

Nonadjacent Counties

The experiences of service sector job growth in nonadjacent counties, though similar to industry-wide trends, show a number of important differences. Total job change in nonadjacent counties mirrored the experience of adjacent rural areas. In contrast, in nonadjacent counties services grew below both the national and metropolitan areas' adjacent rural averages (Table 3-15). Similarly, producer services growth was substantially below rural and adjacent county averages. Although services were a smaller share of total job change in nonadjacent counties, two sectors, health services and eating and drinking establishments, were responsible for 35 percent of all services job growth.

The array of large job-gaining service industries in nonadjacent counties varied from the experience of adjacent counties (Table 3-16). Service industries in nonadjacent rural counties gained jobs in hotels, banks, and oil and gas exploration services. These results reflect the underlying economic structure of rural economies (such as the longstanding importance of oil exploration) and highlight the growing role of tourism in rural

TABLE 3-15

Employment Growth in Nonadjacent Rural Counties, Services and Producer Services Industries, 1974–1985 (absolute and percentage change)

	Absolute Change	*Percentage Change*
Employment	1,271,129	23
Services	1,154,792	40
Producer Services	317,683	67

Source: County Business Patterns 1974 and 1985 enhanced data, University of Washington, Seattle, Geography Department.

TABLE 3-16

Top Ten Service Industries
Experiencing the Largest Employment Job Gains
in Nonadjacent Rural Counties, 1974–1985

Industry Name	*SIC*	*Absolute Change*	*Percentage Change*
Health Services	8000	215,594	67
Eating and Drinking Places	5800	193,730	70
Food Stores	5400	92,492	47
Social Services	8300	56,532	91
Miscellaneous Retail	5900	52,296	37
Employment n.e.c.	9900	49,435	62
Membership Organizations	8600	45,753	61
Hotels & Other Lodging Places	7000	45,750	44
Banking	6000	44,540	43
Non-electrical Machinery	3500	35,788	23

Source: County Business Patterns 1974 and 1985 enhanced data, University of Washington, Seattle, Geography Department.

areas. In significant contrast to rural areas generally, nonadjacent rural counties gained large numbers of new jobs in the Electrical Equipment Industry. These gains are no-doubt associated with the filtering of manufacturing from metropolitan to nonmetropolitan areas.

The composition of services in rural communities points up two important trends: a high dependence on service industries that are tied to the traditional rural economic base (agriculture, mining, and manufacturing) and the insignificant share of service job growth attributable to more advanced services—including producer services. Given the literature on services, the preceding analysis may be too aggregate to identify the development potential of services. As a way of further specifying the role of services in rural counties, the remainder of this chapter explores the relationship between the underlying economic base of rural communities and the structure of services.

Economic Diversity and the Structure of Services

Since the late 1970s, research on rural economic performance has highlighted the diverse nature of rural economies. Along with resource-extractive sectors such as agriculture, timber, and mining, since the 1950s, manufacturing, retirement, and tourism have emerged as important additional sources of rural income. Manufacturing is now a larger rural employer than farming or resource extraction. Clearly, rural America cannot be treated as a homogenous group of economies. We therefore turn to examine the extent to which the service sectors of rural economies differ by the characteristics of their economic bases. At the outset, we hypothesized variations in the range and number of services by county types. The service sector of a manufacturing-dependent county should include a range of services not found in retirement counties (and vice versa). Instead, we find a surprising amount of consistency across rural economies, independent of the counties' economic base.

The Economic Research Service Typology

In 1985 the Economic Research Service (ERS) of the U.S. Department of Agriculture developed a typology of rural economies to summarize the variety of economic experiences of rural areas. This typology[6] characterized rural economies on the basis of their underlying economic dependence in specific sectors as of 1980. The resulting typology identified seven distinct rural economic bases. Four of the seven rural county types recognized economic specializations measuring dominant sources of income attributable to specific sectors. The three others focused on unique sociodemographic and institutional characteristics of the resident rural population. The original typology was constructed using statistical procedures that allow researchers to identify groups of counties with similar income structures.[7] The classification of the seven county groups is based on the following characteristics:

1. Agriculture-dependent counties—Farming contributed a weighted annual average of 20 percent or more of total labor and proprietor income over the period 1975–1979. 702 counties were classified as agriculture-dependent.
2. Manufacturing counties—Manufacturing contributed 30 percent or more of labor and proprietor income in 1979. 678 counties were classified as manufacturing-dependent.
3. Mining dependent counties—Mining contributed more than 20 percent of labor and proprietor income in 1979. 200 counties were classified as mining-dependent.
4. Specialized government counties—Government contributed more than 25 percent of total labor and proprietor income in 1979. 315 counties were classified as specialized government counties.
5. Persistent poverty counties—Per capita family income in a county was in the lowest quartile in each of the years 1950, 1959, 1969, and 1979. 242 counties were designated as persistent poverty counties.
6. Federal lands counties—In these counties, federal lands were 33 percent or more of all land area in 1977. 247 counties were classified as federal lands counties.
7. Destination retirement counties—Between 1970 and 1980 net migration rates of people over 60 were more than 15 percent above expected levels given the resident population over 60 years old in 1980. 515 counties were designated retirement counties.

The county typology classifies all but 370 of the 2443 rural American counties. Although overlaps are evident, 57 percent of all counties belong exclusively to one group. An additional 22 percent are members of two groups, with only 6 percent in three or more groups. Ungrouped counties comprise 15 percent (370) of the total.

Revisions in the Rural Economic Base Typology

In response to changes in rural economies, the Economic Research Service of the U.S. Department of Agriculture updated the assigned categories of rural counties in 1990. Although subsequent analysis in this book uses the original 1985 classification, the reallocation of counties among categories highlights important changes in the circumstances of rural areas.[8] The twin recessions in agriculture of the early 1980s created serious problems for rural areas, and the number of agricultural counties declined significantly. Greater than 200 counties, 28 percent of the total, left the agricultural county classification. Most of these counties moved into the unclassified group, while a small number were reclassified as government-dependent counties.[9] The number of specialized government counties increased significantly from 233 to 358. Because government as a share of all rural employment declined, counties moving into this group shifted in response to a decline in other dominant sectors. Manufacturing, once considered a panacea for rural economic diversification, fell sharply during the 1979–1986 period. The number of manufacturing counties also declined from 621 to 577.[10] Former manufacturing counties moved primarily into the unclassified category, and losses were more likely to reflect declines in manufacturing than excess growth in other sectors. The mining sector also lost jobs over the study period. Most of the reclassified mining counties became unclassified, while a small share moved into the federal lands category. Shifts from the four basic groups resulted in a sharp increase in the number of unclassified counties. More than half of the new unclassified counties were formerly agricultural counties. The growth of unclassified counties resulted from either an increase in the diversity of rural counties, or more, likely, a decline in the original economic base. Implications of recent changes in the economic base of rural areas depend upon the initial interpretation of "diversity" in a rural context. Although rural areas are no longer strictly dependent upon resource extractive sectors, rural reliance on a limited number of sectors persists.[11]

In the next section we begin by describing the structure of services in the different county types. This discussion is coupled with a summary of the economic base of the seven county groups. We then proceed to analyze the structure of services in rural economies.

Services as a Share of Total Rural Employment

The dependence of rural counties on service jobs varies considerably across county type, and is associated with the economic base of individual communities. Variations in the shares of employment in services across county types highlight the nature of the rural service sector. In general, the share of service jobs to total employment is lower in rural areas compared with the nation, 63 versus 68 percent (see Table 3-17). However, the share of employment in services is as high in agricultural, government, and retirement communities as in the nation as a whole, and higher in federal lands counties than in the nation.[12]

Agricultural Counties

In 1980, agricultural counties comprised 27 percent of all rural counties but accounted for only 13 percent of total rural population. In the total of all agricultural counties, more than a third of labor and proprietor income was derived from employment in agriculture. These counties are geographically concentrated in the nation's traditional agricultural region of the Northern Great Plains, along with selected states in the Southeast and South Central regions. Agricultural counties are remote from population centers, suffered large population losses in the 1960s, experienced slow population growth in the 1970s, and then dramatic losses again in the 1980s. Income distribution was uneven, with high per capita and low family incomes. The population was older than the average of all rural counties, with a higher proportion of persons over 65 years old, and there was evidence of significant dependence on transfer income.

TABLE 3-17

Services as a Share of All Employment in Rural County Types, 1985

County Type	*Services Share*
National Average	68
Rural Average	63
Agriculture	68
Manufacturing	49
Mining	55
Government	68
Poverty	55
Federal Lands	76
Retirement	68

Source: University of Texas analysis of County Business Patterns 1974 and 1985 enhanced data, University of Washington, Seattle, Geography Department.

Almost 70 percent of all jobs in agricultural counties are in services. This is above the average for all rural areas and in line with the share of services in the national economy. Location theory suggests that high incomes, threshold population sizes, and the presence of economic activities which attract market-oriented producer services explain larger-than-average service sectors. These factors are relevant here. Incomes in agricultural counties are above average and have been relatively stable in light of overall decline in agricultural employment. Incomes remain relatively high in some cases because federal farm subsidy policies pay farmers for unplanted acreage. These subsidies compensate for lost wages, and a community can maintain reasonable levels of consumer spending—even in the face of agricultural employment decline. Moreover, as shown above, agricultural inputs are more likely than manufacturing or mining inputs to be located in rural areas. Agricultural credit institutions, irrigation systems, farm-product raw materials, and local water transportation are all inputs to agriculture which have concentrated in rural counties, stimulating income growth through import substitution. This pattern is in contrast to the service inputs to mining or manufacturing, which continued to be imported from urban areas. Off-farm income is also a major stabilizing influence in agriculture-dominated counties. Today more than 50 percent of American farms earn the majority of family income off-farm (Kennedy 1991).

Manufacturing Counties

Manufacturing-dependent counties comprise 28 percent of all rural counties and contain 39 percent of total rural population. These counties are more often contiguous to metropolitan areas. More than half of these counties are located in the Southeast, while another one-third are located in the Midwest. Few rural manufacturing counties are located in the Northeast and West, only 15 percent in all. Manufacturing counties are larger and more urbanized, experienced greater-than-average population increases in the 1960s, and average population increases in the 1970s and 1980s.

Despite the size of rural manufacturing counties, the service sector is surprisingly undeveloped compared with the national average. Less than 50 percent of all jobs are in services. There are several explanations for this pattern.

The extent to which manufacturing and services are tightly linked is a hotly debated question in the literature examining our national economic competitiveness. Does the loss in manufacturing employment at the national level also undermine the United States' strength in international competitiveness in services? Are manufacturing and services spatially linked? Do manufacturing enterprises require proximity to their service providers?

The answer appears to be no for rural manufacturing communities. Manufacturing communities exhibit the lowest ratio of services to all jobs. These results reflect a number of unique factors associated with rural manufacturing. A powerful explanation relates to the organizational structure of rural manufacturing and the presence of branch plants. Over the post-WWII period, rural communities were the recipients of branch plants of firms headquartered in America's cities. These establishments typically exhibit few local linkages and rely on the parent corporation for needed business services (Howland and Miller 1990). Another explanation is that the services firms serving the manufacturing sector require a skilled labor force, have a geographically diverse clientele, and are dependent on agglomeration economies for specialized inputs; thus, these firms operate most profitably in urban centers. In either case, it is clear that the service-manufacturing link observed for the nation does not hold in rural manufacturing-dominated counties.

Mining Counties

Mining counties accounted for only 6 percent of total rural population. These counties are concentrated in coal regions of Appalachia and the Midwest, the oil regions of the Southwest, and selected counties in Northern Great Plains states. Mining counties are remote from populated centers yet they are somewhat urbanized. Population growth was high in the 1970s, attributable to increased demand for energy resources. These same counties sustained major population losses in the 1980s, again because of their dependence on the falling international price of energy. These counties have high per capita and family incomes.

Mining counties have service sectors that are smaller than rural and national averages. Similar to manufacturing, mining also fails to draw the service firms that provide inputs to the sector. Most mining activity in the United States is now orchestrated, if not owned outright, by large mining firms. Therefore, mining service functions occur in centers of corporate headquarters. Secondly, mining is increasingly capital intensive with few small operators. This results in low population densities which may never reach the threshold size to support an extensive array of services. In addition, a significant segment of mining community populations consists of individuals who earn income locally but have families that reside in other locations. This, in addition to low average incomes, may help to explain the relatively underdeveloped service sector.

Specialized Government Counties

Thirteen percent of rural counties earn more than 25 percent of their income from government. However, government is a major contributor of income to all rural counties, with 12 percent derived from state and local government sources. Federal government income payments raise the share of total rural income attributable to government to 17 percent. The location of government counties is dispersed among the nation's regions and is based on political decisions rather than market forces. These counties derive income from a variety of government activities including military bases, Indian reservations, state capitals and county seats, parks and forest lands, penal institutions, and educational institutions. Government counties have, on average, larger population settlements and experienced population growth over the 1970–1980 and 1980–1990 periods. Income levels are below average despite rapid population growth and high relative levels of urbanization. Government counties exhibit significant levels of economic diversity, and therefore two-thirds of these counties fall into more then one group. Government counties have a large share of all jobs in services. Like the nation, almost two-thirds of all jobs in government counties are in the service sector.

The specific characteristics of the dominant income source in a county can generate demand for services. For example, state and local political centers attract service inputs necessary for the functioning of government. Legal and financial services and services associated with land claims, tax records, and business licenses are all highly market-oriented activities and concentrate around government administrative centers. Furthermore, state-serving corporations such as public utilities and telecommunications corporations often find it advantageous to locate offices near state capitals. This is particularly the case because these industries are regulated by government, thus they must often petition government for changes in service distribution. Government counties also include military bases, which in turn attract some advanced services that supply research and development for weapons and military communications. This point is underscored when we examine the reason for the location of the only two large rural computer software/systems development firms in Maryland (see Chapter 5). Both establishments were situated near the Patuxent Naval Base to develop advanced defense communications systems.

Poverty Counties

Poverty counties show a chronic incapacity of the local economy to provide a reasonable livelihood for rural residents. These 242 counties have remained below the poverty line for almost four decades. Despite higher-than-average levels of economic diversity (signified by membership in more than one county group), these counties exhibit a persistent pattern of economic stagnation. Poverty counties are geographically concentrated in the Southeast, and are secondarily scattered throughout the Southwest and Northern Great Plains states.

The population in poverty counties is sparsely settled and remote from urban centers. A large portion of poverty counties' populations are members of minority groups. Although African-Americans are disproportionately concentrated in poverty counties, the poverty rate among whites is also high, at five percentage points above the rural average.

Residents of these counties exhibit disadvantages that reduce their employability. Residents of poverty counties exhibit high levels of physical disability and low levels of basic education. Although many residents in poverty counties have jobs, work force participation is characterized by high levels of underemployment. Jobs in poverty counties also pay very low wages. Yet, despite these dismal conditions, per capita transfer payments in poverty counties are lower than the rural average. Because of very low payments from other income sources, however, the share of total income in poverty counties derived from transfer payments is the highest of all rural counties.

In poverty counties the share of jobs in services is lower than the national average. Low service levels are a result of chronic underemployment and low incomes, and despite a large share of residents over the age of 60, their spending capacity differs fundamentally from destination retirement communities' populations. Poverty counties embrace considerable manufacturing employment, but manufacturing wages in these counties are especially low, thus disposable incomes are limited.

Federal Lands Counties

Most federal lands counties are concentrated in the western United States, with scattered locations in Appalachia and the upper Midwest. These counties are distant from population centers, but residents reside in small towns rather than being geographically dispersed. Federal lands counties experienced rapid population increases over the 1970–1980 decade, and income derived from the service sector was high. These counties are the home of large farms and ranches. Federal lands counties are characterized by low population densities and relatively high family incomes. Despite high median family incomes, per capita income is low and poverty levels are high, reflecting a highly unequal income distribution.

The large service base in federal lands counties exists for reasons largely to do with the settlement pattern. Federal lands counties have the highest share of all jobs in services of rural county types (76 percent). In these counties family incomes are above the rural average, and form the basis for a more inclusive service sector. These counties also tend to be remote from population centers with land use restrictions which inhibit multiple use activities. They are often tourist destinations, thus attracting support businesses such as hotels and recreation facilities. These counties also have a small employment base. Therefore, higher proportions of services employment often reflect the absence of other economic activity.

Retirement Counties

Twenty-one percent of all nonmetropolitan counties were classified as destination retirement counties. In these counties, 15 percent or more of the population is over the age of 60.

This is three percentage points above the rural average. Retirement counties are dispersed throughout the nation with geographic concentrations in the Southwest, Florida, and the Upper Great Lakes states. Isolated concentrations of retirement counties are also found in California and Oregon. Retirement counties grew rapidly in the 1960s, 1970s, and 1980s. They tend to be remote from population centers and receive large shares of total income through transfer payments. Income levels are in line with rural averages. The labor force in retirement counties grew rapidly as younger people moved in to take service jobs created by the demands of older residents.

The share of all jobs in services is also high in retirement counties. In important respects retirement communities represent a classic service economy. Income from outside, in the form of government transfer and industry pension payments, supports the local economic base. Retired persons also have considerable disposable income, given that their families are already reared and they likely made large profits on the sale of their homes.

Thus, the resident population brings income into the community without generating jobs in other sectors. Finally, retirement counties include many tourist destinations, and tourists also generate extensive demand for such service activities as eating and drinking, hotel services, and recreation.

Comparison of Rural Services Structure across Seven County Types

Despite a long history of academic emphasis on the manufacturing, mining, and agricultural sectors, services are the major source of rural jobs. There is a high degree of similarity in the structure of services employment across all of the rural county types. At the 2-digit SIC code level, the largest employers in rural counties are services. Only in agriculture, manufacturing, and poverty counties are substantial manufacturing activities among the top ten employment activities (see Table 3-18). Moreover, the same service industries dominate each of the typology categories. Regardless of county type, the three most important 2-digit industries in the economy are health services, eating and drinking establishments, and food stores. The top three service sector rankings mirror the national pattern.[13]

The stability of the structure of employment in rural counties is striking. In Table 3-19 we list the ten sectors that gained the largest number of jobs over the decade. With a few minor exceptions, job gains mirrored the base structure of rural employment. Thus, over a decade of rapid national services growth, rural communities still continued to gain large numbers of new jobs in sectors tied to more traditional sources of income.

Producer services employment growth among different types of rural counties is evident over the decade. Employment changes in this group of industries were extremely modest. Across the seven types of counties, producer services job growth accounted for less than 10 percent of all new jobs. This fraction is substantially below the national average for producer services. Thus, although rates of change were dramatic, there is little evidence that producer services are forming a new export base for rural communities. Given the underrepresentation of these sectors at best we can assume that job additions are import substitutes for services formerly purchased from firms located in metropolitan areas.

Conclusion

To a greater extent than is the case for metropolitan economies, the rural service sector is comprised primarily of services that are dependent on local incomes and population. While it is true that some seemingly residentiary services such as eating and drinking establishments can be an export industry when tourism is a region's economic base, we find that these typically residentiary activities dominate all rural economies, not just tourism and retirement counties.

In addition, with the exception of agriculture-related services, we find little evidence that indirect export services are prominent in rural economies. Indirect exports for the agricultural sectors create rural jobs and wealth, but the basic industry showing the greatest rural growth, manufacturing, is not pulling service inputs with it.

The following three chapters focus in detail on the role of producer services in rural economic development. The preliminary analysis presented in this chapter indicates that rural communities cannot count on advanced services to supplement traditional export-based activities. Case studies suggest that the role of new technologies cuts both ways in rural America. On the one hand, rural communities have access to modern technology that connects them into the global system of information creation and dissemination. On the other hand, continuing advances in technologies facilitate both consolidation and spatial diffusion. Diffusion is no longer confined to the nation's domestic hinterlands. Indeed, firms are pursuing ever more elaborate location strategies to deliver advanced services in a timely and competitive fashion. Rural America plays only a limited role in this new round of spatial diffusion.

TABLE 3-18

Ranking of Largest Ten Industries for Rural County Types (absolute employment): The United States, 1985

Industry Name	*Agri-culture*	*Manu-facturing*	*Mining*	*Govern-ment*	*Poverty*	*Federal Lands*	*Retirement*
Health Serv.	1	1	3	2	2	3	1
Wholesale Trade	2		9	8		6	8
Eating/Drinking	3	2	4	1	4	1	2
Food Processing	4	7					
Food Stores	5	6	5	3	3	7	3
Auto Dealers	6		6	4	6	9	7
Banking	7		10				
Misc. Retail	8		8	5	10	8	6
Misc. Comp. n.e.c.	9						10
Non-elect. Mach.	10	3		6			
Textiles		4					
Apparel		5			1		
Electrical Machinery		8					
Fabricated Metals		9			7		
Lumber and Wood		10			5	5	9
Coal			1				

Oil and Gas	2		8		
General Merchandise	7	7			
Hotels				2	5
Amusement Parks				4	
Special Contractors		9		10	4
Social Services		10			
Utilities			9		

Source: University of Texas analysis of County Business Patterns 1974 and 1985 enhanced data, University of Washington, Seattle, Geography Department.

TABLE 3-19

Ranking of Top Ten Industries in Terms of Absolute Change for Rural County Types
The United States, 1985

SIC	*Agri-culture*	*Manu-facturing*	*Mining*	*Govern-ment*	*Poverty*	*Federal Lands*	*Retirement*
Health Serv.	1	1	1	2	1	3	2
Eating/Drinking	2	2	2	1	2	1	1
Food Stores	3	3	3	4	3	6	3
Banking	4		8	10			
Social Serv.	5	4		5		10	4
Not Classified	6	8	10		10		8
Membership Org.	7	5	9	8			10
Misc. Retail	8	7		6		7	6
Utilities	9		7		4		
Printing/Publishing	10	10					
Educational Serv.		6					
Trucking/Warehouse Serv.		9					
Oil/Gas Extraction			4		5		
Auxiliary Admin.			5				
Wholesaling			6				

Hotels			2	7
Real Estate			4	
Recreation			5	
Contractors		8	8	5
Research and Dev. Labs			9	
Non-electrical Machinery	3	7		9
Electrical Machinery	7			
Transportation Manuf.	9			
Fabricated Metal Prod.		6		
Paper and Allied Prod.		9		

Source: University of Texas analysis of County Business Patterns 1974 and 1985 enhanced data, University of Washington, Seattle, Geography Department.

4

Producer Services: Back Offices, Niche Markets, New Exports?

Although national data show producer services continuing to concentrate in urban America, a number of highly visible firms have moved back-office functions to remote regions. Recent examples include Citibank's check-clearing facility in upstate New York and, as we noted in the introduction, Rosenbluth Travel's data processing facility in Linton, North Dakota. Both popular and professional publications regularly report on high-tech service entrepreneurs relocating to rural communities for a high quality, peaceful lifestyle (Worthington 1991). Is it possible that the anecdotal evidence is correctly picking up a nascent national trend, a flow that fails to show up in our earlier analysis because of spatially and industrially aggregated data?

In this chapter we use the *County Business Patterns* data for the nation and the USEEM microdata covering six states to examine the extent of rural participation in the growth of producer services. Are these back-office and other export-oriented service locations in rural communities idiosyncratic events or the cutting edge of a trend in the dispersal of routine and nonroutine corporate services? To what extent is rural growth in producer services the result of branch spin-offs? Are producer service jobs replacing or complementing rural jobs in the manufacturing, mining, and agricultural sectors?

The *County Business Patterns* data allow us to examine the aggregate of services in rural areas. The microdata file yields information about whether rural employment growth is occurring in branches, subsidiaries, independents, or headquarters facilities. In Chapters 5 and 6 we refine the view even further with two in-depth case studies of producer services industries: computer services and banking.

We devote three chapters to producer services alone because this is the component of the service sector most likely to either produce output that is tradable across jurisdictional boundaries or to promote local income growth through import substitution. Industries included in the producer services category are shown in Table 4-1. This definition is drawn from J. Singlemann (1979) and has been widely used by subsequent scholars (see, for example, Noyelle and Stanback 1983; Daniels 1985).

The model that underlies a conception of services-led growth borrows from the basic Keynesian framework. Equation 1 highlights three modes of regional income growth: income (Y)

TABLE 4-1

Definition of Producer Services: Two-digit Industries Included in Producer Services Category

SIC	*Industry Name*
60	Banking
61	Credit Agencies
62	Security Agencies
63	Insurance Carriers
64	Insurance Agencies, Brokers, and Services
65	Real Estate
66	Combined Real Estate, Insurance, Etc.
67	Holding and Other Investment Offices
73	Business Services
81	Legal Services
86	Membership Organizations
83	Social Services
89	Miscellaneous Professional Services

Source: Singlemann 1979.

grows in region i when there is (1) an increase in exports (X), (2) an increase in local expenditures (E), or (3) a reduction in the proportion of expenditures on imports (M).

$$Y_i = X_i + (E_i - M_i) \tag{1}$$

According to this model, services offer two potential sources of rural growth. They may provide an export base for rural economies (by increasing X) or replace previously imported services (by reducing M). As discussed in Chapter 2, producer services are more likely to act as a basic or export industry than distributive, nonprofit, retail, or consumer services. There are exceptions, of course, and some of these anomalies are highlighted in the chapters that follow. The most widely traded complex corporate services include consulting, banking, insurance, and data processing facilities (Riddle 1986) and accounting, design and engineering, and legal services (Sauvant 1986; Harrington, Macpherson, and Lombard 1991). However, just what proportion of these and other service industries have this potential is unclear. It is often difficult to identify whether a firm, let alone an industry, is export-oriented. For example, a law firm may handle divorce for local residents (a nonbasic service) and corporate law for an out-of-town firm (a basic service).

The prospect for producer services growth outside major metropolitan areas cannot be understood without knowledge of changes in telecommunications technology. Innovations in communications technology are dramatically reducing the cost of crossing space, and many hypothesize they will facilitate the decentralization of service industries (Daniels 1985; Drucker 1989; Hepworth 1989; Kellerman 1985; Smith 1984). Optical fiber developments, two-way videos, fax machines, electronic mail, personal computers, and modem technologies are making it feasible for companies to locate branch offices and back-office functions in remote locations and for small entrepreneurs to live and work in rural areas. According to this argument, improved communications reduce agglomeration economies and liberate establishments from their tight attachment to urban markets and inputs. Observers cite Citibank's credit card handling facility in North Dakota and check-clearing operation in upstate New York as examples. Some scholars go so far as to argue that the home will become the work place, and consumers will not need to leave their homes to make purchases and carry out banking functions (Nilles 1985; Zimmerman 1986).

As we discussed in Chapter two, the models that applied to producer services location assume that services will follow the path of manufacturing, decentralizing to rural areas in search of low-cost land and labor. Whereas Nilles's model hypothesizes employment dispersion, another equally compelling argument is that services' behavior will diverge significantly from that of manufacturing. As suggested in the previous chapter, there is significant evidence to suggest that services will remain spatially concentrated in cities. One reason for this is that services are much more dependent on sophisticated telecommunications technologies than manufacturing was in the past. Investments in this technology are unevenly distributed spatially. Rural areas lag in the necessary investments to link remote areas into the information economy and to attract service firms.

The current telecommunications technology in use in many rural communities is data transmission in analog form and is unreliable and slow, resulting in higher transmission costs. Many rural communities lack digital switching equipment and fiber optic connections which enhance transmission speed and reliability (Price and Blair 1989; Parker et al. 1989; Parker et al. 1992). Installation of digital switching and fiber optic cable needed to enhance competitiveness is justified only if volume of use is high, making these investments uneconomic in many rural areas.

Uneven distribution of telecommunications services is partly attributable to deregulation and the switch to marginal cost pricing in the communications industry. Prior to deregulation, the Bell system set average nationwide rates. The cost of communications systems to rural areas and small towns was therefore cross-subsidized by more profitable high-demand metropolitan routes. Since deregulation, service providers have competed to carve out market shares in heavy traffic inter-city routes by undercutting previous monopoly rates and attracting urban customers with enhanced services. This competitive strategy of "creaming" the most profitable routes has forced AT&T to abandon geographical cross-subsidization and to respond to the competition with marginal cost pricing on the interurban routes and a greater range of services between major cities. The result is that rural and small towns face higher costs because of the higher average costs incurred in serving low population areas, and rural clients will have access to a narrower range of telecommunications options where limited demand does not justify the high fixed costs of state-of-the-art telecommunications investments (Abler and Falk 1981; Langdale 1983).

On the basis of infrastructure limitations, one hypothesis of producer services locational tendencies is that they will not decentralize in mass to nonmetropolitan areas. In fact, given technological constraints, employment in these industries should centralize. Branches and subsidiaries will be deterred from locations where data transmission technologies are inferior. According to this scenario, services will not compensate for the loss of jobs in the goods-producing sectors of peripheral regions.

The National View of Complex Corporate Activities

To set the stage for a detailed discussion of the spatial behavior of producer services within the six study states, we begin by reviewing the results of a shift-share analysis of complex corporate services. The following analysis uses *County Business Patterns* to examine the experience of all counties in accordance with their membership in the ten geographic units of the Economic Research Service urban-rural continuum.

We used shift-share analysis to disaggregate regional job growth into three parts—the change in the region relative to the change in national employment, the mix of both fast and slow growth industries in a region, and regional employment share in sectors growing rapidly at the national level. This accounting technique allowed us to decompose industrial/employment growth in a region.[1]

According to shift-share analysis of 1985 County Business data, all county types experienced growth in complex corporate services relative to total job change at the national level (Table 4-2). The growth of complex corporate services varied significantly in rural counties. The largest relative gains occurred in the most urbanized nonadjacent rural counties. In contrast, the most populated adjacent rural counties' growth rates were below the national corporate service average. While smaller adjacent rural counties experienced growth rates in excess of the national corporate service average, corporate services in smaller nonadjacent counties grew more slowly. These results suggest that the level of complex corporate services in adjacent urbanized rural counties may be influenced by proximity to urban areas. We speculate that because firms can buy services in adjacent urban areas where presumably the diversity of services available and their productivity are high, the size of the local market is diminished. In contrast, distance from an urbanized area may encourage complex corporate services growth—but only in the largest rural nonadjacent counties.

These findings clearly represent mixed results. Corporate services are growing in rural counties. Moreover, there is an obvious trade-off between adjacency and remoteness (a point we made in Chapter 3). Nonetheless, the number of jobs gained over the decade was very small. Although the rates of growth are impressive, the share of job growth attributable to producer services is dwarfed by job expansion in other sectors.

Total and Producer Service Growth by Type of County

Shifting to the six states for which we have establishment-level data, the growth experience of complex corporate services was generally consistent with the national pattern. The USEEM data show that while the service sector is showing strong growth in both metropolitan and rural areas in the aggregate, service employment is centralizing in the six states (see Table 4-3). For example, in the aggregate, producer services are growing more rapidly in metropolitan than in nonmetropolitan counties in the total of the six states, and compared with metropolitam areas, rates of growth of producer services are slower in nonadjacent than in adjacent counties.

Although rural producer service employment growth was slower than in metropolitan areas, nonetheless, it is an important source of new rural jobs. In Table 4-3 we demonstrate the strong growth in producer services in all six states. The growth rate of producer services generally exceeded that of the other four service sector groups.

The process of services centralization varies across the six states. The more rural states such as Virginia and Kansas experienced rapid growth in urban compared with rural areas. The gap between urban and rural producer services growth is also clearly seen by examining the most urbanized states of California, Maryland, Massachusetts, and New York. Whereas rates of producer services growth were more in line with urban trends, nonetheless, the rates of change still favored urban areas.

Differences between adjacent and non-adjacent rural county experiences also are evident in California, Kansas, and Massachusetts. In Massachusetts in particular, the very high growth rate is the result of employment changes occurring on a small employment base. In 1980, there were only 113 producer service employees in nonadjacent rural Massachusetts counties. By 1986, this number had increased to 206. There were 2294 producer service employees in nonadjacent rural counties in California, and 2678 employees in adjacent rural counties in Maryland in 1980.

In Table 4-5 we demonstrate that, relative to the rural share of population, producer services are underrepresented in rural areas. The extent of this underrepresentation did not change between 1980 and 1986.[2]

In nearly all rural areas, the ratio is substantially below .50. Not surprisingly, the ratio is highest for metropolitan counties in New York (which include New York City). There is a pattern of increasing ratios over time in five of the six study states, which is consistent with the centralization of producer services.

TABLE 4-2

Shift-Share Analysis of Employment Change for the Producer Services in Each Urban Rural Area between 1974 and 1985

Urban Rural Category	*Employment in 1974*	*Employment in 1985*	*Absolute Change*	*National Growth*	*Industry Mix Effect*	*Regional Shares Effect*
Core, 1 million and above	5,619,501	8,147,673	2,528,172	1,571,235	1,927,871	−970,934
Fringe, 1 million and above	1,507,022	3,135,253	1,628,231	421,369	517,011	689,851
Fringe, 250,000 to 1 million	2,269,965	3,870,498	1,600,533	634,691	778,753	187,089
Fringe, <250,000	671,105	1,169,116	498,011	187,644	230,235	80,133
Nonmetropolitan >20,000 urban adjacent	253,657	404,556	150,899	70,924	87,022	−7,046
Nonmetropolitan > 20,000 urban nonadjacent	198,564	337,981	139,417	55,519	68,121	15,777
Nonmetropolitan, <20,000 adjacent	221,585	370,052	148,467	61,956	76,019	10,492
Nonmetropolitan, <20,000 nonadjacent	270,924	439,065	168,141	75,751	92,945	−556
Completely rural, adjacent	26,158	439,065	17,746	7,314	8,974	1,458
Completely rural, nonadjacent	52,675	79,211	26,536	14,728	18,071	−6,263

Source: U.S. Department of Commerce, Bureau of the Census, *County Business Patterns*, 1985, 1974. See Appendix 1 for the definition of urban/rural code.

TABLE 4-3

Employment Growth Rates by Type of County, All Services in Six Study States
(Annual Average Percent Change)

	Metropolitan	*Rural Adjacent*	*Rural Nonadjacent*	*Rural Total*
Distributive Services	2.78	0.57	1.56	0.94
Producer Services	5.01	3.94	2.90	3.61
Nonprofit Services	3.57	2.11	3.10	2.46
Retail Services	3.51	2.20	2.49	2.30
Consumer Services	3.53	0.98	0.03	0.71

Source: University of Maryland Analysis of USEEM data, 1980 and 1986. Using the 1983 definition of metropolitan/non-metropolitan counties.

TABLE 4-4

Employment Growth Rate for Producer Services in Metropolitan and Nonmetropolitan Areas, by Type Of County, 1980–1986: Annual Average Percent Change

State	*Metropolitan*	*Rural Adjacent*	*Rural Nonadjacent*	*Rural Total*
California	5.4	1.8	9.3	2.8
Kansas	7.9	1.1	4.0	3.2
Maryland	8.6	15.6	1.4	6.6
Massachusetts	6.1	5.6	13.7	5.8
New York	5.1	4.7	.0	4.4
Virginia	9.7	6.1	1.8	4.1

TABLE 4-5

Ratio of Producer Service Employment to Population Relative to the National Ratio, 1980 and 1986

	Metropolitan		*Rural Adjacent*		*Rural Nonadjacent*	
	1980	*1986*	*1980*	*1986*	*1980*	*1986*
California	1.13	1.03	0.35	0.26	0.27	0.39
Kansas	0.88	0.95	0.32	0.27	0.39	0.38
Maryland	1.04	1.17	0.33	0.48	0.61	0.49
Massachusetts	1.21	1.28	0.56	0.53	0.42	0.51
New York	1.41	1.42	0.36	0.36	0.31	0.24
Virginia	1.07	1.21	0.22	0.22	0.35	0.30

Source: University of Maryland analysis of USEEM data, 1980 and 1986.

When the data are disaggregated by city size, there is a clear trend toward service decentralization within metropolitan counties (see Table 4-6). Employment growth is lowest in the cities of 1 million population and greatest in the smaller cities in metropolitan counties. There is also a pattern of faster growth in the larger rural towns. Total service employment and producer service employment is growing faster in the larger rural towns than in the largest cities, 1 million population and above (see Table 4-7). These results should not come as a surprise given the job and population loss experienced in the nation's major metropolitan areas over the last 20 years.

Patterns of Growth in Export-Oriented Producer Services

In light of the mixed results seen in the previous section, we now turn to a more disaggregated view of the growth experience of producer services most frequently thought to export be-

TABLE 4-6

Annual Average Employment Growth Rates by City Size in All Services in Six Study States: Annual Average Percent Change

City Size	*Metropolitan/ Rural*	*Percent Growth*
ABOVE 1,000,000	MSA	1.56
500,000–999,999	MSA	3.83
250,000–499,999	MSA	2.61
100,000–249,999	MSA	3.89
50,000–99,999	MSA	4.20
25,000–49,999	MSA	5.45
10,000–24,999	MSA	5.35
5,000–9,999	MSA	4.00
2,500–4,999	MSA	3.02
25,000 and up	RURAL	2.59
10,000–24,999	RURAL	2.89
5,000–9,999	RURAL	2.77
2,500–4,999	RURAL	1.99

Source: University of Maryland Analysis of USEEM data, 1980 to 1986. Using 1983 definition of metropolitan/non-metropolitan counties.

TABLE 4-7

Producer Service Employment Growth Rates
by City Size in All Six Study States:
Annual Average Percent Change

City Size	*CA*	*KS*	*MD*	*MA*	*NY*	*VA*	*Total*
MSA	4.65	6.45	6.92	5.17	4.41	7.72	4.98
RURAL	2.57	2.90	5.55	4.95	3.89	3.63	3.60
Metropolitan							
ABOVE 1,000,000	−1.87	—	—	—	3.31	—	2.04
500,000–999,999	4.36	—	5.78	4.94	—	—	4.76
250,000–499,999	7.02	7.28	—	—	3.71	3.97	5.62
100,000–249,999	5.78	2.16	—	4.68	5.53	6.44	5.62
50,000–99,999	6.33	6.66	3.71	4.81	3.42	13.16	5.74
25,000–49,999	8.37	6.95	8.30	6.64	9.56	−.68	8.02
10,000–24,999	8.53	2.45	3.12	6.09	5.63	12.39	7.12
5,000–9,999	8.20	10.37	6.24	10.14	6.58	1.35	6.05
2,500–4,999	14.01	8.00	5.59	.72	4.22	11.13	6.20

Rural							
25,000 and up	.00	3.23	.00	10.96	6.77	14.88	6.43
10,000–24,999	4.17	5.70	.02	5.23	4.07	3.48	4.11
5,000–9,999	4.93	7.67	13.47	5.86	5.86	4.10	5.85
2,500–4,999	4.38	4.66	3.59	4.14	3.34	3.71	3.86

Source: University of Maryland Analysis of USEEM data, 1980 to 1986. Using 1983 definition of Metropolitan/Nonmetropolitan counties.

yond local boundaries. This analysis further verifies the fact that while rural areas have benefited from marginal changes in producer services growth, still the scope of decentralization is largely confined to smaller metropolitan and more suburban locations. Four industries are repeatedly cited as export-oriented services: Advertising, mailing and reproduction, management consulting, and computer and data processing. A further examination of these industries determines the extent to which they are decentralizing (see Table 4-8). Whereas all earlier analysis focused on rates of employment change, Table 4-8 compares the 1980 and 1986 share of state employment in each region. This approach avoids the problem of large percentage changes that result from small increases (or decreases) on a small employment base. Again, we see the pattern of employment concentration in metropolitan counties and, with few exceptions, this employment has centralized very slightly over the 1980 to 1986 period. The only case in which employment appears to have decentralized to any significant extent to nonmetropolitan counties is in the mailing and reproduction services. For example, in Virginia, the share of employment in mailing and reproduction services in adjacent nonmetropolitan Virginia counties rose from 2.2 to 8 percent of state employment. According to this more refined assessment, the services most likely to be export-oriented show very little tendency to shift to rural counties. As we agreed in Chapter 3, although rural counties appear to be participating in the national shift to a service-based economy, the composition of this shift differs markedly between urban and rural areas.

What about Import Substituting Service Industries?

Clearly not all producer services are pure export-oriented activities. As we noted in the discussion in Chapter 2, many of the more sophisticated service industries produce for both local consumption and/or export. Banking, insurance, accounting, and legal services are all likely to be market-oriented activities in rural areas. Their decentralization to rural areas would most likely promote rural growth through import substitution. In Table 4-9 we report the distribution and change in distribution of these activities between 1980 and 1986. As hypothesized, all four of these activities are more decentralized than advertising, mailing and reproduction, data processing, and engineering and architecture. And yet, a cross-sectional view of these more market-oriented industries provides a static assessment of their locational tendencies. In most of the six study states these more market-oriented service activities became more concentrated in the metropolitan counties over the 1980 to 1986 period.

The service variant of the innovation diffusion model discussed in Chapter 2 suggests that rural service growth will take place as large companies site export-oriented branch establishments in rural communities. In the next section we review the accuracy of this prediction.

The share of each region's employment in independent firms, headquarters, subsidiaries, and branches is reported in Table 4-10. The percentages represent the share of each region's producer service employment in independents, headquarters, subsidiaries, and branches.[3]

Across the states, rural producer service firms are more likely to be independents than are urban producer service firms. Nearly one-half or more of rural producer service employees work in independent firms. For example, in California in 1980, 66 percent of producer service employees in adjacent rural counties work in independents, and 60 percent of employees in nonadjacent counties work in independent firms. Twenty-two percent of the work force in adjacent counties in California work in branch plants. The comparable figure in nonadjacent counties is 40 percent. Comparable proportions of rural employees work in branch plants across all of the states (except Kansas). Kansas has a particularly low dependence on rural branch plant employment and a high reliance on employment in single plant operations.

A story consistent with these and earlier findings is that producer services are moving down the urban hierarchy. From an early concentration in the largest metropolitan areas of the

TABLE 4-8

Decentralization of Export-Oriented Services, Share of State Employment by Region (percent)

	Computer and Advertising [731]			*Engineering/ Mailing/Reproduction [733]*			*Data Processing [737]*			*Architecture [891]*		
	Metro	*Rural Adj*	*Rural Nonad*	*Metro*	*Rural Adj*	*Rural Nonad*	*Metro*	*Rural Adj*	*Rural Nonad*	*Metro*	*Rural Adj*	*Rural Nonad*
California												
1980	99.6	.3	.1	99.4	.5	.1	99.8	.1	.1	98.6	1.2	.2
1986	99.6	.3	.1	99.4	.5	.1	99.8	.2	0	98.9	1.0	.2
Kansas												
1980	82.8	4.5	12.8	81.4	11.7	7.0	90.5	2.8	6.7	67.5	3.3	29.2
1986	84.0	1.3	14.7	87.0	4.2	8.8	93.5	2.7	3.9	73.3	3.0	23.2
Maryland												
1980	98.2	.2	1.6	97.3	2.0	.7	97.8	2.1	.2	96.4	2.2	1.4
1986	98.0	.4	1.7	97.4	2.1	.6	97.7	2.1	.2	95.3	3.8	1.0
Massachusetts												
1980	98.1	1.9	0	99.0	1.0	0	99.4	.6	0	99.4	1.0	0
1986	98.5	1.5	0	99.2	.8	0	99.4	.6	0	98.2	1.8	0

New York												
1980	99.2	.8	0	99.5	.5	0	94.8	5.2	0	98.0	1.9	.1
1986	99.3	.7	0	99.2	.8	0	98.8	1.2	0	98.3	1.7	0
Virginia												
1980	96.8	1.4	1.8	96.2	2.2	1.6	96.0	3.4	.6	93.7	4.1	2.3
1986	98.0	.8	1.2	90.4	8.5	1.1	95.2	2.3	2.5	96.4	2.3	1.3

Source: University of Maryland Analysis of USEEM data, 1980 and 1986. Using the 1983 definition of metropolitan/non-metropolitan counties.

TABLE 4-9

The Spatial Distribution Employment of More Market-Oriented Producer Services

	Banking 60			*Insurance 63*			*Accounting 8931*			*Legal 81*		
	Metro	*Rural Adj*	*Rural Nonadj*	*Metro*	*Rural Adj*	*Rural Nonadj*	*Metro*	*Rural Adj*	*Rural Nonadj*	*Metro*	*Rural Adj*	*Rural Nonadj*
California												
1980	96.2	3.4	.4	99.5	.5	.0	99.1	.7	.2	99.4	.6	.1
1986	97.2	2.5	.3	99.5	.4	.1	99.8	1.0	.2	99.2	.7	.1
Kansas												
1980	44.6	17.5	37.9	77.5	2.9	19.6	60.6	18.9	20.6	71.7	12.9	15.4
1986	52.3	15.1	32.6	72.3	3.4	24.2	69.7	9.9	20.4	84.6	5.6	9.8
Maryland												
1980	98.4	.3	1.2	98.7	.1	1.2	97.8	1.1	1.1	97.8	.6	1.6
1986	92.8	4.0	3.3	99.3	.1	.6	96.6	1.3	2.1	97.7	.7	1.7
Massachusetts												
1980	97.0	2.9	.1	99.9	.1	.0	98.5	1.5	.6	98.9	1.1	.0
1986	97.6	2.3	.1	98.9	1.1	.0	99.5	.5	.0	99.0	1.0	.0

New York												
1980	93.6	6.0	.3	99.5	.5	.0	97.9	1.5	.6	98.8	1.15	.1
1986	94.7	5.1	.1	99.1	.9	.0	98.2	1.2	.6	99.1	.8	.1
Virginia												
1980	81.0	9.5	9.5	98.5	.9	.7	90.7	3.6	5.7	93.7	2.9	3.4
1986	82.7	10.5	6.9	98.4	.7	.9	88.5	8.5	2.9	94.6	2.5	2.9

Source: University of Maryland analysis of USEEM data, 1980 and 1986. Using the 1983 definition of metropolitan/nonmetropolitan.

United States, branches move first to the urban fringe of the largest cities. In a second phase, services decentralize to second- and third-order urban centers throughout the country and to rural areas surrounding the first-order cities. The hinterlands of the medium-size urban centers such as Kansas City are bypassed altogether, and the producer services which evolve are locally owned independent enterprises. Verifying this pattern, in California and New York there is evidence of a relatively high proportion of rural producer service employment in branch plants. In New York, 29 percent of adjacent and 39 percent of nonadjacent counties' producer services employment is in branch plants, as compared to only 16 percent of MSA employment in branch plants. This suggests some branch plant dependence in both of the states with the largest cities. In Maryland, Massachusetts, and Virginia, the shares are roughly even across regions, and in Kansas there is a much smaller share of rural producer service employment in branch plants than is the case for MSAs.

Between 1980 and 1986, changes in rural dependence on corporate branch plant employment varied across six states. For example, in 1980 New York had 39 percent of its nonadjacent counties' corporate service employment in branch plants. In 1986, the percentage was still 39 percent. In both Virginia and Maryland there was an increase in employment in branch plants in adjacent rural counties. This finding, along with earlier evidence of decentralization of producer export services, suggests that the innovation-diffusion model for services could apply to metropolitan-adjacent rural counties of Maryland and Virginia.

In Table 4-10 we report the levels and relative increases in the categories of rural employment in branch plants, but do not provide rates of employment growth or decline. For example, employment in independents may be created at the same rate as employment in branch plants. In Table 4-11 we exclude this possibility by showing employment growth in producer services by type of firm, including branches and subsidiaries or independents and headquarters. It is clear from Table 4-10 that independents dominate the independent headquarters category, and branches dominate the branches/subsidiary category.[4]

In Table 4-11 we indicate that independents are major contributors to rural producer services growth. In California, Massachusetts, Kansas, and New York the growth rate of independents is greater than branch plants. In Maryland and Virginia a higher proportion of growth is due to the growth of branches and subsidiaries.[5]

Banking is a major contributor to the employment base of the producer services sector. Because of deregulation in the banking industry and the rapid growth of branch banking in rural counties, changes in the sector may therefore dominate the branch/subsidiary categories and overshadow the role of independents as the major share of growth in rural producer services. Whereas banking may include back-office, export- oriented functions, the major share of this activity is most likely to be market-oriented functions, serving local businesses and final consumers. Establishments in banking (SIC codes 60, 61, and 62) were eliminated from the producer services category to determine the sources of rural service growth in the remaining business services. The results in Table 4-12 show that without banking, independents/headquarters increase their importance as a contributor to rural producer service growth. For example, without banking, independents and headquarters created 69 percent of the rural employment between 1980 and 1986, while branches and subsidiaries were responsible for only 31 percent of the growth. In New York, independents/headquarters accounted for 73 percent of job growth and in Virginia, independents/ headquarters accounted for 65 percent of rural corporate services growth. The sources of banking growth are reported in Table 4-13 for the states with establishment populations of 250 or above.

As hypothesized, branch banking is growing in rural areas at the expense of locally owned banks. The reasons, advantages, and disadvantages of the growth of rural branch banking is a topic we explore in detail in Chapter 6.

Conclusion

Three conclusions and one hypothesized explanation can be drawn from the previous two chapters. First, although ser-

TABLE 4-10

Share of Each Region's Producer Service Employment in Independent, Headquarters, Subsidiary, and Branch Establishments (percent), 1980 and 1986

Industry Category	*Independent*			*Headquarters*			*Subsidiary*			*Branch*			*Total*		
	MSA	*Rural Adj.*	*Rural Non-adj.*	*MSA*	*Rural Adj.*	*Rural Non-adj.*	*MSA*	*Rural Adj.*	*Rural Non-adj.*	*MSA*	*Rural Adj.*	*Rural Non-adj.*	*MSA*	*Rural Adj.*	*Rural Non-adj.*
California															
1980	55	66	60	29	11	0	2	2	0	13	22	40	100	100	100
1986	54	64	72	24	11	3	6	20	0	16	6	24	100	100	100
Kansas															
1980	50	66	59	22	19	26	6	8	6	23	8	10	100	100	100
1986	43	63	54	18	22	18	12	8	18	27	8	10	100	100	100
Maryland															
1980	42	48	49	18	16	14	10	1	2	30	36	35	100	100	100
1986	38	41	54	18	10	19	12	5	3	32	44	25	100	100	100
Massachusetts															
1980	34	62	64	25	10	32	13	4	0	28	24	4	100	100	100
1986	37	62	71	28	17	21	13	4	0	23	17	8	100	100	100

New York															
1980	40	51	53	30	20	9	14	1	0	16	29	39	100	100	100
1986	37	47	48	25	20	13	18	4	1	21	30	39	100	100	100
Virginia															
1980	43	48	47	21	20	15	10	5	6	26	27	32	100	100	100
1986	36	48	56	18	12	12	14	4	3	32	36	28	100	100	100

Source: University of Maryland analysis of USEEM data 1986. Using the 1988 definition of metropolitan/non-metropolitan counties.

TABLE 4-11

Sources of Employment Growth, Branches and Subsidiaries versus Independents and Headquarters, Rural Producer Services Annual Average Percent Change, 1980–1986

	CA	*KA*	*MD*	*MA*	*NY*	*VA*
Branches and Subsidiaries	1.0	1.2	3.9	2.0	1.5	1.8
Independents and Headquarters	2.4	1.8	2.9	3.1	1.8	1.6
State Total	3.4	3.0	6.8	5.1	3.3	3.4

Source: University of Maryland analysis of USEEM data, 1980 and 1986.

TABLE 4-12

Sources of Employment Growth, Branches and Subsidiaries versus Independents and Headquarters, Rural Producer Services Minus Banking Services, Annual Average Percent Change, 1980–1986

	CA	*KA*	*MD*	*MA*	*NY*	*VA*
Branches and Subsidiaries	.7	1.8	4.4	2.2	.8	1.5
Independents and Headquarters	2.8	4.1	2.8	3.6	2.2	2.8
State Total	3.5	5.9	7.2	5.8	3.0	4.3

Source: University of Maryland Analysis of USEEM data, 1980 and 1986.

vices and producer services are growing relatively rapidly in rural economies, this growth continues to lag behind that of metropolitan counties. Whereas there is evidence that services (in total, and producer services, in particular) are decentralizing, this movement out of the largest metropolitan areas is primarily limited to the urban fringe and smaller urban centers. Services and producer services are growing relatively rapidly in

TABLE 4-13

Sources of Employment Growth, Branches and Subsidiaries versus Independents and Headquarters, Banking Services, Annual Average Percent Change, 1980–1986

	CA	*KA*	*MA*	*NY*	*VA*
Branches and Subsidiaries	1.9	.6	2.1	5.1	1.3
Independents and Headquarters	1.2	−1.6	0.0	−.3	−.3
State Total	3.1	−1.0	2.1	4.8	1.0

Source: University of Maryland Analysis of USEEM data, 1980 and 1986.

rural economies, yet this growth continues to lag behind that of metropolitan counties.

Second, although previous research provides convincing evidence that some services are tradable across regions and nations, there is little support for the hypothesis that export-oriented services are decentralizing to rural areas. Rural counties contain a small proportion of producer services relative to their shares of population, and, with few exceptions, their employment-to-population ratio relative to the nation declined or remained constant between 1980 and 1986.

Third, there is very limited evidence that branch plants are major contributors to producer services growth in rural areas. The major share of rural corporate services employment is in independent firms, and for most of our case study states, the rural share of corporate service employment in branch plants has remained stable over the 1980 to 1986 time period.

There is also evidence of slower, but respectable producer service growth in the largest cities in rural communities. Therefore, the standard innovation-diffusion model in which headquarters spin off branch plants to distant locations does not accurately capture rural services growth trends. For the most part, independents, not branch plants, are responsible for this rural growth.

5

Rural Computer Services in an International Economy

In the previous chapter we reviewed the aggregate evidence surrounding the growth of producer services in rural areas. We concluded that whereas some decentralization is occurring, expectations about widespread diffusion of producer services through the formation of branch plants has been limited. These results run counter to more anecdotal evidence about producer service industries' tendencies to decentralize. Therefore, in Chapters 5 and 6 we look specifically at two industries: computer services and banking. We selected these industries for two reasons. In the case of computer services, the industry is considered geographically footloose with a highly divisible labor process; rural areas are therefore thought to be attractive to labor-intensive data processing key-entry activities. The banking services industry is a mainstay employer in rural communities. Yet, deregulation, both geographically and by product, has caused considerable consolidation. In the next chapter we will examine how this as well as the introduction of labor-saving telecommunications-intensive technology is altering banking service provision and job levels in rural areas.

Computer Services: The Expectation

The popular press, along with a number of researchers, highlights computer services' potential as a source for rural development. These reports have emphasized the potential for job creation by entrepreneurial software programmers seeking the rural lifestyle (Drucker 1989; Worthington 1991). But is this popular image supported by evidence?

No. Despite the much-touted decentralization of skilled software jobs, few rural firms in the computer services industry fall into this advanced services category. The large rural computer service industry employers are data entry firms. Although the data entry business is not a major employer in rural America, it is a big player in a number of rural communities. Firms in this industry select rural locations for their low-wage, hard-working labor force. Rural data entry operators currently enjoy a market niche for quick turnaround (i.e., less than one week) data entry from handwritten documents. Will rural firms be able to hold onto this niche? Is this an activity other rural areas can duplicate? What government strategies might improve the competitiveness of these rural establishments vis à vis foreign competition? These questions are addressed in this chapter and later in the conclusions.

In the first section, we review the distribution of the computer services industry in rural economies. In the second section we examine the importance of computer software development and programming services to rural development. In the third and final portion, we evaluate the long-run viability for rural data entry and processing. This analysis is based on USEEM data for 1980 and 1986 for six study states, California, Kansas, Maryland, Massachusetts, New York, and Virginia;[1] telephone interviews; and on-site interviews.

Overview of Rural Computer Services

Until 1986, computer services (SIC 737) was divided into two distinct 4-digit industries: computer software development and programming (SIC 7372) and data preparation and processing (SIC 7374). Computer services not elsewhere classified (7379) was a third category, and it included a heterogeneous mix of business lines.[2]

Computer services are highly concentrated in urban centers, more concentrated than is population (see Figures 5-1,

5-2, 5-3, and 5-4). Programming activities (SIC 7372) are more concentrated than data preparation and processing services (SIC 7374). This result is not surprising since programming activities are more likely to be market-oriented and require higher-skilled labor. As implied in the figures and outlined in Table 5-1, the absolute number as well as the proportion of computer services establishments in adjacent and nonadjacent rural counties is small. Despite newspaper reports celebrating the decentralization of computer firms, these results show that decentralization is not a major trend.

Although SIC 7372 is dominated by independent establishments, rural businesses are more likely to be independently owned than are urban establishments (see Table 5-2). Yet, there are exceptions. For example, rural and urban areas in Maryland have nearly equal shares of independent establishments.

Whereas establishments in this industry are small, rural firms tend to be smaller than the state-wide average (see Table 5-3). Again, there are exceptions in the study states. In particular, rural establishments in Maryland and Virginia, two states with large rural data entry operations, are larger. Differences in size of establishment in these two states may be explained by their geographic proximity with the nation's largest military-industrial complex.

Computer Programming in Rural Economies

To understand underlying trends in the location of computer programming firms, and in particular any nascent tendencies to decentralize, we undertook a telephone survey of 28 rural establishments in SIC 7372. Although the number of phone interviews is small, this sample captures 50 percent of all rural computer programming firms in existence in 1986 and 1991 in the six study states. The establishments were identified from the USEEM data, which provided information on line of business, exact address, and telephone number.

Recall from Table 5-1 that the total population of rural computer programming businesses in the six study states was

FIGURE 5-1

EMPLOYMENT SHARE BY LOCATION
COMPUTER PROGRAMMING

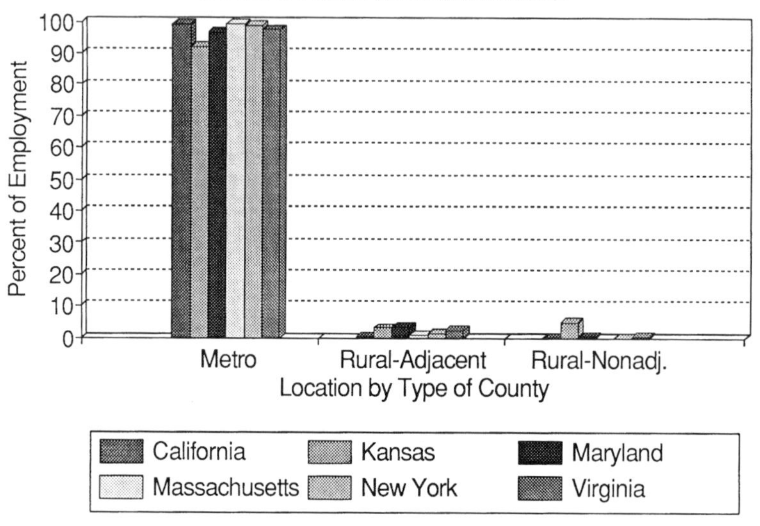

FIGURE 5-2

EMPLOYMENT SHARE BY LOCATION, 1986
DATA PROCESSING AND ENTRY

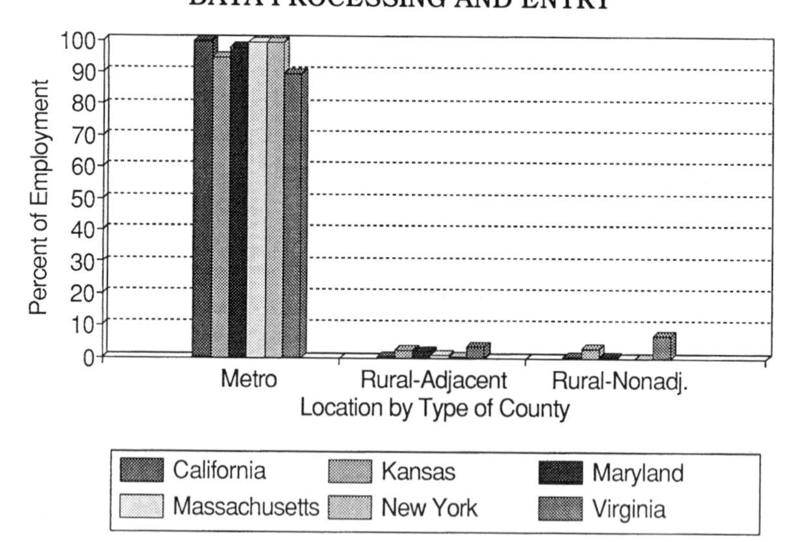

FIGURE 5-3

EMPLOYMENT SHARE BY LOCATION, 1986
FIRMS NOT ELSEWHERE CLASSIFIED

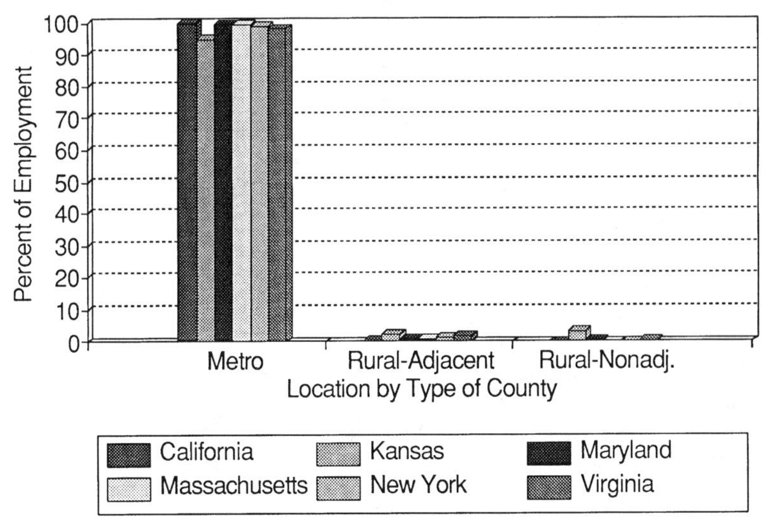

FIGURE 5-4

POPULATION SHARE BY LOCATION, 1986
METROPOLITAN/NONMETROPOLITAN

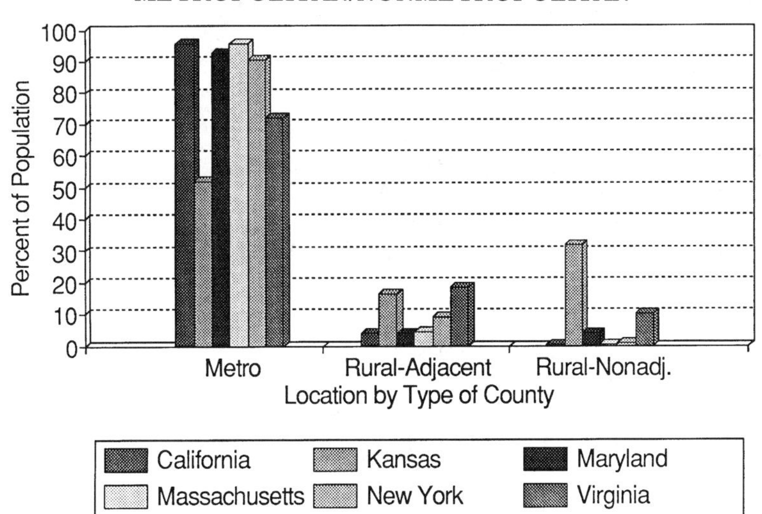

TABLE 5-1

Total Number of Establishments and Employment in Rural Counties, Computer Services, SIC 737, 1986

	California		*Kansas*		*Maryland*		*Massachusetts*		*New York*		*Virginia*	
	Est	*Emp*	*Est*	*Emp*	*Est*	*Emp*	*Est*	*Emp*	*Est*	*Emp*	*Est*	*Emp*
Programming	3	165	18	198	9	326	14	110	34	221	29	483
Entry/Processing	8	38	15	106	3	263	5	57	13	87	8	447
Not Classified	13	46	9	20	8	35	5	26	23	569	16	88

Source: University of Maryland analysis of USEEM Data, 1986.

TABLE 5-2

Percent of Independently Owned Establishments , Comparison of Rural and All Establishments, Computer Services, SIC 737, 1986

	California		*Kansas*		*Maryland*		*Massachusetts*		*New York*		*Virginia*	
	All	*Rural*	*All*	*Rural*	*All*	*Rural*	*All*	*Rural*	*All*	*Rural*	*All*	*Rural*
Programming	78.1	77.4	77.8	75.6	66.7	67.1	85.7	73.6	94.1	82.8	82.8	60.7
Entry/Processing	87.5	61.9	80.0	61.4	33.3	56.5	80.0	54.2	76.9	77.3	87.5	59.5
Not Classified	100.0	80.9	100.0	81.0	75.0	72.8	100.0	81.0	95.7	77.8	81.3	68.1

Source: University of Maryland analysis of USEEM data, 1986.

TABLE 5-3

Mean Establishment Size in Rural Counties and All Counties, Computer Services, SIC 737, 1986

	California		*Kansas*		*Maryland*		*Massachusetts*		*New York*		*Virginia*	
	All	*Rural*	*All*	*Rural*	*All*	*Rural*	*All*	*Rural*	*All*	*Rural*	*All*	*Rural*
Programming	16.4	5.2	21.2	11.0	23.7	36.2	21.2	7.8	6.5	14.9	35.5	16.7
Entry/Processing	37.1	4.8	28.6	7.1	73.1	87.7	38.9	11.4	49.0	6.7	46.2	55.9
Not Classified	14.1	3.5	7.6	2.2	15.7	4.4	20.5	5.2	24.7	24.7	13.4	5.5

Source: University of Maryland analysis of USEEM Data, 1986.

only 107 in 1986, thus we achieved a coverage rate of approximately 25 percent. The sample is biased toward survivor firms, those in existence in 1986 and still operating in early 1991. The dissolution rate for these operations is high, with more than 50 percent of the contacted establishments out of business by 1991. The profile then is of successful rural computer software businesses.

The interview questions centered on the reasons for the choice of business location, advantages and disadvantages of a rural site, and the location of markets. The underlying theoretical framework was that (1) computer services are export-oriented services that can provide an independent source of income growth for rural communities, and (2) improvements in telecommunications technologies, desire for the rural lifestyle, and growth in military spending (which benefits rural communities and stimulates market demand for computer software), would all accelerate the decentralization of computer programming services.

Our interviews indicate that the activities of these firms include the writing of software programs for sale to manufacturers, government, utilities, and banks. A number of the establishments subcontract to larger firms such as IBM and Data General. For example, one rural firm acts as a subcontractor providing computer graphics for other software developers. Client-rural firm interactions are taken care of by telephone, facsimile, or a single meeting. With one exception, the tasks are high-skilled. The one low-skilled operation involves the copying and packaging of software programs developed in the firm's Atlanta headquarters.

The results, presented in Figures 5-5 through 5-9, indicate the importance of noneconomic factors. The majority (nearly 75 percent) of the entrepreneurs selected a rural area because it was their hometown or because the area offered a high quality of life. Proximity to a university and to a targeted market were other draws for software development and programming firms. The markets referenced were, in all three cases, military bases.

FIGURE 5-5

REASON FOR SELECTING LOCATION
25% SAMPLE OF 1986 ESTABLISHMENTS

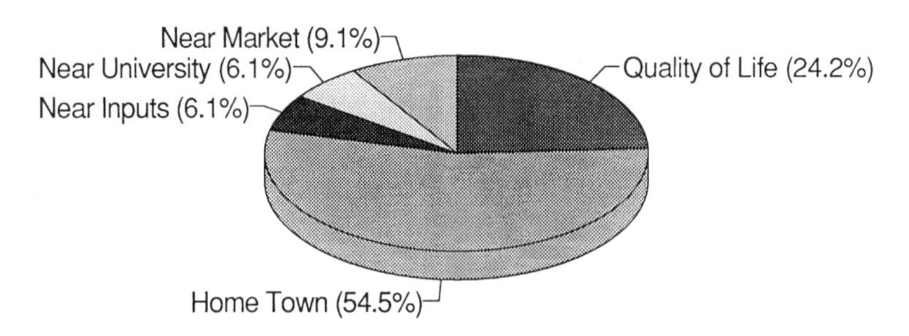

Source: University of Maryland telephone interviews.

FIGURE 5-6

ADVANTAGE OF LOCATION
25% SAMPLE OF 1986 ESTABLISHMENTS

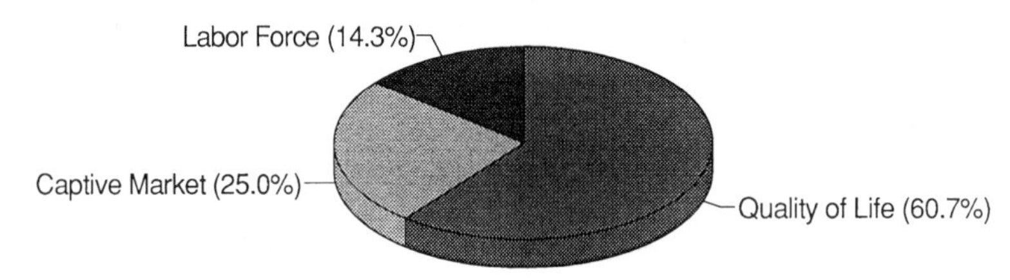

Source: University of Maryland telephone interviews.

FIGURE 5-7

DISADVANTAGES OF RURAL LOCATION
25% SAMPLE OF 1986 ESTABLISHMENTS

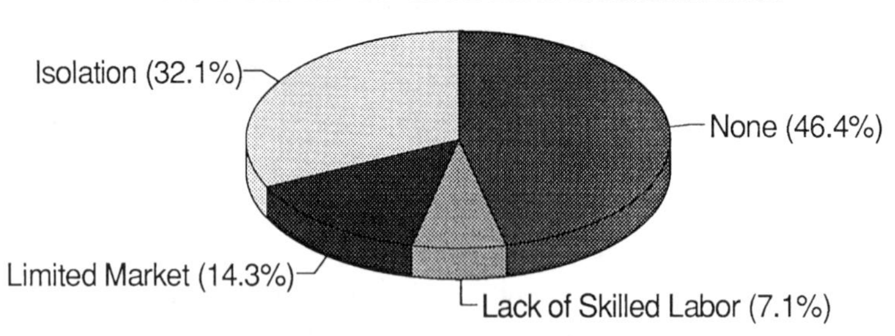

Source: University of Maryland telephone interviews.

FIGURE 5-8

LOCATION OF MARKETS
25% SAMPLE OF 1986 ESTABLISHMENTS

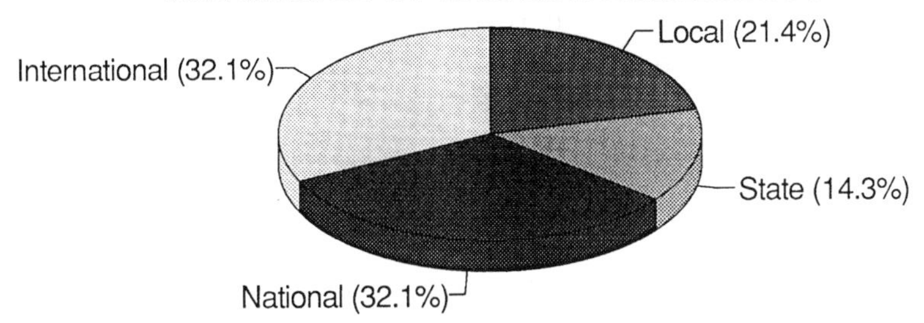

Source: University of Maryland telephone interviews.

FIGURE 5-9

DO YOU HAVE PLANS TO RELOCATE?
25% SAMPLE OF 1986 ESTABLISHMENTS

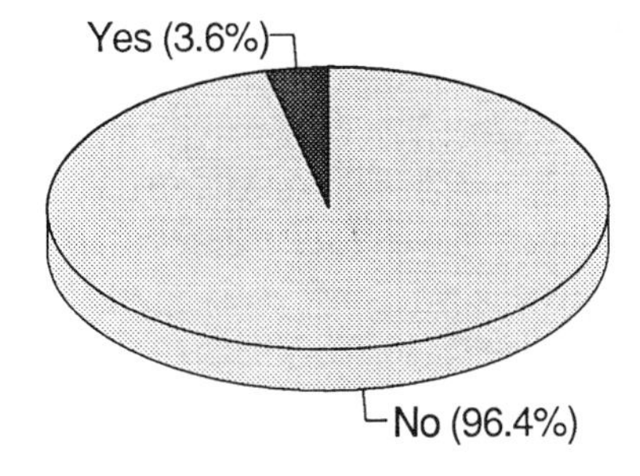

Source: University of Maryland telephone interviews.

The survey supports the popular view that quality of life issues are important for those few computer programming firms that chose rural locations. Nearly 61 percent of the respondents stated an improved quality of life was the single most important advantage of their location. Several respondents, one as far away as California, reported moving from New York City seeking a cleaner and quieter atmosphere. One quarter of the respondents drew some business from local markets, and a few felt that a captive local market or lack of competition was the single most important locational advantage of rural areas. Firms noting a captive market were either serving the military or local businesses. For example, one entrepreneur developed his business by helping local firms implement and adapt specialized accounting and inventory software. Yet, with these exceptions aside, the majority of firms are export-oriented (75 percent).

Although 46 percent of the firms interviewed reported no disadvantages associated with their location, 32 percent described isolation from both industry innovations and airports as handicaps. Only 7 percent cited lack of skilled labor, a commonly assumed shortcoming of rural locations. The lack of importance of access to skilled labor can be explained by the fact that the firms are small and hire few additional technical workers. Eleven of the twenty-eight establishments had four or fewer employees. The largest establishment (20 employees) of the group was not a software developer. Rather, it was a low skilled operation that assembled and packaged existing software for retail sales.

Although we expected export-oriented firms to be more likely to note disadvantages related to a rural location, this was not the case. Nearly the same percentage (46 percent) of export-oriented as local market-oriented firms claimed there were no disadvantages associated with a remote location.

These results offer little encouragement to rural counties already experiencing large employment losses, particularly agriculture, mining, and poverty counties. The counties most likely to attract high-technology services are those hosting a military base or university, or those possessing natural amenities and high quality of life. Counties in this latter category are generally the least economically distressed because these areas already attract tourists and retirees.

Rural development and telecommunications scholars (Parker et al. 1992) debate the extent to which telecommunications is a facilitator of rural job growth. Our interviews indicate that telecommunications technology is not capable of leading growth, but when a rural site is desirable for other reasons—a hometown connection or the draw of a high quality of life—the availability of advanced communications technologies makes a distant site feasible.

Data Entry and Processing in Rural Economies

Firms in the data entry and processing industry are large rural employers and provide an important source of employment in a number of remote rural counties. In fact, with 1800 workers, rural-based Appalachian Computer Services (ACS) is the largest American employer of data entry workers. Industry location decisions are, for the most part, motivated by the calculus of economic rationality, and at present rural firms have a solid market niche in quick turnaround jobs, especially those requiring key-in from handwritten documents.

Despite current market strength, the long-run prospects for rural data entry jobs are in question. Within the decade, technological change will facilitate the off-shore transmission of documents to be entered into machine-readable form, and telecommunications investments by a number of low-wage countries will speed up the return of completed jobs. Both of these changes will reduce the competitive advantage of rural U.S. firms. Furthermore, rural data entry firms tend to be undiversified and situated in remote locations for one reason: a low-wage, hard-working labor force. As the industry continues to reduce its labor input through the adoption of scanning technology, the rural advantage will deteriorate.

Analysis of this industry is based on on-site and telephone interviews with heads of rural, urban, and suburban data entry and processing firms, off-shore data processing facilities in Barbados and Europe, producers of telecommunications, optical scanning and imaging equipment, and secondary source material.[3]

We had a number of rationales for selecting both the places in which to conduct interviews and the organizations we ultimately selected for in-depth discussion. Barbados was selected as one off-shore case study site because of its successful and active government program to attract data entry operations. As of December 1989, the Barbados Industrial Development Corporation had subsidized ten foreign data entry firms employing a total of 1,200 workers. Saztec, in Ardrossan, Scotland, was the site of a second off-shore interview. We selected this facility for evaluation because, like rural American firms, it is located in a peripheral area of a developed country. Finally, we interviewed producers of telecommunications, optical scanning, and imaging equipment to understand the current and near future state-of-the-art technologies relevant to this industry.

Rural Data Entry and Processing Firms: The National Context

Differences between the activities of rural and urban establishments in this industry highlight the role rural economies play in the national economy (see Lipietz 1982; Scott 1988; and Henderson 1990 for detailed discussions of contemporary industry location). Urban firms in this industry provide nonroutine, knowledge-intensive services. Although most of these high-level computer services are labor-intensive, the need for both face-to-face contact with clients and a highly trained labor force necessitate an urban location. Firms within this industry are moving toward vertical specialization, or the offering of new and more specialized services that require intensive company-client interaction. The creation of new markets and the development of more sophisticated products act as the glue bonding service firms to urban centers.

In contrast, rural firms tend to conduct low-end functions—labor-intensive but low-skilled data entry. We did not observe substantial skill shortages in rural areas nor did firms indicate that they had plans for making substantial skill investments in remote areas. Instead we found substantial evidence suggesting that America's rural communities are in direct wage cost competition with the labor forces of developing countries. There is almost no evidence that this industry will be a major source for jobs in rural America in the coming decade.

Rural establishments dominate the data entry business in the United States. Where an urban establishment employs data entry workers, this activity is supplementary to other lines of business or is declining over time as a portion of the operation. Due to the labor-intensive nature of data entry and higher urban than rural labor costs, urban establishments are simply not competitive in the data entry business. Urban firms with data entry operations complain about the difficulty of retaining workers. Data entry work is tedious and stressful, requiring long hours at a video display terminal, and the urban labor force has other employment options. Rural firms noted a lack of competition from urban data operations.

Saztec is a multinational data entry firm with an urban presence in Dayton, Ohio and Kansas City, Missouri. The company has additional facilities in Manila, Philippines and Ardrossan, Scotland. The Dayton facility employs five data entry workers for jobs too small to send overseas. The Kansas City facility employs 180 workers to do complex keying tasks requiring close contact with clients to check specifications or questionable data. This facility also handles tasks requiring 24-hour turnaround. However, the major share of Saztec's data entry work goes off-shore (Hamilton 1990).

Urban firms in the industry are more likely to earn the major share of their revenues from data processing or computer-related software development. Although firms performing software development would usually be classified under SIC 7372, the interviewed firms reported that data processing was their main line of business or they had started as time-sharing or data entry/processing establishments and had only recently branched into programming.

Acknowledging the limited number of functions performed by rural firms is critical to understanding the current and future role of rural economies in relation to the computer services industry. Whereas rural establishments tend to be almost solely dependent on data entry activities, urban establishments generally operate several lines of business. For example, Automated Business Systems (ABS), a small suburban firm in Maryland, started as a data entry business but now earns the largest proportion of its revenues from a contract to maintain computers in a local school system. Automated Data Processing (ADP) is the second largest data processing company in the United States, with $1.4 billion in sales in 1987. ADP's traditional line of business is payroll and tax processing, however, ADP is moving away from processing payrolls into the provision of more specialized services such as tax consulting combined with payroll processing. Other firms in this industry such as Computer Services Corporation (CSC) and General Electric (GE) began as computer time-sharing companies. With the introduction of personal computers in the early 1980s, time-sharing companies diversified to offer other specialized software and computer systems development services. Trade journals confirm that these patterns are typical across the industry. Data processing firms are moving toward vertical specialization and are offering new, and often more specialized services to existing clients (Fersko-Weiss 1987; Unites States Congress 1987).

As telecommunications technologies improve, data processing, at first glance, may appear to be an industry ready to disperse. Our results indicate this is not the case. Trends toward more specialized services, increasing skills requirements, and diversification are anchoring these firms to urban areas even more than in the past. Specialized services require close proximity to customers and a highly trained labor force. Both factors imply a continued and increasingly strong attachment to urban areas. ADP provides a good example of a business that could conceivably move some of its operations to rural areas, but probably will not. An ADP client delivers payroll time sheets by courier to the ADP plant or information is sent over telephone lines into the ADP computers. ADP processes the information and prints employee paychecks, which are then delivered by courier to both large and small customers. Therefore, proximity to markets is still crucial. The equipment for printing checks is still too expensive for individual employers to purchase. However, as the price of this technology drops, the printing could eventually be done at the customer's site, further reducing the need for spatial proximity between the data processing firm and its customers. Although reduction in price for check-printing technologies would free ADP from its tight attachment to the urban market, other industry changes counteract this tendency.

Recent changes suggest that firms like ADP will not decentralize, even as the cost of on-site printers drops. Because ADP is moving away from simple data processing and toward developing solutions to specific client needs, proximity to clients is becoming increasingly important. Moreover, since data processing is not a labor-intensive, low-skilled operation, the company is not disadvantaged by its urban location. Secondary sources also confirm an industry-wide movement away from routine services toward more specialized jobs, and thus a greater need to be located in urban areas. For example, in February 1990, Nippon Telephone and Telegraph Corporation announced plans to open its first overseas data center in Jersey City, New Jersey. "Locating in Jersey City makes excellent business sense," said Mr. Tamura, General Manager, noting that it gives the company "unbeatable access to the largest potential clients" (Armbruster 1990).

In short, these urban firms tend to be highly client-oriented, and clients are concentrated in urban markets. As a reason for an urban location, client orientation was ranked above access to a skilled labor force. In fact, for large contracts computer service companies will open new branches and pay to move highly skilled employees in order to be near a prominent customer. As the industry moves toward more specialized software solutions, it is likely to be more rather than less anchored in urban areas.

How Do Data Entry Firms Operate in Rural Areas?

Although there is variation across firms, for the most part information to be translated into machine-readable form is delivered in hard copy by the U.S. Mail, Federal Express, or courier. Each of the firms runs its own courier service from surrounding metropolitan areas and airports. The mostly female labor force manually keys in and verifies data at computer work stations. The completed jobs are then returned to the client on tape or disk or by telephone line. ACS transmits 99 percent of final product via phone lines. The smaller companies are more likely to ship tapes. Some examples of work carried out by these firms include the keying in of publisher mailing lists, doctors' patient records, appliance warrantee information, medical claim forms, credit card receipts, data bases, and book manuscripts.

Rural data entry firms are located in remote locations; ACS is a two-hour drive out of Lexington, Kentucky; TDEC is situated in Oakland, Maryland, approximately three and one-half hours outside of Washington, D.C.; Highland Data is in Blue Grass, Virginia, approximately two and one-half hours outside of Roanoke in the Allegheny Mountains.

Moreover, these are not small operations. ACS is the largest domestic data entry firm in the United States, and all of the above firms employ more than 50 workers in each of their rural facilities. In all instances, sites were selected for their labor force characteristics, low wages, and labor availability. Remote sites offer not only a hard-working, low-cost labor force, but also distance from manufacturing. Proximity to manufacturing, which is higher paying but cyclically sensitive, can lead to high quit rates during upswings in the business cycle.

Two examples illustrate the process by which a rural location is chosen. Highland Data was started by a woman whose husband worked in the data processing industry, and who, through this connection, assessed demand for data entry services. She was familiar with Blue Grass, Virginia as a vacation spot. The recent closure of a nearby sewing factory suggested an available labor force, and the closure of a public school provided a potential facility.

Appalachian Computer Services began providing data management and processing for a local county's tax bills. After years of struggle and an insufficient market for data management and processing services, the company backed into the area for which there was the greatest demand and for which the company was particularly competitive: data entry.

None of these companies was started by individuals seeking a rural lifestyle. In fact, most owners do not live in the rural communities where their facilities are located. Managers and industry observers claim demand for data entry services is strong, and all of these firms have recently expanded and/or are currently considering expansions.

Although wage rate differences between rural and suburban areas are important, the key draw to a rural location is the reliability of the work force. Labor quality (not simply low wage levels) is a major reason firms are attracted to rural locations. Data entry jobs rarely have long-running contracts. Rather, each job is fixed in length and must be done correctly and on time or clients will go elsewhere for their next job. This means that labor force reliability is key. According to one manager, "We don't get a second chance to do the job right."

In Virginia, hourly wages for low-skilled workers are the same in rural and urban areas. Rural workers are considered more dependable. Reinforcing the importance of a captive and reliable work force, one manager argued that unions pose a threat primarily because of the increased potential for walkouts and strikes. Higher wages accompanying unionization were considered secondary concerns.

Most data entry jobs begin at minimum wage. For example, until April 1991, when the minimum wage was increased to $4.25 per hour, salaries began at the minimum wage of $3.80 an hour in Kentucky and Virginia. Over time, management anticipates adjusting to higher wage bills by replacing labor with technology or by shifting more of the work off-shore.

Wage rates are further determined by worker productivity, measured by keyboard stroke speed and accuracy. For example, in one firm the average wage is $5.80 an hour, with a few workers earning as high as $16.00 an hour. Fringe benefits include paid holidays, vacations, and health insurance. Many employees work part time with the part-time/full-time ratio varying by firm. Part-time work serves both the needs of the firm and, in some cases, the needs of the employee. Since contracts are generally short term, but require rapid turnaround, labor demand is variable. Hiring part-time workers gives the firm flexibility in meeting fluctuations in contracts. Although many workers prefer full-time work, others claim part-time work better meshes with the demands of a family. Shift work is not uncommon, since night work permits faster turnaround. A job can be delivered in the evening and be returned to the client the next day.

Managers mentioned a number of disadvantages to a rural location. An initially surprising disadvantage mentioned by all firms was the difficulty in acquiring additional labor after startup. All firm managers indicated that the rural labor pool was rapidly tapped; expansions had to be satisfied through the opening of branch operations in nearby towns. Three of the four companies opened one or more branches to meet additional demand. A fourth company operated a sister establishment offshore.

Another disadvantage mentioned frequently is distance from clients. Sales and marketing functions require ongoing face-to-face contact with current and potential clients. Two of the four companies have dealt with this problem by having sales offices in metropolitan areas. However, even in these cases managers mentioned the difficulty of bringing a prospective client to the site to see the facility. For a third, the smallest firm, a sales representative makes frequent calls on firms located in the metropolitan area.

Distance from other professionals in the field also was mentioned as a disadvantage. Keeping up with the competition, changes in technology, and changes in the market are more problematic when contact with others in the industry is limited to once-a-year professional meetings. Remoteness is more serious than some managers may recognize. A number of managers were unaware of new technologies pertinent to the data entry and transmission business.

The absence of broad band telecommunications technology was *not* considered a major disadvantage by the interviewed rural firms. Although rural data entry firms shipped the major share of their data on tape or disk, all but one transmitted some information by telephone lines back to clients. Traditional telephone service with copper wiring is the norm in these communities. The largest rural company was an exception, with one dedicated fiber optic link-up from its rural headquarters. These findings contradict claims that fiber optic cables and digital switching are a necessity for rural participation in the new information economy. Enhanced telecommunications infrastructure, made possible by digital switching and fiber optic cable, permit the faster and clearer transmission of voice, video, and data information, and although these advances are most likely critical to the future competitiveness of rural computer services firms, they are not key to the current day-to-day operations. We discuss this issue in more detail below.

The Future of Data Entry Work in Rural Areas

Rural areas' existing competitive advantage lies in the data entry business. However, the outsourcing of data entry functions, optical scanning, point of transaction data entry, and offshore data entry all point to impending massive change for the industry. Although there are countervailing trends, such as increased outsourcing of data entry functions, technological change poses potential threats to the competitiveness of rural data entry operations.

Industry-wide trends suggest that outsourcing of data entry is becoming increasingly common as data users are faced with cost-cutting pressures resulting from increased foreign competition and the current economic downturn. According to one manager, a client recently began outsourcing to reduce costs associated with fringe benefits paid to in-house data entry workers. The company offered a generous benefits package to the high-skilled work force in order to attract them to the firm. These same generous benefits filtered down to low-wage and low-skilled data entry workers. In a move to cut costs, the company found it cheaper to eliminate its in-house data entry work force and outsource to a rural data entry company. One bank reports savings of $1 million per year in computer-related costs since outsourcing its data processing tasks (Fersko-Weiss 1987). A slowing economy is expected to accelerate the developing trend toward outsourcing of both data entry and data processing facilities. This trend is partly responsible for the current strong market for and decentralization of rural data entry services.

The development of optical scanning leads to a firm's side-stepping manual data entry entirely. Innovation in barcoding technology has eliminated the need for vast numbers of manual data entry workers. Nonetheless, there are still an immense number of tasks that do not lend themselves to barcode scanning.

Optical Character Recognition (OCR) technologies permit the mechanical translation of documents into machine-readable form. However, in its current configuration the technology has limitations. First, scanning documents that contain font changes results in error rates above 10 percent. At one rural firm, the claim was made that a document could be keyed in and verified faster and cheaper than the document could be mechanically scanned, edited, and corrected. Although this company had purchased costly scanning equipment, the machinery sat idle.

Second, scanning technologies are limited in their ability to read handwritten entries. Machines with Intelligent Character Recognition (ICR) are designed to read handwritten documents, but error rates currently run about 50 percent. This error rate is too high to make ICR use economically feasible. Experts suggest that, barring an unforeseen technological breakthrough, accurate machine-scanning of handwrittendocuments is still years away.

Third, scanning technology is expensive and in many cases must be designed specifically to read the document being entered. Because most data entry jobs are short-term contracts, rarely does one job justify the cost of a specially designed scanner. According to the estimates of Haley Collings,

Account Representative for Xerox Imaging Systems, commercial scanning equipment costs in excess of $25,000 for both hardware and software. One of the firms interviewed, however, does use scanning technology. This company has a long-running contract with a number of banks to translate credit card receipts into machine-readable form. The scanner reads customers' credit card numbers, but the amount of purchase and date, which are handwritten, are keypunched manually. For the foreseeable future, as long as optical character recognition technologies are limited to typeset documents (even then, not all typed documents), there will continue to be a market niche for manual data entry.

Another threat to manual data entry jobs is "point of transaction" data entry. Increasingly, information is entered into machine-readable form at the point of transaction, displacing the demand for specialized key entry workers. For example, merchants are moving toward credit card transactions for which information is entered into the computer at the point of sale.[4] Insurance underwriters not only write and sell policies, they enter information directly into the computer, eliminating data entry worker positions (Baran 1985). Doctors are submitting medical insurance claims on computer disks, and many courts have switched to recording legal cases directly into computer-decipherable form. These changes reduce demand for manual key entry. At the same time, demand for computer-readable data is growing as information flow between industries intensifies and computers are applied to new situations and in new problem solutions. Industry observers have yet to quantify the net impact of these two contradictory trends. Nonetheless, in the long run, the need for data entry workers will most likely decline.

The most immediate danger to rural data entry firms is offshore data entry. This threat captured national attention when American Airlines closed its data processing facility in Tulsa, Oklahoma in 1984 and moved 500 jobs to Barbados. Barbados, Jamaica, Ireland, the Philippines, Taiwan, Sri Lanka, and China are now all attracting data entry jobs from the United States. Between 1982 and 1987, Jamaica attracted approximately 3,000 data entry jobs (Kuzela 1987). Saztec has a labor force of 750 in the Philippines. Between 1980 and 1985,. 40 companies in the United States, Japan, and England sent their data entry work overseas. Barbados has attracted 11 data entry operations in the last decade.

Rural Data Entry in the International Market

A primary attraction of off-shore data entry is labor availability and low wages. The Office of Technology Assessment estimates that off-shore wages range from one-fourth to one-fifth of U.S. wages, with the lowest wages found in Asia (Ludlum 1986). This ratio holds true when comparing foreign wages with rural U.S. labor as well. Barbadian data entry operators, for example, earn an average of $2.55 an hour, compared to a current minimum of $4.25 in rural areas of the United States. In the case of American Airlines, approximately 900 pounds of used airline tickets are delivered daily by air to Caribbean Data Services, an American Airlines subsidiary in Barbados. Employees sort tickets and enter information into computer terminals. American Airlines estimates that, with all costs included, salaries are about $6.00 an hour less in Barbados than in the United States. The company estimates a $3.5 million savings per year due to the move (Beers 1985).

Another equally important advantage of off-shore operations over rural American locations is the availability of labor. Barbados, as well as other Third World countries, offers large pools of unemployed and underemployed labor. Therefore, a single plant is not constrained from achieving technological economies of scale. One American firm operating in Barbados claimed it opened a branch in this Caribbean country not only for the lower cost of labor but for the larger qualified labor pool. The company operates in several rural communities in the United States. In recent years, however, attempts to expand in the rural locations have resulted in the tapping of a poorly educated, less reliable labor pool. Even allowing for the wider commuting sheds of rural workers, managers of data entry facilities in rural areas of the United States find that the labor pool is exhausted relatively quickly. Expansions then require new facilities in new towns, with all of the inherent expenses of duplicating infrastructure.

All off-shore managers of U.S.-headquartered firms in Barbados concurred that foreign workers are as reliable and accurate as the best rural workers in the United States. Although competitors in the data entry industry are not limited to English-speaking countries, major players remain in the English-speaking Caribbean, with Barbados and Jamaica attracting the greatest numbers of jobs. In addition to the language advantage, the people of Barbados and Jamaica have high literacy rates. The illiteracy rate in Barbados is only .7 percent, lower than that of the United States.[5] The illiteracy rate in Jamaica is 3.9 percent (Pelzman and Schoepfle 1988). All of the off-shore firms interviewed reiterated their satisfaction with the skills and work ethic of the local labor force. Although English-speaking countries have an advantage, China also provides data entry services. For example, Pier 1 Imports uses Chinese labor to input catalogue lists.

Lack of minimum wage laws and less stringent worker safety restrictions are additional attractions for firms moving overseas. More lenient environmental regulations are not as much an issue for the "cleaner" service industries as they are for manufacturing. Health benefits are socialized, further reducing costs to business.

Whereas labor costs in Third World countries are substantially lower than rural wages in the United States, at this point rural data entry firms still hold a competitive market niche. The turnaround time for off-shore jobs is longer, usually about one week. Although estimates on the turnaround time from foreign data entry sites vary, most off-shore data entry falls into what is called "retrospective work," work that can wait for two weeks (Myers 1986). The quickest turnaround possible from Asia is five days. The quickest turnaround currently possible from the Caribbean is 48 hours. When necessary, some rural U.S. sites can return data in 12 hours.

Fortunately for rural firms, the market for quick turnaround jobs is currently robust and growing. For example, Mead Data Central is a major user of data entry work in the creation of their Nexis/Lexis on-line legal data base. Mead Data Central now requires quicker job turnaround than in the past. When they had a monopoly in the legal database business, delays in putting court decisions on-line were not a problem, and much of their work went to the Philippines. Competition from other providers has forced Mead Data to have legal decisions on-line within 24 hours. Consequently, data entry jobs are no longer sent off-shore. For faster turnaround, rural domestic firms are more competitive. In a second example of the strength of domestic relative to foreign production, one rural-headquartered company, Appalachian Computer Services, recently closed its Jamaica branch because it lacked sufficient work volume permitting longer than a 24-hour turnaround time.

A second market niche for rural firms in the more developed countries combines some intellectual processing and knowledge of Western cultures combined with data entry. For example, a job cataloguing the music library for the British Broadcasting Company was allocated to the Philippines. Results were unsatisfactory because workers were unable to distinguish between song titles and composers or performers. The Ardrossan, Scotland branch of Saztec justifies its higher salaries by combining indexing and bibliographic reference tasks with data entry. The fact remains, however, that although the present market for domestic manual data entry is strong, the best predictions are that in the 1990s, off-shore data entry firms pose a serious threat to rural U.S. operations.

Foreign Competition in the 1990s

In the long run, innovations in imaging technology and massive investments in state-of-the-art telecommunications technologies threaten rural America's currently secure data capture market niches. Whereas small rural firms primarily rely on Federal Express, couriers, and the U.S. Mail service to deliver data, some smaller firms also use telephone lines. Using current copper cable lines, data transmission is slow and relatively costly. And, while these communication linkages are not considered insurmountable barriers to developing new markets for expansion, as more sophisticated linkages become common, these rural firms will suffer a technological disadvantage.

At present, the cost of installing points of presence[6] are beyond the budget of all but the very largest private firms. Unfortunately, at the same time that rural areas in the United States are lagging in telecommunications investments, foreign governments—particularly in Barbados and Jamaica—are undertaking massive investments in telecommunications technologies in an aggressive attempt to attract U.S. data entry firms and orders.

Over the next decades, companies operating abroad will be increasingly competitive in the data entry business for jobs requiring shorter turnaround time. The speed with which off-shore data entry dominates the market depends on improvements in imaging equipment. When data can be imaged by satellite or telephone line across long distances, off-shore sites will offer as quick a turnaround as rural areas in the United States.

Imaging technologies differ from Optical Character Recognition scanners in that the former produces a photo image which can then be transmitted by cable or satellite over long distances. The text is not in computer-decipherable form. Facsimile machines are the most common example. Imaging technologies allow data entry workers in remote sites to read material directly from a computer screen or hard copy and enter it manually into machine-readable form. At present, the delays and costs of transferring hard copy information to overseas data entry sites curb the off-shore movement of data entry work. Imaging technology that enables the quick, accurate, and inexpensive transmission of pictures will shrink delays to the hours required to send an image, keypunch the data, and return the data on-line. High-speed imaging would also dramatically reduce document transport costs.

Rapid transfer of documents through telecommunication channels will eliminate the "quick turnaround" advantage of rural firms and displace jobs in rural America. At present, imaging technology is expensive and slow, and most data entry firms still transfer hard copy. However, several firms are experimenting with the on-line transmission of images. One alternative currently being tested by two U.S. firms is to transfer document images to computer tape in the United States and ship the tape abroad, thereby saving the mailing or document transit costs. The same two firms are also retooling domestic sites to become centers for collecting documents and imaging them to tape or over dedicated high-speed lines to branch operations in the Caribbean. The keyed-in documents are then returned directly to the client. If this technique spreads,then routine rural data entry operations would become noncompetitive. Smaller rural data entry firms which could not afford to buy the technology or to establish a Caribbean facility would be put out of business.

At present, high-speed imaging technology is too costly for any but the largest data entry firms. One firm manager estimates that the cost of purchasing document imaging, sending, and receiving equipment for a Caribbean-U.S. link-up is $85,000. However, industry researchers believe that imaging equipment will follow the path of all other computer technologies: enhanced speed and quality accompanied by falling prices. Projections are that within the decade, high-speed document imaging will be feasible on a large scale. Once this occurs, the market niche for rural firms—quick turnaround—will disappear.

A number of Caribbean countries are making massive investments in telecommunications technologies in order to attract the more routine U.S. services, such as data entry and telemarketing. In 1988, a joint venture between AT&T, Cable and Wireless PLC of the United Kingdom, and Telecommunications of Jamaica invested $8 million to install image transmitters and satellite transmission at Montego Bay, Jamaica (Thurston 1990). The station now offers digital international long-distance, 800 number services, and switched and dedicated high-speed data circuits up to 1.5 megabytes. Barbados External Telecommunications (BET) provides direct access to the global space communications system via earth station to satellite, and a microwave link to communications networks in the United States and the Atlantic underwater cables. BET also leases fiber optic dedicated lines with digital switching to companies requiring continuously available circuits, such as data entry companies. Whereas only a few of the local companies currently take advantage of returning data by telecommunications channels, lack of telecommunications access is not a barrier to further growth. These communications links are quickly surpassing the links available between urban and rural regions of the United States and further threaten the ability of rural areas to maintain data entry jobs.

The Rural Response to Changing Markets

Several firms are already adjusting to the changing market. One firm is moving into ancillary lines of business, such as document management and storage, and simple data processing. One example is in the credit card operations of Appalachian Computer Services. Credit card sales are increasingly being entered into computer-readable form at the point of sale. This company now provides a document storage and retrieval system for all of these transactions. A record of all transactions is stored on microfilm, and originals are stored on-site for 120 days. For bank clients, records of transactions are supplied when purchases are challenged by credit customers. The company also provides clients who purchase data entry services with simple data processing and editing services. For example, the company matches entry and exit data on all foreign travelers to the United States and has edited applications for citizenship under the Immigration and Naturalization Reform Act of 1987.

Several of these firms are adjusting to the competitive challenge by purchasing branch operations in the Caribbean. In one case, documents will be imaged at the domestic rural site and mailed off-shore for keypunching. A second firm is purchasing imaging technology that will transmit 18,000 pages every 24 hours to a branch in Jamaica. According to the vice president of this firm, the domestic operation could eventually become a document receiving and transmitting center, with the major share of key punching carried out in Jamaica.

Conclusion

Although examples of high-technology computer services can be found, the small number of firms indicates that the decentralization of software programming enterprises to rural areas is not a major trend. Consistent with popular wisdom, however, quality-of-life factors figure prominently in the location decisions of rural computer programming firms.

Similar to the pattern observed for manufacturing, rural areas have attracted the low-skilled, labor-intensive portion of the computer services industry—primarily data entry. There is little evidence that urban firms in the data entry/processing industry will decentralize on a grand scale in the foreseeable future. A trend toward vertical specialization and the offering of more advanced, client-specific, complex services limits the prospects of spatial filtering. The capital-intensive nature of data processing further limits dispersal. Similarly, advances in scanning technologies and barcoding are reducing the importance of labor availability, reliability, and cost, diminishing the advantages of leaving high-labor-cost urban markets.

Simultaneously, rural firms are threatened by off-shore data entry operations in countries with lower wage rates and solid educational systems. Intensified foreign competition or changes in technology could easily weaken rural American firms' quick turnaround advantage and undermine the sole reason for a domestic rural location.

The unidimensional function of most rural data entry establishments makes them and their communities particularly vulnerable to changes in markets. Because of the isolated location of most of these firms and the lack of alternative job prospects for rural workers, economic losses could be severe for residents of the surrounding communities.

In contrast, urban establishments are more likely to operate several lines of business, thus changes in any one line are less devastating. Moreover, urban firms are centered in metropolitan markets for numerous reasons, including access to clients, the ease of acquiring skilled labor, and access to specialized inputs. Thus, market adjustments are much less likely to result in a change in optimal location.

6

The Changing Face of Banking in Rural Communities

The financial service sector in rural areas has undergone radical restructuring over the past 15 years, and from all accounts it will continue to experience change through the 1990s. Driving these structural changes is increased market competition propelled by the twin forces of governmental deregulation and technological advancement. Deregulation is opening local markets to regional and national competitors while automation and advanced telecommunications are revolutionizing information handling, thus altering occupational profiles (Baran 1986). The combined effects of deregulation and technological change are restructuring decision-making processes and institutional hierarchies at the local level (Baran 1985). Nowhere have these phenomena been more evident than in the commercial banking industry.

Spatial manifestation of deregulation and the technological revolution in rural banking services is characterized by two trends—consolidation of community-based rural banks into medium and large[1] institutions, and acquisition of resulting bank holding companies by regional bank organizations (RBOs).[2] Between 1980 and 1986 the number of local, one-county banks dropped by 11 percent while multi-county banking firms jumped by 52 percent (Milkove and Sullivan 1990). The bank holding companies into which these banks have been absorbed are generally urban-based. Indeed, the number of rural offices of urban holding companies increased by 1,473 or 38 percent.

Numerous studies based on government data and other aggregate supply measures attempt to evaluate the implications of consolidation on the delivery of financial services and the availability of credit. However, because of the scale and the rapid pace of industry consolidation, even recent data sources reflect an industry profile that no longer exists.[3] Flawed though they may be, these data and previous research based on them provide a starting point for evaluating the distribution of banking activity by regions and establishment sizes and for identifying critical issues. By developing a case study methodology, we were able to enliven our examination of ongoing industry consolidation. In short, we synthesized previous research with current empirical observations of the evolving institutions that have been critically reshaping the industry, the RBOs.

Institutional consolidation in rural banking sectors has been heralded by deregulation proponents for its potential to increase credit availability and expand the breadth and sophistication of financial services, as well as provide new employment opportunities in remote areas. Yet, these gains rest on the assumption that additional services would be automatically assured by the presence of a banking facility—particularly one affiliated with a large institution. Proponents also maintain that consolidation is the rational consequence of market forces directing investment and providing services in the most efficient fashion. Mergers and acquisitions are pursued in order to achieve economies of scale, and they thereby increase operational efficiency (Heimstra 1990).

However, many bankers and industry specialists disagree with these positive views of banking deregulation. Although the available data on employment in financial services industries show increased numbers of jobs in rural areas through the mid-1980s, more current empirical evidence based on industry analysis and case studies suggests that industry consolidation may have dampened the effect of such employment growth.

In addition, as stated earlier, the potential gains from decentralization of metropolitan-based institutions' back-office operations may also have been overstated. In terms of gains to financial service users, assurances that the resources of larger operations are downstreamed to local establishments are also not empirically verified. Thus, debate about deregulation has largely centered on how local service delivery from new competitors compares with that of the banks they replace. If services do vary, do differences affect the availability of credit at the local level? Anecdotal evidence suggests they do.

A hypothetical example may point out potential pitfalls of industrial restructuring. In 1980, a rural entrepreneur who wanted to obtain a small unsecured short-term loan could walk into a local independent bank and meet face-to-face with a commercial loan officer. The bank officer would make an in-house decision about extending credit based on knowledge of the borrower's character and general business history as well as local economic conditions.

Today, this same rural retailer, entering the same bank building, might have a dramatically different experience. First of all, the financial institution would no longer be an independent bank but a branch of a large, distantly based RBO. Also, the customer would not meet directly with a credit approval officer. Rather, he/she would be required to complete a loan application that would be forwarded to a regional loan office for processing. Since acquisition, the bank's market orientation has shifted from providing a full range of commercial and retail services toward offering standardized consumer financial products. The local office is ill-equipped to handle small business loan requests. It may be that the only option available is a second mortgage on the borrower's family home.

Although this may be an extreme example, it does illustrate the potential negative impacts of bank restructuring on rural enterprises. Businesses and small agricultural operations rely on local banks for their credit needs. In a recent study by Deborah Markley (1990) of small businesses and rural banks in New England, it was found that local commercial banks provide between 55 and 66 percent of all credit received by small business in rural areas. Nationwide, small rural-based banks were equally important agricultural lenders (supplying 49 percent of all bank credit to agricultural enterprises in 1989) (Mikesell and Marlor 1991).

In light of these local linkages, it is obviously important to explore the extent of consolidation of small banks and the modus operandi of the large regional bank organizations that are acquiring them. Although it is generally known that consolidation is occurring, what has not been examined are the motivations behind regional bank organizations' encroachment into rural markets and the effect of their market orientation and service delivery mechanisms on rural business.

Thus, this chapter addresses what may be a general oversight in our perceptions of the effects of recent bank deregulation and regional bank consolidation. We highlight recent changes in the ownership, operations, and market orientation of banking establishments in rural areas. Through case studies and interviews, we describe trends of changing occupational profiles within banking offices, rationalization of operations, and standardization of products. This description is based on careful scrutiny of trade literature on regional bank organizations as well as interviews with local-level bankers.

Competitive Context Steers Structural Changes and Market Orientation

Between 1986 and 1989, the total number of nonmetropolitan banks dropped from 7,569 to 6,968 or nearly 8 percent (Mikesell 1989; Mikesell and Marlor 1991). Smaller nonmetropolitan banks accounted for this entire decrease. Although failures caused some of the decline of rural banks, the bulk of the change was due to mergers and acquisitions.

While the number of small banks was decreasing, the number of medium-sized banks in rural areas jumped from 654 to 832 between 1986 and 1989. Multi-bank holding companies also increased significantly (see Table 6-1). The large bank sector grew by only five institutions, however, this sector's mean asset base swelled by over 15 percent (see Table 6-2). As this growth in asset base has developed substantially faster than growth in the rest of the nonmetropolitan market, much of it appears to have resulted from acquired institutions. Although not as dramatic, medium-sized banks' mean asset base also grew, suggesting that most multi-bank holding company formation accommodated the consolidation of small banks into larger entities.

Nationwide, bank expansion has recently proceeded mainly by deregulation-facilitated merger and acquisition. Although this process may be slowing slightly, as Table 6-3 reflects, the FDIC approved 721 mergers between 1987 and 1989. Among the reasons cited for this corporate strategy by banks is that the Depository Institutions Deregulation Monetary Control Act of 1980 (DIDMCA) and the Depository Institutions Act of 1982 phased out Regulation Q interest rate ceilings. Prior to DIDMCA, banks were forced to compete on the basis of service (which largely translated to convenience and thus numerous branch facilities). Allowing banks to compete in terms of interest rates paid on deposits, in addition to the development of ATMs, eliminated a major structural impetus for de novo branch expansion.[4]

While branch facilities remain deposit collectors, their new attraction is to become marketing arms for the parent organization. Absorbing an existing firm provides an instant and reasonably assured market share in a community. Moreover, geographic expansion by acquisition also has made deregulation more palatable to the small local banks, whose equity value has risen due to the larger market for their stock. Independent banks may actually seek to be acquired. As one rural banker in Montana commented recently, the possibility of her bank's being acquired was attractive because it would allow the owners to liquidate their investment and reap a substantial profit.

Historically, states have allowed several varieties of branch banking, as reflected in Figure 6–1. Some states tolerate unrestricted branching throughout the state. However, many limit the number and/or geographic dispersion of branch locations. The alternative form is to allow branch banking through acquisition or merger. Beginning in the late 1970s, many states initiated deregulation of the industry by allowing

TABLE 6-1

Nonmetropolitan and Metropolitan Bank Characteristics: Geographic Location, Size, Age, and Ownership (1986 and 1989)

	Nonmetropolitan		*Metropolitan*	
	Number of Banks in 1986	*Number of Banks in 1989*	*Number of Banks in 1986*	*Number of Banks in 1989*
Bank Size:[a]				
Very small	3,231	2,571	1,499	1,137
Small	3,675	3,551	2,861	2,426
SNBs[b]	6,906	6,122		
Medium	654	832	1,758	1,767
Large	9	14	321	359
Age:[c]				
New	374	360	1,294	1,220
Mature	7,195	6,608	5,145	4,469

Holding Company (HC) Type:[d]				
Non-HC or one bank HC	5,854	5,196	3,862	3,518
Limited multi-bank HC	1,002	1,148	990	856
Large multi-bank HC	713	624	1,587	1,315
Total	7,569	6,968	6,439	5,689

[a] Very small banks have total assets of $25 million or less; small banks have between $25 million and $100 million in total assets; medium banks have between $100 million and $1 billion in total assets; and large banks have more than $1 billion in total assets.

[b] SNBs are smaller nonmetropolitan banks and include very small and small nonmetropolitan banks.

[c] New banks are one to six years old and include replacement banks for those that have failed. Mature banks are over six years old.

[d] An HC is a nonbank firm that owns controlling interest in one or more banks. Limited multi-bank HCs own between two and nine banks whose total assets do not exceed $1 billion. Large multi-bank HCs own more than nine banks and have assets in excess of $1 billion.

Sources: Derived Mikesell and Marlor 1991, and Mikesell 1989.

TABLE 6-2

Nonmetropolitan Bank Characteristics: Asset Concentration by Firm Size (1986 and 1989)

	Asset Concentration 1986 (in thousands)			
	Number of Banks	*Mean Asset Base*	*Subtotal*	*Percent of Total Assets*
Nonmetropolitan Banks				
Very small	3,231	14,571	47,078,901	13.53%
Small	3,675	48,703	178,983,525	51.43%
SNBs	6,906		226,064,996	64.96%
Medium	654	165,845	108,462,630	31.17%
Large	9	1,499,351	13,494,159	3.87%
Total Nonmetropolitan	7,569		348,019,215	100.00%
Total U.S.	14,008		2,902,578,992	

Nonmetropolitan Banks				
Very small	2,571	15,135	38,912,085	10.15%
Small	3,551	50,038	177,684,938	46.35%
SNBs	6,122	35,380	216,597,023	56.50%
Medium	832	171,300	142,521,600	37.17%
Large	14	1,733,614	24,270,596	6.33%
Total Nonmetropolitan	6,968		383,389,219	100.00%
Total U.S.	12,657		2,373,221,232	

Sources: Derived from Mikesell and Marlor 1991, and Mikesell 1989.

TABLE 6-3

FDIC-Approved Mergers 1987–1989

	1989	*1988*	*1987*
Mergers			
Approved	200	287	234
Denied	0	1	0

Source: Federal Deposit Insurance Corporation 1990.

multi-bank holding companies to pursue this latter option. The impact was quite noteworthy. In Florida, for example, 70 banks were absorbed as subsidiaries of holding companies in 1977–78, the year legislation allowing limited branch banking by merger was enacted (Milkove and Sullivan 1990).

States in the Midwest and the South that historically prohibited branch banking and had densely populated rural areas also have large numbers of small banks. These small institutions are particularly vulnerable to consolidation. As state legislatures have removed barriers to branch banking, a rash of merger activity has unfolded. As we indicate in Table 6-4, these regions accounted for nearly 88 percent of the total decline in nonmetropolitan banking firms between 1986 and 1989.

The trend in bank consolidation has not been limited by state boundaries. In 1980, ten interstate banking firms operated offices in rural counties; by 1986, the number had increased to 51. At year-end 1986, there were 320 nonmetropolitan commercial banks affiliated with interstate banking operations. The number of bank offices has increased equally dramatically—from 556 in 1980 to 2,347 in 1986 (Milkove and Sullivan 1990).

Regional consolidation has progressed at a brisk pace. Regional banks have capitalized on the weaknesses of their larger brethren, the major money-center banks, and exploited new acquisition opportunities created by removal of geographic barriers. While the New York and Chicago money center-banks have retrenched, sold assets, trimmed operations, and raised equity in order to recoup enormous write-offs of third-world debt, junk

FIGURE 6–1

STATE BRANCH BANKING LAWS AS OF 1986

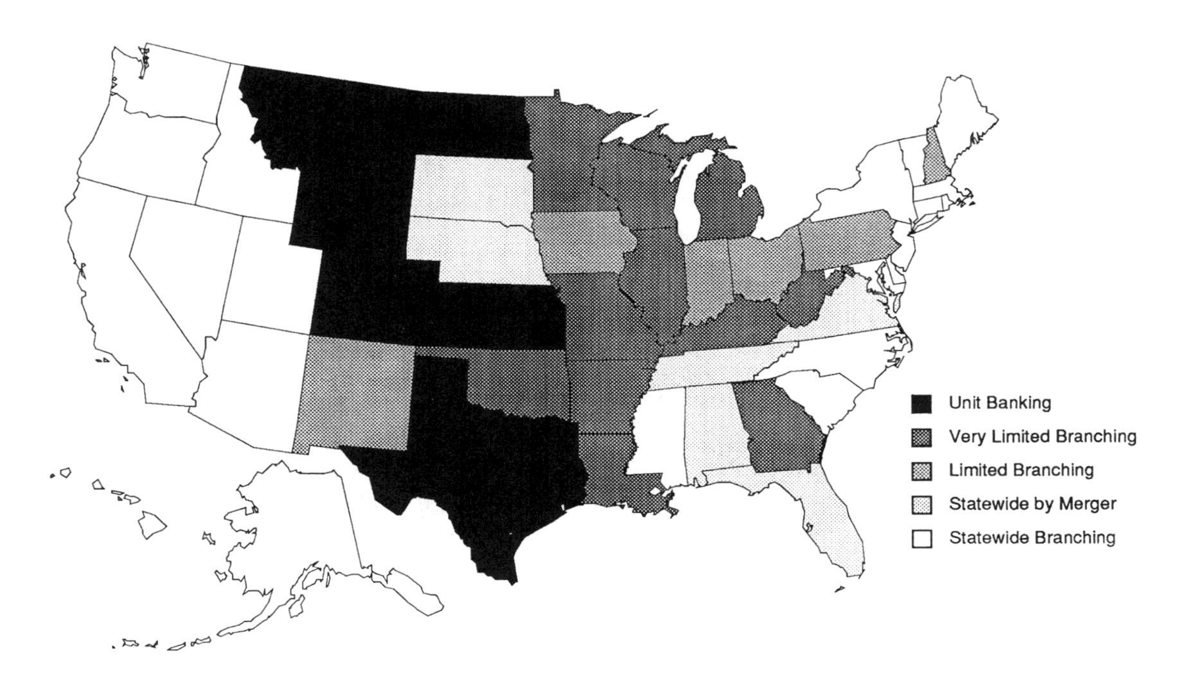

Source: Milkove and Sullivan 1990.

TABLE 6-4

Nonmetropolitan Bank Characteristics: Changes in Firms by Geographic Location (1986 and 1989)

	Number of Banks in 1986	*Number of Banks in 1989*	*Percent of Total Change*
Region			
West	628	581	7.82%
Midwest	3,922	3,580	56.91%
South	2,777	2,588	31.45%
Northeast	242	219	3.82%
Total	7,569	6,968	100.00%

Sources: Derived from Mikesell and Marlor 1991.

bonds, and real estate losses, banks such as NCNB (Charlotte, NC), Norwest (Minneapolis, MN), and Banc One (Columbus, OH) have been able to solidify their regional positions (Bates 1991). In short, economic circumstances have destroyed the traditional subservient relationship of the regional banks to the money-center banks. As reflected in Table 6-5, many of today's regional banks that have acquired rural independent banks at rapid rates since deregulation are now as large or larger than some of the money-center banks.

Therefore, in the next section we examine the institutional structures and the operations of three major regional bank organizations during the late 1980s and early 1990s. The objective is to determine the intermediate and longer-term strategies of each of these regional giants, then to describe how these plans have been being implemented at the local level.

The Case Studies

In this section we examine three of the leading regional bank organizations to illustrate distinctive and evolving approaches to banking that will affect services in widely dispersed

TABLE 6-5

Ten Largest U.S. Bank Holding Companies
(1980 and 1990) (in billions)

	1980 Total Assets		*1990 Total Assets*
Citicorp (NY)	$115	Citicorp (NY)	$216
BankAmerica (SF)	112	BankAmerica (SF)	110
Chase Manhattan (NY)	76	Chase Manhattan (NY)	98
Manufacturers Hanover (NY)	56	J. P. Morgan (NY)	93
J. P. Morgan (NY)	52	Security Pacific (LA)	84
Continental Illinois (C)	42	Chemical (NY)	73
Chemical (NY)	41	NCNB (CH)	65
Bankers Trust (NY)	34	Bankers Trust (NY)	63
First Interstate (LA)	32	Manufacturers Hanover (NY)	61
First Chicago (C)	29	Wells Fargo (SF)	56

(C) Chicago; (CH) Charlotte; (LA) Los Angeles; (NY) New York; (SF) San Francisco

Sources: Arnold Danielson 1991, and Meehan and Woolley 1991.

markets. We present detailed case studies of First Interstate Bancorp, NCNB Corporation, and Norwest Bank Corporation to show their corporate growth strategies, the extent of growth, and the RBOs' organizational characteristics that affect the breadth and availability of credit for the rural business customers of their new remote offices. See Figure 6-2 for the three banks' market areas. The mid-1980s to the early 1990s were a period of considerable restructuring in the banking industry.

First Interstate Bancorp[5]

Based in Los Angeles, at year-end 1990, First Interstate Bancorp ranked as the ninth largest bank holding company in the United States. Through its 28 subsidiary banks it currently operates over 1,040 offices in 14 states. Table 6-6 reflects the RBO's principal subsidiaries and their respective asset bases. In addition, First Interstate has franchise arrangements with 39 franchise banks possessing 143 branches in ten states where otherwise it has no operations.[6]

First Interstate's banking operations are carried out by very different entities in equally distinct ways. Franchise operations are conducted by independent banks which use the First Interstate logo and name. These banks also market many of First Interstate Bank of California's (the RBO's flagship bank) retail products. First Interstate Bank of California encompasses a sprawling branch network, and affiliate banks outside the state have operated as independent subsidiaries.

TABLE 6-6

First Interstate Bancorp:
Major Bank Subsidiaries

	Total Assets
First Interstate Bank of California	$19.1 billion
First Interstate Bank of Arizona	6.7 billion
First Interstate Bank of Oregon	5.9 billion
First Interstate Bank of Texas	5.4 billion

Source: Thompson 1991.

FIGURE 6–2

GOEGRAPHICAL REACH OF CASE STUDY BANKS

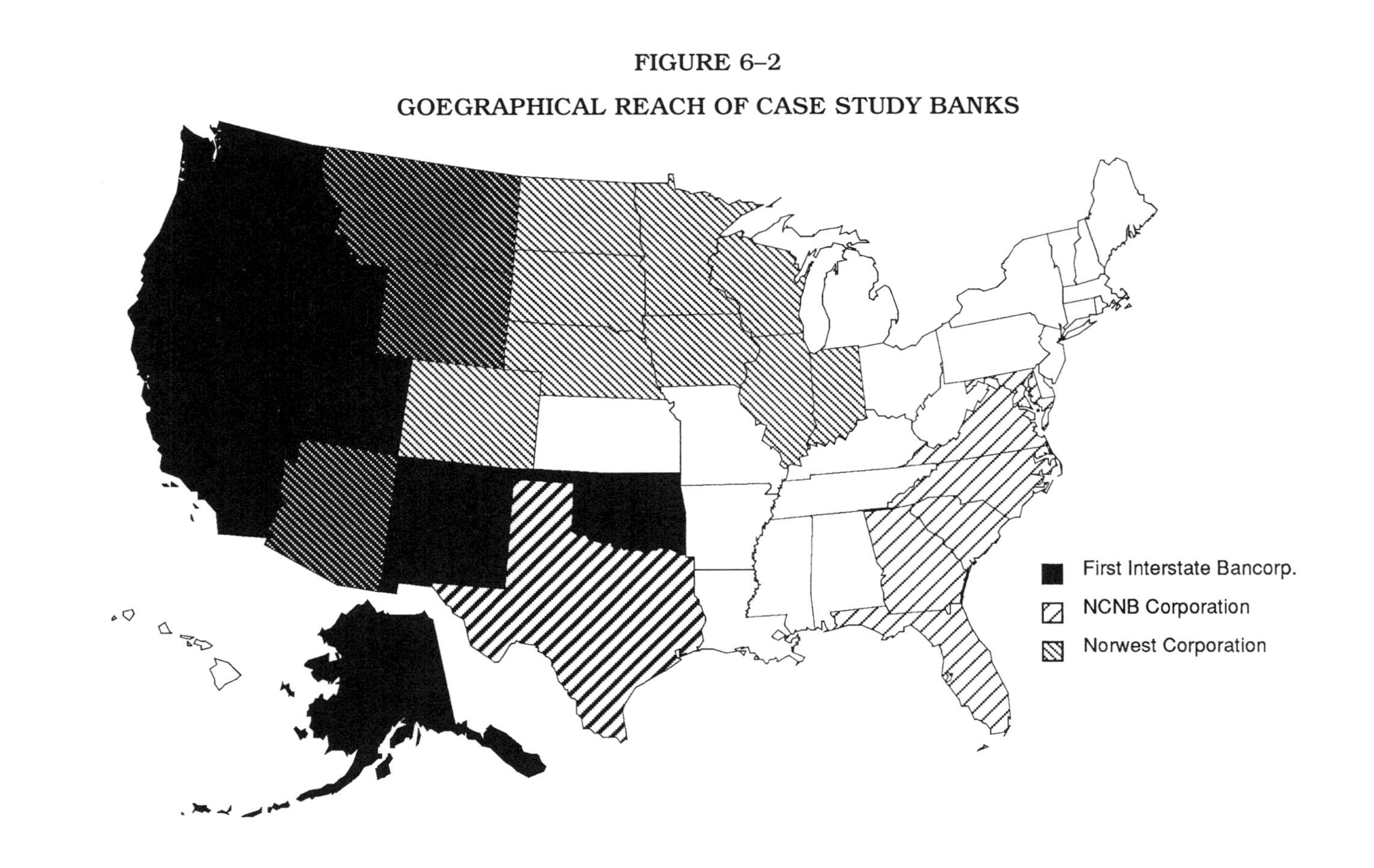

Wholesale and retail banking. In 1985 retail and wholesale banking operations were separated in First Interstate Bank of California. Under the current organizational structure at the lead bank, virtually all commercial borrowings are handled by business bankers (commercial loan officers) who work out of business banking centers or satellite offices. These centers often service large territories. For example, communities near the Oregon border are serviced by the business banking center in Marysville, more than 200 miles to the south. There is a satellite office in Redding (at which two business bankers are based), but this is still more than 70 miles away. The business bankers travel throughout the region to meet with existing or prospective customers and discuss their credit needs and financial service requirements.

Every retail branch is assigned a business banker who responds to commercial credit requests. The business banker's role is also to solicit new commercial accounts through calling programs. In addition to his/her marketing function, the business banker is responsible for analyzing credit proposals and packaging them for the approval process. Depending on the size, type, and complexity of a loan request, approval is made at increasingly higher levels of the corporate hierarchy.

Financial condition and operating results.[7] The combination of a weakening West Coast economy and First Interstate's acquisitions in Texas and Arizona have severely impacted the RBO's consolidated financial condition and operating results. As reflected in Table 6-7, earnings deteriorated sharply after 1986 due to steep loan loss provisions in 1987 and 1989. Whereas at first glance it appears that earnings healthily rebounded in 1990, over half of net income was generated by changes in accounting practices and the sale of assets, including the company's consumer lending subsidiary and portfolios of credit card receivables and mortgage servicing. As much as another $1.5 billion of assets are currently for sale, including banks in Colorado and New Mexico.

Other financial measures indicate some improvement in the company's overall financial condition. As part of the com-

TABLE 6-7

First Interstate Bancorp:
Consolidated Profitability Profile

	1990	*1989*	*1988*	*1987*	*1986*
Net Interest Income	$2,355	$2,506	$2,476	$2,224	$2,252
Provision for Loan Loss	499	1,204	590	1,254	475
Other Income	1,204	1,158	971	825	893
Overhead Expenses	2,562	2,545	2,539	2,379	2,045
Net Income	469	(124)	129	(604)	322

Source: Wong 1991.

pany's restructuring plan, total assets declined by 13.3 percent in 1990, primarily due to a contraction in total outstanding loans. Sixty percent of this decrease reflected a drop in commercial lending. Nonperforming loans decreased by 22 percent from year-end 1989, but still totalled $928 million or 2.6 percent of total loans. Approximately 50 percent are real estate–related borrowings. Moreover, real estate acquired in satisfaction of loans and other foreclosures total nearly $2.8 billion. The 1990 provision for credit losses dropped to $499 million. By year-end, reserves set aside for credit losses stood at $1,011 million or 109 percent of nonperforming loans.

Being the weakest player in the California market, several industry analysts predicted early on that a strong "marriage partner" was First Interstate's best long-term option for survival (Meehan 1991). The potentially enormous impact of the BoA/Security Pacific merger also meant that the company had little choice. True to form, merger plans were announced in the fall of 1991 with Wells Fargo & Company. Although combination of the two organizations amassed a 21 percent share of the total California market, it was still dwarfed by the new BoA's 44 percent market share.

Unlike the BoA/Security Pacific merger, both First Interstate and Wells Fargo have high concentrations of real estate and corporate buyout loans. Whereas First Interstate's management claimed to have passed the worst point of working itself out from under the heap of bad loans, Wells Fargo had just begun to falter (Bates 1991). In June of 1991 it announced a huge $350 million set aside in the second quarter for possible bad loans. Wells Fargo is also highly leveraged, and $17 billion of its total portfolio falls into the riskiest of loan categories. This amount is roughly five times the RBO's equity, which is regarded as a very high leverage ratio in the industry and an indication of unusually high risk (Bates 1991).

Under such conditions, First Interstate/Wells Fargo's long-run growth options may be out-of-state. Although Wells Fargo has not moved banking operations out of California, First Interstate already has an extensive interstate network of branches, affiliates, and franchise arrangements throughout the West. But its weak financial position has not provided much financial ability to continue expansion into alternative markets. Instead, bank has attempted to streamline operations following the pattern established in California. Credit and other operational functions have been centralized, and retail and wholesale lending operations have been segregated.

Previously, the non-California subsidiary banks operated relatively autonomously. As of 1992, the non-California affiliates were lumped into three regional groups. In the words of Chairman Carson, "We are a banking company that spans a broad geographic area—we do not propose to operate as a company of banks" (First Interstate Bancorp., 1991, p. 5). Most operational and many credit approval processes have been moved to regional centers. Already, credit decision making has recently undergone standardization in terms of analytical format and criteria applied for decision approvals. The objectives are to cut costs and to achieve a more conservative risk profile for the company.

Current provision of credit at nonmetropolitan Offices.[8] Regardless of management's plans to restructure the RBO's subsidiaries outside the flagship bank, currently there are substantial differences in operations between affiliates in the most remote areas of the First Interstate organization and those closer to home. First Interstate Bank of California's branches do not have commercial loan officers on-site. Conversely, affiliates generally have several. Affiliates reported that they have as much as 85 percent in-house lending authority. However, they generally complained of decreasing latitude in decision-making and structuring credits. First Interstate Bank of California's branches usually process all credit requests via a regional Business Banking office.[9] Although loan portfolio comparisons are not possible, overall outstandings were reported to be lower than several years ago, while competition universally was reported to be higher. This was despite the fact that the number of local competitors had frequently decreased (usually due to S&L

failures). Finally, both branch and affiliate personnel reported that more of their time was spent in marketing functions today than several years ago.

Strategic goals and local translation. First Interstate is under severe pressure to cut operating costs. Indeed, it must do so in order to survive. To meet these immediate critical objectives, it is rationalizing operations throughout the bank organization.[10] Credit decisions are being separated from marketing functions in order to increase efficiency and lower costs.

Complementing this operational trajectory, the merger with Wells Fargo is an attempt to create scale economies by increasing operating volume. The combination means elimination of redundant facilities and personnel. Finally, the BoA/Security Pacific merger required First Interstate and Wells Fargo to target their resources to areas where they had traditionally been the strongest. The largest single component of both banks' business is retail operations. Given the recent poor experiences of both banks with real estate lending, and in Well Fargo's case leveraged buyouts, it will not be surprising if they focus their limited resources on consumer business—at least in the short term.

NCNB Corporation

The modern day NCNB Corporation[11] was formed in 1968 to acquire North Carolina National Bank. From 1968 to 1979, NCNB diversified into activities such as mortgage banking and commercial finance, while the flagship bank, NCNB National Bank of North Carolina, expanded geographically statewide primarily through acquisitions. By 1979, NCNB had gained a 20 percent market share of deposits in North Carolina (as had two other banks), so to expand NCNB had to look beyond North Carolina borders.

NCNB's began its out-of-state expansion by acquiring banks in Florida, California, Virginia, and Maryland. The RBO also capitalized on the S&L crisis and the collapse of the energy and real estate industries which wiped out nearly all of the large Texas banks. By the mid-1980s, there were virtually no major state institutions capable of providing the capital infusion, and some argued the managerial expertise, required to restore the failed or failing institutions. Using the window of opportunity opened by federal and state regulators to interstate acquisitions in Texas, NCNB doubled its asset base by purchasing several large financially troubled Texas institutions.

The decade-long acquisition campaign increased NCNB's total assets from $7.7 billion in 1981 to $66 billion in 1991. However, the holding company did not stop to digest this phenomenal growth. The merger with C&S/Sovran Corp., renamed Nationsbank, nearly doubled NCNB's size again. The resulting realignment of the top banks, taking into account the other mega-mergers (BoA/Security Pacific and Manufacturers Hanover Trust/Chemical Bank), moved NCNB from the seventh largest RBO to the fourth largest position, with total assets in the neighborhood of $116 billion.

Finally, nonbank diversification also continued into the 1990s. Most significantly, in 1990, the bank purchased a $460 million credit card processing portfolio from Chevy Chase Federal Savings Bank and an $8.0 billion mortgage servicing portfolio from Fundamental Mortgage Corp. These major nonbank acquisitions have greatly enhanced the bank's position in both of these consumer market segments.

Operating structure.[12] Based in Charlotte, North Carolina, NCNB operates 923 offices throughout the south and in Texas. Each of these offices is a branch of one of the RBO's state-level bank subsidiaries. Table 6-8 reflects the size and regional market share (in terms of deposits) of each bank subsidiary. Although procedures and organizational structure are relatively uniform throughout all seven banks, each entity's operations and managerial hierarchy remain segregated.

NCNB has radically reorganized its organizational structure by dividing its basic banking business into two parts. The Corporate Bank now serves large corporate clients that have sales in excess of $100 million. The General Bank serves retail and commercial customers. Within the General Bank, managerial and credit functions were further subdivided according to consumer or commercial orientation. Consumer Banking in-

TABLE 6-8

NCNB Major Bank Subsidiaries:
Asset Base and Representative Deposit Market Shares

Subsidiaries	*1990 Asset Base*[a]	*1989 Market Share*[b]
NCNB National Bank of North Carolina	$19,070	20.8%
NCNB National Bank of Florida	12,186	8.3%
NCNB National Bank (Georgia)	603	N/A
NCNB National Bank of South Carolina	4,789	14.2%
NCNB National Bank of Maryland	331	N/A
NCNB Texas National Bank	32,753	20.4%
CNB Virginia	11	N/A

[a] Asset base designated in millions.
[b] Market share designated in terms of deposits.

Source: Hanley 1991.

cludes individuals and small businesses (companies with annual sales less than $1 million). Commercial Banking encompasses businesses with sales between $1 million and $10 million that use commercial credit. Personnel have been subsequently shifted to regional or subregional locations from which credit functions for Commercial Banking and Corporate Banking are performed. This operating structure has been replicated in each of the subsidiary banks.

Credit review and quality control.[13] In 1990, we saw increasing focus on tightening the credit approval process and the standardization of policies and risk assessment. Increasingly, line-operating functions are being separated from credit review functions. Credit officers are assigned to the individual consumer, commercial, and corporate areas of each subsidiary bank. These officers report directly to the holding company's Chairman of Credit Policy, who being on equal footing with the subsidiary bank presidents, reports directly to the Chairman of the holding company.

Credit approval is signature-based, meaning that various line and credit personnel accept direct responsibility for loan extensions. Individual approval authority ranges according to the type of business, seniority of personnel, and the market. Approval from a loan officer and a credit policy officer is required for loans over $1 million; however, recently smaller credits have come under increasing scrutiny. Moreover, the company has tied incentive compensation to controlling credit quality as well as meeting other production-oriented goals.

NCNB and market opportunities. NCNB's extraordinary growth in the 1980s was facilitated by its exploitation of weaknesses of other institutions in the industry. NCNB targeted acquisition candidates struggling under portfolios of problem loans, while major competitors in the Northeast and Chicago were too preoccupied with their own internal loan problems to challenge NCNB's actions. Moreover, favorable acquisition deals struck with the FDIC for assistance ameliorated costs associated with assuming the assets of insolvent institutions.

In his letter to the shareholders from the RBO's 1990 annual report, NCNB Chairman McColl continued this fact, stating that management's overall goal was to:

> position NCNB to take advantage of the dislocation underway in the financial services industry. We expect substantial consolidation to occur in the near future, and we intend to participate in it. (NCNB Corporation, 1991, p. 5)

The creation of NationsBank represents the exploitation of such opportunities. Indeed, clash of corporate cultures blocking the consolidation of C&S/Sovran, and mounting evidence of a problem real estate loan portfolio may have engendered C&S/Sovran management's willingness to accept NCNB's overture.

The creation of Nationsbank also poses enormous management problems. NCNB managerial resources are already stretched thin by the herculean task of operationally merging the Texas acquisitions into the NCNB system, and currently C&S/Sovran is mired in internal organizational squabbles over the integration of technologies and marketing efforts (Meehan 1991). Yet, the plum analysts estimate is that the new Nationsbank could net as much as $300 million in cost savings in the first two years of operation (Cline 1991).

In short, success of the NCNB-C&S/Sovran merger hinges on the ability of the new entity to rationalize operations. Joining of the two RBOs greatly increases scale economies in credit card processing, trust operations, and mortgage servicing; however, divergent technologies and other operations must be integrated (Roosevelt 1991). Consolidation of widely overlapping retail branch networks in Florida and South Carolina means substantially paring down the number of facilities and corresponding operating costs. Even before the merger was announced, C&S/Sovran had projected a 4 percent reduction in work force in 1991 (Business Wire Inc. 1990).

Finally, there remains the question of how the organizational structure for Nationsbank will be established. Given the rigorous standardization NCNB has imposed on previous merger and acquisition partners, it is reasonable to assume that it will attempt to continue this same course of action. NCNB's arrival on the scene may inspire a compromise between the divergent elements in C&S/Sovran. On the other hand, it may forge an alliance against NCNB, particularly if large numbers of mid- and upper-level staff jobs are being threatened. Although NCNB's previous growth has come largely from acquisitions, this merger of equals poses a danger similar to that of the C&S/Sovran combination, where consolidation of operations have been stalled by internal discord and management indecision.

Provision of credit at local nonmetropolitan offices.[14] The findings from interviews with branch officials mirrored the strategic objectives of streamlining operations. None of the branch managers interviewed claimed to have any personnel devoted mainly to commercial credit functions. Rather, a commercial loan office, generally in a nearby larger community, was assigned to serve most of the branch office's smaller commercial customers' credit needs. Although several offices maintained small portfolios of commercial and agricultural loans, this practice was being phased out. In such cases, branch managers performed dual functions in administration and credit approval processes. However, most viewed their positions as evolving toward a marketing orientation in which their main function in the future would be routing customers to the appropriate service group within the bank.[15]

Norwest Corporation

Norwest Corporation[16] is organized as a multi-bank holding company whose operations can be divided into five major areas: community banking, corporate banking, consumer finance, residential mortgage originations, and full-line insurance. Subsidiaries operate independently, and decision-making processes are generally decentralized. Operating managers are given far more responsibility than in similar organizations of Norwest's size.

The RBO aggregates its 340 community banks operating in 11 states into three geographic regions. In Table 6-9 we provide the geographic breakdown and market shares in each of these territories. Lending is primarily geared to consumers, small businesses, and middle market commercial borrowers. Each community bank operates as an independent profit center and must achieve a minimum of 1.05 percent return on assets (ROA).[17] Although a community bank's loan portfolio is subject to credit reviews, the means by which this level of profitability is achieved is left largely to the community bank president. Certain operating functions, such as data processing and cash management, are centralized, but decisions regarding business mixes and employment remain at the local level. Credit review is maintained on a regional basis with each state comprising a separate region for review purposes, and the RBO assigns a credit review officer to each region. It also enforces control by audits of each region's risk-rating methodology (Hemel 1991).

Corporate banking is concentrated in the head office and a few regional bank centers. Most of the focus of corporate banking is on the generation of fee income from cash management, institutional trust services, and international trade services. Indeed, the emphasis today is on providing lending only to fee-based customers.

Norwest Financial is a consumer finance company with 663 offices in 46 states (Thompson Financial Networks 1991). It has proven to be the driving force behind the RBO's earnings growth throughout the 1980s. Operations are decentralized, with underwriting criteria completely determined by the local office manager. Average loan size is $3,000 and the customer base is almost exclusively retail. Previously, the holding company had attempted to coordinate community banking operations and consumer finance, but abandoned the top-down efforts when they proved ineffectual (Hemel 1991).

With 270 offices, Norwest Mortgage is the fifth largest mortgage originator in the United States. Operations are divided relatively equally between retail and wholesale operations (for which portfolios are purchased from smaller thrifts). Like community bank presidents, Norwest Mortgage office managers assume considerable responsibility for pricing loans and are paid

TABLE 6-9

Norwest Corporation:
Organization of Community Banking System
and Market Share

Region/State	*% of Deposits*	*Market Rank*
North Central		
Minnesota	25.2%	1
Wisconsin	4.1%	5
Illinois	N/A	
Indiana	N/A	
Total offices - 172		
South Central		
Iowa	8.2%	1
Nebraska	8.2%	3
Total offices - 55		
Western		
Montana	11.2%	2
Wyoming	10.6%	2
North Dakota	14.4%	1
South Dakota	23.2%	1
Colorado	21.7%	1
Arizona	N/A	
Total offices - 108		

Source: Deans 1991.

on the basis of profitability versus volume (Hemel 1991). There appears to be considerable coordination between community banks and the mortgage affiliate in cross-selling services.

Norwest Insurance is the largest domestic RBO-owned insurance agency, and it ranks twelfth overall in the insurance industry. Selling all lines of insurance, its current industry mix is 65 percent consumer, 35 percent commercial. Norwest Insurance has 3,100 agents who are often placed directly into community banks (Deans 1991).

The norwest competitive edge. Investment analysts have attributed Norwest's growth to a refocusing of the company's business toward consumer and small business lending, a new emphasis on technology-based and fee-generating products, and the geographic and sectoral extension of the company's operating base by acquisitions (Scholl 1991). The high proportion of consumer and small business lending has contributed to stable loan growth and relatively wide operating margins (Thompson 1991). Having a portfolio of small loans is also much less risky than having a few larger loans.

Investments in technology have generated sizable increases in fee income for the RBO. Such increases diversify income sources and smooth out earnings, which for banks tend to gyrate with interest rates and inflation. Technological investments have also capitalized on newly created economies of scale resulting from Norwest's recent acquisitions. Conversely, Norwest's investment in a new retail banking software system being developed by Banc One is geared toward minimizing costs associated with acquisitions (Gullo 1991).

Finally, Norwest has capitalized on its relative financial strength to expand its geographic horizons into neighboring states. Its largest acquisition to date, United Banks of Colorado, provided an immediate and dominant presence in the state as well as boosted the RBO's overall size by 20 percent. However, its less-noted and smaller acquisitions throughout the Upper Midwest may in the end be of equal importance.

Norwest's focus on community banking throughout the small towns which dot the Upper Midwest has provided it with very large market share in these communities. Norwest enjoys lower funding rates, low advertising expenses, high customer retention, high employee retention, and low labor costs (Hemel 1991). The downside of this geographic orientation is that the local economies of these communities are frequently agriculture-dependent. Although Norwest bases its agricultural lending on cash flows and has decreased its aggregate agricultural lending, the company would no doubt be negatively impacted by another economic downturn in this sector.

In sum, Norwest is constructing a regional network of affiliated banks while simultaneously nurturing a host of financial service subsidiaries. The network provides a guaranteed market for the financial services subsidiaries' products and services. Indeed, more than one investment analyst has dubbed Norwest the "Walmart" of the banking industry (Hemel 1991; Jaffe 1991). Today, Norwest customers can go to their local branch and have their usual banking needs fulfilled, buy stock, take out an insurance policy, and obtain a home loan complete with title insurance.

Small towns and credit.[18] The affiliate bank presidents interviewed reported increases in total loans outstanding over the past several years but no major changes in the mix of their portfolios. These are generally made up of consumer loans (ranked first), followed by commercial loans, and then at a distant third, agricultural loans. Most of the new services provided were retail-oriented. However, a newly assimilated affiliate reported that his small bank now offers a number of services geared to ranchers, such as commodity hedging services and a software package that assists in determining breakeven stocking levels. There did not appear to be any recent major change in their autonomy or any centralization of decision-making capabilities. There was, however, a consensus on increased accountability and general standardization of credit approval criteria.

Doing business in small communities has been a profitable enterprise for Norwest, but attempting to determine whether the host communities have benefitted equally is far more daunting a task. We can say that the RBO's market orientation targets small businesses. From a structural standpoint, the local offices have great flexibility determining their customer bases. Moreover, they are staffed with credit officers. The fact that their compensation is based on performance could positively or negatively impact credit availability. Although loan officers are rewarded for generating business, they do control the types of loans placed, and they have considerable disincentives to take on nonstandard risks.

As is already clear, Norwest, First Interstate, and NCNB have consciously molded their institutions and operating procedures. In each case, management has made deliberate decisions affecting how and where banking services are performed. In the next section we compare these strategic decisions and their implementation and draw conclusions regarding their impacts.

Discussion of the Case Studies and Their Implications

The case study profiles highlight three very different bank holding companies. Although the RBOs' circumstances and responses to the emerging consolidated environment vary, there are some discernable broad trends that have significant implications for the availability of commercial credit to rural businesses. Such trends may also have significant impacts on both the employment structure within rural banking facilities as well as on other rural financial services providers. Companywide trajectories associated with market expansion that encourage standardization of operating procedures and rationalization of facilities and personnel will impact rural small businesses and employment. In this section we will compare and contrast the RBOs' strategic reorganization, drawing upon specific anecdotal findings obtained from the interviews conducted with RBO bank managers and other industry specialists.

Standardization of Operating Procedures

Standardization of operating procedures is generally referred to as the application of uniform formats for processing information in back office operations. But increasingly, procedural standardization has come to also include the process by which credit decisions are made (Baran 1986). Indeed, in the previously outlined case studies, NCNB and First Interstate both epitomize organizations undergoing drastic top-down standardization. However, their respective motivations result from profoundly different circumstances.

NCNB is a company on the move. Aggressively acquiring vast banking networks throughout the South and Southwest, its strategic actions are proactive. Standardization is the means by which NCNB digests its acquisitions, integrating them into the NCNB organization, and centralizing control over their operations. Uniform operating procedures through-out the RBO's diverse holdings also create scale economies for various financial services sectors such as mortgage banking and credit card processing. Furthermore, if regulators remove the final barriers to nationwide banking, NCNB is ready to fully consolidate operations across state borders and give full meaning to its new name, NationsBank.

Like NCNB's, First Interstate's management avidly adheres to the standardization school. Yet for First Interstate, the reasons for its actions are not to promote growth. Indeed, while NCNB is doubling in size every three years, First Interstate is contracting. Plagued with years of extraordinary losses, struggling under large portfolios of nonperforming loans in Texas and Arizona, and now facing the onslaught of an overwhelmingly powerful competitor in its primary market, First Interstate is reacting to its tenuous position. The California RBO is desperately attempting to restore profitability by cutting operating expenditures. The immediate objectives are to eliminate nonessential personnel and to increase the efficiency of its remaining labor force.

In contrast to either NCNB or First Interstate, Norwest has maintained a diversity of functions at the establishment level. Its prevailing corporate philosophy is to maximize profitability by providing establishment-level personnel with the appropriate mix of resources and incentives to meet corporate profit goals. Nevertheless, as with the other two RBOs, standardization has occurred in Norwest's backoffice operations, and today most information processing functions of local offices are outsourced to regional servicing centers. Financial products themselves are also standardized, but the marketing methods employed and the product mix of each local office vary greatly.

Furthermore, in terms of credit review, Norwest's approach is quite different. Whereas NCNB and First Interstate formalize the credit review process from Charlotte or Los Angeles, at Norwest each region develops its own credit review criteria. Governmental regulations and the RBO's corporate oversight impose parameters within which credits are evaluated; however, the resulting methodological approaches to reviewing the loans of affiliate offices are much less uniform than at many regional RBOs.

Rationalization

Perhaps more than any other reason, rationalization is the justification invoked for bank mergers today (Padley 1991; Milligan 1991). Certainly it has figured prominently in NCNB and First Interstate's recent merger plans. In both cases, overlapping markets with their respective merger partners means substantial duplication of branch facilities and personnel. These cutbacks are projected to translate into enormous cost savings, but to reduce the number of local financial institutions (and offices) and employees in rural communities. For NCNB, the merger with C&S/Sovran will solidify the RBO's dominant market position in the Southeast. Conversely, whereas First Interstate's merger with Wells Fargo will improve operating efficiency, at best it enables the new entity to minimize losses in market share and competitive strength vis-à-vis the BoA/Security Pacific combination.

Again, Norwest differs from NCNB and First Interstate. Rationalization has generally played a lesser role in its overall corporate strategy. In part, this may be due to the fact that the unit banking tradition of the Upper Midwest has discouraged the formation of large regional banking organizations (among which Norwest is the first). Without other large organizations competing in the same marketplaces, rationalizing operations can usually only marginally improve profitability. Purchasing a unit bank means there is only one bank to close, and that generally involves paying a premium. Moreover, operationally merging banks is costly. At least with larger transactions, scale economies can be achieved in the consolidation process. Nonetheless, it should be noted that Norwest actively pursues a strategy that centralizes back-office operations into regional processing centers.

In spite of differences among the three case studies, the fundamental objective of rationalization is to reduce employment and overhead costs. Some have argued that such reductions in rural employment at branch locations are offset by the metropolitan-based RBOs' decentralization of data processing and other back-office functions to rural areas. However, as noted in Chapter 5, recent historical analysis of USEEM data of export- and non-export-based employment does not confirm this hypothesis.

How Locations Are Affected by Industry Consolidation

Two themes run through the following discussion of local impacts. The first has to do with transaction costs and the second with market networks. Transaction costs are important because they are a primary component of the final cost of credit or financial services, thus they partly determine the availability of local credit. Market networks are the conduits through which financial products are sold. Their construction and orientation determine how, for, and to whom financial products are designed and delivered. Changes in transaction costs and market orientation also may inpact other small rural financial service providers.

In our examination of RBOs' local banking establisments, one observation was universal—excluding commercial banking centers, all of the offices were retail-oriented. Even the presidents of the largest affiliate banks often spend more time on retail marketing efforts than on developing business in other market sectors. In all three cases, financial products are developed and packaged at regional or corporate headquarters and then channeled to the local offices for sale. Such services include personal credit facilities and credit cards, electronic bill paying and tax filing, numerous investment options, and insurance brokerage.

A major factor driving the RBOs' retail orientation is the size of the market. Regional RBOs target larger consumer groups in order to spread the total costs associated with providing the particular service or product over as broad a base as possible—thereby reducing per unit transaction costs (Rose 1987). In contrast, when they provide services or credit to commercial borrowers, the customer pool shrinks exponentially, and per unit transaction costs skyrocket. Although most bankers are reluctant to discuss their cost structure, the amount of a loan must range from $75,000 to $100,000 in order for transaction costs to be covered and a reasonable rate of return earned on the credit. Large banks, having more overhead, have even higher thresholds, perhaps as high as $250,000, below which credit extensions are unprofitable or do not generate a sufficient rate of return.[19] So it appears that the cost structure of larger RBOs may be incapable of profitably accommodating small loans. Small business borrowings simply do not generate enough revenue to cover the RBO's transaction costs and yield a sufficient rate of return.

Establishment interviews and corporate profiles of the three RBOs indicate that strategic response to controlling transaction costs has varied widely. NCNB and First Interstate have consolidated commercial credit functions under special personnel, relationship managers or business bankers. The notion is that specialization increases efficiency and thereby drives down costs. Norwest, on the other hand, relies on the individual expertise of the affiliate's management and a system of rewards and punishment to maximize personnel efficiency. In both approaches there are pitfalls for the small business borrower.

For NCNB and First Interstate, specialization implies fewer line officers, hence lower overhead expenditures. It may also translate to a reduction in the scope of business development efforts, since the loan officer's time must be concentrated in the most profitable market sectors. As we have shown, these do not include small business loans. Moreover, where a loan officer's market territory is large, his/her time and knowledge of localities is likely to be limited, and the potential of the smaller customer not being targeted for service may increase. The alternative servicing level is the retail branch, but as it is primarily consumer-oriented, the chances of it providing satisfactory commercial service are compromised.

By contrast, the small borrower may receive a more familiar welcome at the Norwest office. Norwest's management is allegedly driven harder and is more motivated to make a deal. Yet, as with the NCNB and First Interstate loan officers, the local manager must weigh the time spent to complete small business loans against marketing products which generate more profit, such as consumer financial products and services.

From the banker's view, consumer loans have an additional advantage. Often, as in the case of auto loans or home equity loans, they are secured. Conversely, the most important type of credit for small business is the unsecured short-term loan which bears a greater credit risk. As Norwest community bank managers' compensation is based on meeting overall portfolio credit standards (in addition to certain profitability measures), there may be a built-in disincentive to lend to small borrowers.

RBO expansion into affiliated financial services may impact rural independent firms or franchise establishments as well as independent banks. Financial product deregulation has allowed large banking organizations to enter mass retail markets with new standardized financial products in insurance, brokerage, investment services, and many other areas. For some RBOs—in particular First Interstate and NCNB—this phenomenon has facilitated increased segmentation of operations along consumer versus commercial banking activities. Regardless of the institutional flavor of the local office, enormous scale economies allow the RBOs to compete in newly deregulated financial services sectors where local independent banks have neither the financial nor the human resources to enter. Moreover, the competitive advantage enjoyed by RBOs may impact other financial service providers in rural communities as well. In a limited local market, small independent firms or franchise establishments simply may not be able to survive in the face of a larger competitor. Hence, product deregulation may enable large banking institutions to consolidate numerous financial services under a single corporate umbrella, for example, the Sears-Discover Card-Allstate-Dean Witter conglomerate, and offer them through a single retail-oriented outlet. Potentially, the provision of additional financial services could benefit a community, but at a cost to the local entrepreneurial community. Indeed, more than firm loss may occur. The incorporation of financial services into one location may reduce overall employment requirements and diminish the potential for new firm formation.

Yet, there are some mitigating features to the bleak scenarios that we have just portrayed. For one, there are more nonmetropolitan bank offices and more nonmetropolitan counties being serviced by a larger number of offices than prior to the rash of deregulatory moves in the early and mid-1980s. Even if these offices do not provide commercial banking services onsite, theoretically they should be able to direct the small businessperson to the appropriate business office. Moreover, there appear to be some overlapping capabilities or functions between retail and commercial lending specializations. For example, a retail branch manager at First Interstate described various ways in which he had used consumer loan instruments to finance small business borrowings, for example, a second mortgage for a local merchant to buy equipment for his shop.

The application of technology has in some cases yielded commercial products geared specifically for small businesses. First Interstate has created a special overdraft facility for small business borrowing less than $20,000 which operates like an overdraft protection on a consumer checking account. While automating much of the loan booking functions, the credit approval process for each overdraft facility remains intact. Hence, overall transaction costs have not been majorly affected. In fact, the effective interest rates (including fees) on these facilities tend to be substantially higher than standard small business borrowing rates but, according to First Interstate, such access to credit is well worth the additional expense.

Finally, all three RBOs support or have incorporated into their organizations as subsidiaries, enterprises which are geared to providing credit and often technical assistance to very small businesses. NCNB's major state banks all have subsidiaries targeting women or minority-owned businesses. However, the activities of these enterprises are focused on urban centers. Norwest, on the other hand, has capitalized a private small-business development corporation which finances entrepreneurs in rural northern Minnesota, many of whom are referred by the local Norwest affiliate. Admirable though these endeavors may be, their operations are geared to particular locations. Their geographic isolation and relatively small scale of operations do not address the pervasive structural problems facing small businesses throughout rural America.

The Impact of Competition on Credit for Small Business

To some degree the argument that small-business borrowers fall between the cracks rests on the notion that a lack of competition drains the incentive for bankers to target less-profitable businesses such as small enterprises. However, in most of the markets where we interviewed bank managers or presidents, there appeared to be considerable bank and nonbank competition. Indeed, interviewees often stated that their respective markets were over-banked. This confirms what many industry analysts have maintained; that there should be a reduction in the total number of banks (Deans 1991). It also confirms that for banks in slow-growing markets (most nonmetropolitan communities), the only way for banks to grow is often by absorbing their competitors.

Nevertheless, many analysts have argued that the market is sufficiently broad to provide market niches for small banks serving nonmetropolitan communities (Milkove and Sullivan 1990; Danielson 1991). Theoretically, these niches could also encompass small-business borrowers. Yet, recent history does not provide great reassurance for small independent bankers (Padley 1991). To reiterate a point made earlier, over the past few years considerable consolidation has occurred among the smaller banks in nonmetropolitan areas, and most believe the process will continue (Milkove and Sullivan 1990; McCall and McFadyen 1986). One Norwest banker admitted that he saw little room in his community for the remaining independent bank. Indeed, if the most profitable sectors of the local bank market are captured by the regional branch or affiliate offices, independent banks will be concentrated sectorially, and in those sectors that are most volatile and marginally profitable, such as agriculture. Under such tenuous conditions, small banks are easily subject to failure. In the long run, local independent banks' ability to serve as the primary source of credit for small businesses will probably decline.

Little assistance appears to be forthcoming from other nonbank competitors. Depository institutions such as S&Ls and credit unions that compete with banks for retail business have historically shown little interest in commercial lending. When they have branched away from their retail bases, as the S&L crisis illustrated, they have been largely ineffective.

Other public and private sector institutions appear to be reorienting investment strategies and tightening credit requirements—thereby reducing the aggregate amount of credit available in rural areas. Credit policies for quasi-public sector entities such as the Farm Credit System are now far more restricted than in earlier periods. Scheduled reductions in federal agricultural subsidies that will reduce net farm income can only further add to the negative impact on local businesses in agricultural communities. Trends in federal agricultural lending are likely to exacerbate this credit crunch. The increasing reliance on loan guarantees in recent years rather than more traditional direct credit extensions may reduce credit availability as the transaction costs to banks to service this type of loan are great because procedures are cumbersome and time consuming.

Finally, the decline in mortgage lending by insurance companies also has grave consequences for rural communities and small businesses. For the near term, real estate projects in rural areas increasingly may have to compete for financing with projects in more rapidly growing suburban areas. This may dash hopes for developing retirement- or tourism-related industries, and it means more pressure on funds available for long-term financing.

Conclusion

In this chapter we have examined the broad evolutionary trends in the U.S. banking industry to evaluate how they impact on employment and the provision of critical financial services to rural communities. Using the example of three leading RBOs, we illustrated how each has standardized operating procedures, rationalized operations, and expanded into new geographic and product markets. Comparison of the cases reveals how small-business borrowers may be impacted by such comprehensive corporate maneuvering. For example, transaction costs establish thresholds which may potentially price some small-business borrowers out of the market. Moreover, RBO attempts to reduce transaction costs related to personnel specialization and increasing rationalization of operations may limit access to commercial loan officers and reduce employment and business opportunities in rural communities. Clearly these changes and trends toward increasing deregulation and implementation of merger agreements have specific and thus far inadequately explored implications for the availability of credit in rural places.

7

THE TRANSFORMATION OF THE RESIDENTIARY SECTOR: FROM LOCAL SERVICES TO BRANCH OPERATIONS

As we noted in Chapter 3, recent growth of the service sector in rural America has largely been comprised of jobs in residentiary activities. These services both shape our collective image of small town life and are essential to local economic vitality and well-being. During the past 15 years, innovations in transportation, telecommunications, distribution and marketing, and business profit-maximizing strategies have revolutionized retail and consumer service delivery. Products and consumers now travel further faster. Rural residents have access to a greater variety of goods, often at lower prices than in the past.

For many rural communities this transformation has not been without cost. Locally owned storefronts have been replaced by chain establishments, and in some instances "Main Street" shopping areas have been entirely deserted in favor of regional retail and service centers. When rural residents bypass local merchants and travel out-of-town to shop, small town central business districts lose their vitality, and the least mobile residents lose access to critical services. When branch facilities of remotely operated companies displace locally owned businesses, local profit income is lost, and local leadership infrastructure is diminished. There is also some evidence that over the decade of the 1980s, employment expansion in the retail sector was manifested in the growth of part-time jobs.

This phenomenon may be exacerbating the economic instability of rural residents.

In this chapter we examine rural residentiary services in order to illustrate how current trends in service employment growth and ownership affect both the rural economy and the welfare of rural residents. We focus on services that have traditionally been the least likely to be directly exported, namely retail and consumer service activities. Through an examination of employment trends we observe the extent to which residentiary services are centralizing or decentralizing. We also examine how ownership changes are altering the composition of rural retail and consumer services.

The conceptual framework most commonly applied to understand the geography of the residentiary sector is based upon a model of spatial hierarchy. Central place theory asserts that availability of services is a function of the population size of a place. The larger an urban settlement, the more complex and varied the range of available services will be. Thus, services found in large urban settlements include activities that reach minimum costs at high levels of output (convention centers) and require immense market areas to yield sufficient demand (sophisticated medical services). Smaller, more remote areas support a narrow complement of services that require frequent access (grocery stores) and lower economies of scale to maintain profitability or viability (Christaller 1966; Clark 1982).

This model is useful in verifying very broad statements about the spatial distribution of essential goods and services, such as gas stations and convenience stores. However, central place theory has less applicability in an increasingly interconnected city system in which sophisticated telecommunications and transportation capabilities make possible levels of local specialization in excess of that dictated by strictly size of place (Pred 1975). Changing business practices that are assisted by advancing technology and reductions in transportation costs allow residentiary services providers (in particular retailers) to achieve increasing economies of scale in the provision of goods and services. Due to large-scale buying, standardized floor layouts and displays, generic advertising and promotion programs, and computerized inventory management, chain retailers are reaching minimum average costs at much larger levels of sales than in the past. Retail establishments requiring larger market areas, while offering lower prices and wider selection of goods, are syphoning off local expenditures and displacing highly localized small "mom and pop" operations of smaller towns. The proliferation of franchising further erodes the market share of locally owned establishments by providing proprietors of chain-affiliated establishments with access to economies of buying, distribution, and advertising associated with the central organization. Thus, while rural America today is more connected with the outside world than in the past, the price of connectivity may be less local control over the shape of the local economy.

Our analysis in this chapter will suggest that over the last decade many residentiary service functions have moved up the spatial hierarchy as multi-unit business organizations have proliferated and profited heavily by accumulating demand across space and satisfying it from centralized locations. Increasingly, the residentiary sector of small town rural America is in serious trouble, as residents travel longer distances to enjoy a broader variety of goods at lower costs.

Retail Services

The retailing sector, responsible for nearly one-quarter of rural jobs, is the largest rural employer. Nationally, the retail sector is a dynamic job creator, and rural America reflects aggregate trends. Between 1975 and 1985, retailing provided nearly 750,000 new rural jobs, yet metropolitan areas are still capturing the major share of national retail growth.

During the 1980s the greatest growth in retailing was in specialty merchandising—sales of unique, less-standardized products. As a result, agglomeration economies, the benefits that accrue from concentrating in larger shopping centers, have figured prominently in location decisions. Currently, successful shopping centers include one or more department stores and a large number of specialty shops. Smaller shopping districts, both in rural communities and urban neighborhoods, are increasingly less competitive and tend to be by-passed by local residents who are willing to travel to regional shopping areas. The impact of this trend has been to strengthen larger retail centers at the expense of smaller ones.

Our data support these hypothesized tendencies. Retail growth is spatially uneven, with more urbanized communities outside of central city cores experiencing the greatest growth. National data permit an overview of retail growth by county size and type. We use employment change, growth rates, and shift-share analysis (Table 7-1) to describe spatial variations in retail employment.

As our shift-share analysis of residentiary services indicates, national retail employment growth is vibrant, and there has been an absolute increase in retail employment in all county categories (columns three and four). A favorable industry mix indicates strong rural retail growth (column five). In other words, rural areas had a high proportion of retail industries that exhibited strong national growth. Again, this pattern prevails across all county types. The industry mix component of the shift-share analysis includes retail activities disaggregated to their 2-digit Standard Industrial Classification codes. Rapid-growth national retail industries that have been important to rural economies include food stores, eating and drinking places, and miscellaneous retail activities.

Despite a favorable industry mix, several county types exhibited local growth rates behind that of the nation. Here, central counties of the largest cities have much in common with the most rural counties. Both core cities, 1 million population and above, and nonmetropolitan counties with less than 20,000 urbanized population exhibited slower than national-level retail employment growth. For example, had local retail employment grown at a rate comparable with that of the

TABLE 7-1

Shift-Share Analysis of Employment Change for the Retail Service Industry in Each Urban Rural Area between 1974 and 1985

Urban Rural Category	*(1) Employment in 1974*	*(2) Employment in 1985*	*(3) Absolute Change*	*(4) National Growth Effect*	*(5) Industry Mix Effect*	*(6) Regional Shares Effect*	*(7) Annual Average Growth Rate*
Core, 1 million and above	3,832,334	4,753,383	921,049	1,071,536	272,769	−423,256	2.2
Fringe, 1 million and above	1,948,095	2,931,106	983,011	544,695	138,657	299,659	4.1
Fringe, 250,000 to 1 million	2,771,542	3,809,569	1,038,027	774,934	197,266	65,827	3.2
Fringe, < 250,000	1,135,877	1,622,574	486,697	317,596	80,847	88,255	3.6
Nonmetropolitan, > 20,000 urban adjacent	483,376	658,760	175,384	135,154	34,404	5,826	3.1
Nonmetropolitan, > 20,000 urban nonadjacent	420,846	585,119	164,273	117,670	29,954	16,649	3.3
Nonmetropolitan, < 20,000 adjacent	508,272	676,794	168,522	142,115	36,177	−9,769	2.9
Nonmetropolitan, < 20,000 non-adjacent	626,377	812,953	186,576	175,138	44,583	−33,144	2.6
Completely rural, adjacent	60,458	78,316	17,858	16,904	4,303	−3,349	2.6
Completely rural, nonadjacent	113,663	146,838	33,175	31,781	8,090	−6,696	2.6

Source: U.S. Department of Commerce Bureau of the Census, *County Business Patterns* 1985, 1974.

nation, the least urbanized rural counties (not adjacent to metropolitan counties) would have gained almost 7,000 additional jobs (column seven).

Slower than average retail growth in lower population rural counties is due to trends toward specialty retailing, increasing scale economies of multi-establishment retailers, and lower transportation costs which facilitate geographic concentration of supply. Relatively lower rural income growth and population losses also contributed to the tendency toward retail centralization.

County-level data are too aggregate to afford a precise picture of shifts in retail employment across the city-size hierarchy. Therefore we also examined the USEEM data for a more disaggregated picture of six states.[1] Although we have gained geographic detail below the county level, we have unfortunately sacrificed the breadth of a nationwide picture (Table 7-2).

As discussed earlier, the USEEM data are reported at the establishment level, and (because no data are suppressed) information can be aggregated for even the smallest employment centers. By using addresses, we assigned each establishment to its town/city, and then grouped towns/cities by their 1980 population size. Retail employment changes were then calculated for each population grouping. Results are generally consistent with the predictions of central place theory, other researchers' findings, empirical evidence, as well as our county-level analysis for the entire United States.

Retail employment growth is generally slower in small towns than in larger places. Rural towns of 2,500 to 5,000 population in New York, and towns of 2,500 population and below in Kansas, Maryland, and New York actually experienced declines in retail employment. Data for Massachusetts are not available because there are too few towns in these size categories to yield reliable results. The smallest urban Kansas towns (less than 2,500 population) also exhibited employment losses.

Retail employment growth is greatest in medium-sized metropolitan communities, which include suburban nodes. In particular, growth is greatest in urban communities sized 10,000 to 50,000. Greater retail employment growth in larger rural towns is a pattern found by other researchers such as Stone (1987), who examined retailing sales in rural communities in Iowa over the 1979 to 1986 period. Stone found that retail growth declined in rural Iowa towns with populations below 5,000. Anding et al.'s (1990) results are similar. This work reports that between 1960 and 1989, only the metropolitan centers, primary regional, and secondary regional shopping centers in the Midwest increased their share of all retail establishments. The lowest three classes of trade centers, including the smallest settlements and minimum and full convenience centers, were less important retail trade destinations in 1989 than they had been in 1960.

The greatest rural retailing growth shows up in communities that are not adjacent to metropolitan counties (see Tables 7-1 and 7-3). Adjacency appears to dampen rural retailing vitality, presumably because residents in these counties tend to commute to nearby urban centers to take advantage of a broader array of specialized products and more competitive prices. Recent research by Deller and Holden (1991) supports our findings. They also found that rural retail centers existing in the shadows of metropolitan markets have difficulty competing.

Import Substitution

In metropolitan-adjacent rural counties, retail employment losses exceeded population losses (or gains were slower than population gains). This further suggests that rural customers are traveling to urban retail centers to purchase goods and services. The ratio of service employment to population in each county, relative to the ratio of service employment to population for the nation, provides an indication of the extent to which a local population is served by local services. This measure is defined below.

$$(E^i_r/P_r)/(E^i_{us}/P_{us})$$

TABLE 7-2

Annual Average Retail Services Employment Growth Rates by City Size in Six Study States: Annual Average Percent Change 1980 to 1986

City Size	*Metropolitan/ Rural*	*CA*	*KA*	*MD*	*MA*	*NY*	*VA*	*Total*
	MSA	3.64	3.98	4.17	3.17	2.69	5.48	3.49
	Rural	3.82	1.68	3.12	2.8	5.88	2.84	2.29
ABOVE 1,000,000	MSA	−1.37	—	—	—	2.21	—	1.05
500,000–999,999	MSA	4.62	—	1.44	.09	—	—	−2.90
250,000–499,999	MSA	2.06	2.14	—	—	1.20	6.67	2.66
100,000–249,999	MSA	4.05	3.21	—	3.10	3.59	4.17	3.89
50,000–99,999	MSA	3.26	2.89	1.67	2.34	1.37	4.07	2.92
25,000–49,999	MSA	4.43	7.04	5.70	4.82	3.49	6.10	4.57
10,000–24,999	MSA	5.69	3.34	5.87	3.71	2.88	6.89	4.47
5,000–9,999	MSA	3.70	3.48	4.67	5.85	3.57	1.11	3.74
2,500–4,999	MSA	2.58	−3.26	4.65	3.77	1.99	.49	2.17

25,000 and up	RURAL	.0	3.25	.0	7.13	1.85	6.16	3.30
10,000–24,999	RURAL	3.67	2.90	4.69	2.72	2.07	4.96	3.34
5,000–9,999	RURAL	4.74	2.93	4.01	4.38	2.39	.45	3.03
2,500–4,999	RURAL	3.17	.13	2.86	.09	−.84	4.38	1.50
< 2,500	RURAL	3.70	−1.05	−.58	.na	−.63	1.13	.18

Source: University of Maryland Analysis of USEEM data, 1980 to 1986. Using 1983 definition of metropolitan/nonmetropolitan counties.

TABLE 7-3

Retail Employment Growth Rate in Metropolitan and Nonmetropolitan Areas, 1980–1986 (Annual Average Percent Change)

	Metropolitan	Rural *Adjacent*	Rural *Nonadjacent*	Rural *Total*
California	4.1	4.6	2.6	4.3
Kansas	4.5	2.2	1.6	1.7
Maryland	4.7	2.4	4.3	3.4
Massachusetts	3.5	2.9	9.0	3.1
New York	2.9	.8	2.5	.9
Virginia	6.5	2.6	3.7	3.1

Source: University of Maryland analysis of USEEM data, 1980 and 1986.

where

E	= employment
P	= population
i	= service industry
r	= county
us	= United States

A quotient of 1 indicates that the region has the same ratio of service employment to population as the nation. Similarly, a quotient of greater than 1 indicates a greater ratio of service employment to population than the nation and suggests that a region supplies services to populations living outside the region. An increase in quotients between 1980 and 1986 would indicate an increase in rural service self-sufficiency or exports. A reduction could reflect the fact that rural residents are traveling further to make their purchases. A strong retail base may in some instances be explained by tourist expenditures rather than expenditures by locals. This is most likely the explanation for the high ratio found for nonadjacent counties in Massachusetts. Nantucket dominates this category and is a popular tourist and vacation spot.

This measure has shortcomings. A decline in the quotient could signify a loss in rural incomes relative to urban incomes. Data for the 1982–1986 period indicate that urban income growth exceeded rural income growth by more than 80 percent (Ghelfi and Majchrowicz, 1990), and this fact would contribute to reductions in employment/population quotients. Another weakness of this measure is its assumption of similar technologies and productivity levels across regions. For example, declines in quotients could be caused by the adoption of labor-saving technologies in one region. The national ratio in the denominator controls for the widespread adoption of labor-enhancing or displacing technological change.

As expected, the employment/population ratios are close to 1 in all locations, urban and rural. This indicates that rural areas are mostly self-sufficient in retail trade (see Table 7-4).

TABLE 7-4

Ratio of Retail Employment to Population Relative to the National Ratio, 1980 and 1986

	Metropolitan			*Rural Adjacent*			*Rural Nonadjacent*		
	1980	*1986*	*Ch*	*1980*	*1986*	*Ch*	*1980*	*1986*	*Ch*
California	0.91	0.91	+	0.92	0.88	–	0.85	0.94	+
Kansas	0.91	0.98	+	0.76	0.79	+	1.00	1.00	0
Maryland	0.89	0.98	+	0.35	0.32	–	1.12	1.20	+
Massachusetts	0.98	1.07	+	1.48	1.41	–	2.33	2.77	+
New York	0.81	0.86	+	0.77	0.73	–	0.70	0.74	+
Virginia	0.86	0.99	+	0.57	0.57	0	0.89	0.97	+

Ch = Change

Source: University of Maryland analysis of USEEM data, 1980 and 1986.

Retail trade includes such activities as general merchandise stores, food stores, auto dealers, apparel stores, furniture and home furnishings, and eating and drinking establishments.

In general, the quotients dropped in adjacent rural counties, a pattern that is consistent with the argument that rural residents close to metropolitan economies are traveling further to metropolitan areas to shop. The increase in the ratios for metropolitan counties is consistent with this story. Notably, the ratios are higher for the nonadjacent than the adjacent counties, and they are higher over time, indicating greater retail self-sufficiency in the most remote locations and increasing self-sufficiency over time.

Trends in Ownership

The most striking change in rural retailing between 1980 and 1986 was the penetration of branch retailers into rural counties and the dramatic decline of rural retailing employment in independently owned firms (Table 7-5). For example, in Kansas in 1980, nearly 70 percent of retail employment in nonadjacent rural counties was in independently owned firms.

TABLE 7-5

Share of Each Region's Employment in Independent, Headquarters, Subsidiary, and Branch Establishments (percent), 1980 and 1986

	Independent			*Headquarters*			*Subsidiary*			*Branch*			*Total*		
Year	*MSA*	*Rural Adj.*	*Rural Non-adj.*	*MSA*	*Rural Adj.*	*Rural Non-adj.*	*MSA*	*Rural Adj.*	*Rural Non-adj.*	*MSA*	*Rural Adj.*	*Rural Non-adj.*	*MSA*	*Rural Adj.*	*Rural Non-adj.*
							California								
1980	56	77	75	13	10	13	3	0	2	28	13	11	100	100	100
1986	48	65	67	11	10	11	2	1	1	39	24	21	100	100	100
							Kansas								
1980	55	72	70	15	11	9	4	2	1	26	15	20	100	100	100
1986	45	58	59	9	4	2	2	40	33	30	100	100	100	100	100
							Maryland								
1980	9	11	69	12	12	14	4	1	3	29	10	14	100	100	100
1986	55	77	58	10	11	9	3	2	4	36	19	30	100	100	100
							Massachusetts								
1980	51	68	88	12	8	4	4	1	—	21	10	8	100	100	100
1986	63	81	84	11	7	13	4	1	—	30	21	3	100	100	100
							New York								
1980	56	70	76	12	8	6	7	2	1	15	14	17	100	100	100
1986	66	76	63	10	8	5	5	1	1	25	24	32	100	100	100
							Virginia								
1980	60	67	71	13	7	9	5	2	1	29	17	19	100	100	100
1986	53	74	59	10	7	9	3	1	1	44	34	32	100	100	100

Source: University of Maryland analysis of USEEM data, 1980 and 1986.

By 1986, these establishments accounted for only 59 percent. Simultaneously, the share of retailing employment in branch establishments increased from 20 percent to 30 percent. In adjacent Kansas counties, the share of retailing employment in branches jumped from 15 percent in 1980 to 33 percent in 1986. This pattern was found in all of the six states.

Branch retailing grew at the expense of independent retailers. For example, retail service employment in rural Kansas counties grew by 1.8 percent. All of this growth was accounted for by branches and subsidiaries. Employment in the independents/headquarters category declined by .7 percent, while branch employment grew at an annual average rate of 2.5 percent per year (Table 7-6).

What does the growth of branch retailing imply for the welfare of the rural work force? In the retailing industry, rural workers employed by firms with 1,000 employees or more are more likely to work part time than are the rural employees of retailing firms with 25 employees or less. Our analysis of the 1990 Current Population Survey shows that 38 percent of rural workers in the less-than-25-employee-firm category worked part time. In the size category of 1,000-employee firms, 49 per-

TABLE 7-6

Sources of Employment Growth,
Branches and Subsidiaries versus Independents and Headquarters Rural Retail Services,
Annual Average Percent Change, 1980 to 1986

	CA	*KA*	*MD*	*MA*	*NY*	*VA*
Branches and Subsidiaries	2.4	2.5	2.6	2.3	1.9	3.3
Independents and Headquarters	1.4	−.7	.6	.8	−.8	−.5
State Total	3.8	1.8	3.2	3.1	1.1	2.8

Source: University of Maryland Analysis of USEEM data, 1980 and 1986.

cent of all rural employees worked part time. Although this breakdown is not a perfect surrogate for employment in branches and independents, the results are suggestive. Twenty-seven percent of the 2,358 rural employees in retail firms with fewer than 25 employees were noted as self-employed, compared to 1 percent of the 1,609 rural workers in retailing firms sized above 1,000 employees.

The prevalence of part-time work in a rural economy has several negative ramifications for local residents. Part-time work generally pays a lower hourly wage than does full-time. In addition, employees are usually ineligible for unemployment benefits should they be laid off. Part-time workers do not typically receive medical insurance benefits. And labor forces in which many workers are employed part time (with a resulting reduction in the reported unemployment rate) may not be as attractive to potential new industry as another community in which the unemployment rate is high.

Case Study: Olney, Illinois

The following case study of retailing change in the rural communities surrounding Olney, Illinois illustrates the impacts that community size, proximity to a metropolitan center, and large retail chain outlets can have on traditional rural retail operations. Olney is a southern Illinois community located in rural Richland County. Richland County is not adjacent to a metropolitan area, and Olney had a 1990 population of 8,500. Its economic base is diverse and includes agriculture, oil mining, manufacturing, a regional health center, and a junior college. The surrounding counties, Jasper and Edwards, are smaller places and are also not adjacent to metropolitan areas. In 1990, the approximate population of Newton (in Jasper County) was 3,000 and of Albion (in Edwards County) was 2,100.

In 1978, a Walmart discount store opened outside Olney's traditional downtown. Impacts were felt almost immediately. Within the first year of the retailer's opening, several downtown stores, including a five-and-dime, a hardware store, and a pharmacy, all closed their doors. And although a second pharmacy moved into the fringe mall housing the Walmart, there were additional downtown closures over the next few years (though not all local business failures were precipitated by Walmart's arrival).

More recently, Olney's downtown has recovered somewhat despite the fact that local population is declining. Since 1986, five new specialty stores have opened and offer higher-quality merchandise (such as fine jewelry and apparel) that does not compete directly with Walmart.

Walmart's presence is reflected in Richland County economic statistics. Olney Township comprises nearly 65 percent of Richland County's population, and Richland County's overall retail growth has been 1.86 percent per year—faster than the surrounding counties (even though Edwards County experienced more rapid income growth). The greatest local growth is concentrated in general merchandising, with average increases of 15.59 percent per year throughout the 1980s. While Richland County's population has declined and the county's mean effective buying income has increased only slightly, general merchandise sales growth has been substantially higher than for either neighboring Jasper or Edwards Counties. The combination of town size, nonadjacency, presence of Walmart, and lower transportation costs have strengthened Olney's retail position in the region.

The three communities demonstrate a major limitation of central place theory. Rather than a neat hierarchy of places, small communities can specialize in a retail area. For example, furniture, eating and drinking places, and automotive sales grew fastest in Jasper County, even though its major town center, Newton, is smaller than Olney (Table 7-7).

Summary

Retail trade is growing rapidly at the national level, and whereas all county size categories display this vitality, the slowest growth occurred in the smallest rural places. Suburban areas and medium-size urban centers have been the biggest

TABLE 7-7

Change in Population, Income, and Retail Sales, 1981–1990 for Three Counties in Southern Illinois

	Richland	*Jasper*	*Edwards*
Population	−0.81%	−3.10%	−1.00%
Income	3.15%	−0.75%	3.48%
Retail Sales	1.86%	1.47%	0.84%
Grocery Stores	−5.45%	0.00%	7.10%
Eating/Drinking	1.50%	3.02%	−5.53%
General Merch.	15.59%	5.44%	5.71%
Furniture	−1.84%	3.64%	0.19%
Automotive	4.06%	5.26%	−8.87%
Pharmacies	9.67%	NA	NA

Source: Richland County Chamber of Commerce.

winners of increased retail services sector growth. Spatial variations in retail employment growth offer opportunities for medium-size rural communities, particularly those not adjacent to metropolitan centers. As rural residents travel further to shop, medium size nodes can capture a larger share of regional dollars. Increasingly, the decisions made by large chain retailers such as Walmart will determine the locations of these regional nodes.

Across both urban and rural locations there are dramatic shifts in retail ownership patterns. Small, locally owned retail businesses are rapidly vanishing and being replaced by branches of large, multi-branch specialty retailers. Although these retailers offer a wider range of goods at lower prices for the consumer, there may be negative consequences for the quality of local jobs, local circulation of profits, and the ultimate identity and vitality of rural downtowns.

Consumer Services

Consumer services include hotels and other lodging places, personal services (such as dry cleaners, barber shops, etc.), auto repair and other repair services, motion pictures, amusement and recreation services, and private household services. Reflecting rapid national growth in consumer services, all county types experienced positive consumer employment growth (Table 7-8). However, suburban fringe and smaller urban counties experienced more rapid growth than that of the nation in these sectors. This trend can be explained by: (1) falling transportation costs, which in accordance with the central place model results in individuals traveling further to shop; (2) declining retail trade in the smallest towns as rural shoppers elect to frequent regional shopping nodes that offer consumer services; and (3) declining rural population and income.

Again, we use the USEEM data to analyze employment growth by city size. Losses of consumer services are particularly evident in rural Kansas, New York, and Massachusetts. California and Virginia are both states with sizable rural tourism and retirement growth, and both states show steady consumer growth across most rural communities. In Kansas, where retirement and tourism development are probably least likely to occur, there are declines in consumer service employment across all rural size classes (see Table 7-9). Consumer service growth is greatest in metropolitan centers sized 10,000 to 24,999.

Consumer services in metropolitan-adjacent, yet completely rural counties grew at a pace more rapid than that of the nation. This pattern shows up in both our national county-level analysis (Table 7-8) and in the establishment-based six-state analysis (Table 7-10).

Trends in Ownership

While there are differences across consumer service activities, in general these are not activities which have seen growing economies to scale or increasing employment concentrations in branches. For the most part, consumer services continue to be carried out by small, independent firms (see Table 7-11). This pattern is more exaggerated for rural communities, where, for example, about 80 percent of rural Kansas consumer service employment is in independent firms. Across the states, employment losses are occurring in branches as well as in independents (see Table 7-12).

The process of ownership consolidation seen in the retail sector was not evident in consumer services. This was somewhat surprising in light of anecdotal evidence that suggests there has been significant augmentation of consumer services functions through innovations in distribution and marketing. For example, the USEEM data does not distinguish between independent and franchise operations. It may be that consumer services are erroneously identified as independent establishments when they are in fact part of a larger franchise business operation. Some of the decline seen in the consumer services category, in particular in the smallest rural places, may reflect the incorporation of formerly independent operations such as film finishing, video rentals, and dry cleaning into retail operations. Finally, declines in consumer services may also reflect the geographic consolidation of retail functions which draw other consumer operations to centralized locations.

Conclusion

Rural and urban economies have both reflected rapid national growth in retail and consumer service employment. But rural and central city economies received smaller shares of this growth than did suburbs and medium-sized cities. Both consumer and retail service employment growth is particularly weak in the smallest rural communities, with a number of states showing employment declines in rural towns sized 5,000 population and below. Population and income losses are, in part, responsible. Increases in market threshold and range have occurred in retail services, moving these activities up the city-size hierarchy.

There are notable long-run equity concerns associated with these trends. As higher-income households travel further to take advantage of the wider range of services available in larger communities, smaller centers decline. The range of services remaining locally available to those who are less mobile,

TABLE 7-8

Shift-Share Analysis of Employment Change for the Mainly Consumer Service Industry in Each Urban Rural Area between 1974 and 1985

County Type	*(1)* *Employment in 1974*	*(2)* *Employment in 1985*	*(3)* *Absolute Change*	*(4)* *National Effect*	*(5)* *Industry Mix Effect*	*(6)* *Regional Shares Effect*	*(7)* *Annual Average Percent Change*
Core, 1 million and above	998,442	1,292,740	294,298	279,168	95,559	−80,430	2.35
Fringe, 1 million and above	324,443	533,889	209,446	90,716	31,052	87,679	4.53
250,000 to 1 million	614,253	879,632	265,379	171,748	58,789	34,842	3.27
Metropolitan < 250,000	229,486	322,753	93,267	64,165	21,964	7,138	3.10
Nonmetropolitan, >20,000 urban adjacent	87,062	108,328	21,266	24,343	8,333	−11,409	1.99
Nonmetropolitan, >20,000 urban nonadjacent	91,490	116,953	25,463	25,581	8,756	−8,874	2.23
Nonmetropolitan, < 20,000 adjacent	87,346	105,813	18,467	24,422	8,360	−14,315	1.74
Nonmetropolitan, < 20,000 nonadjacent	123,905	155,202	31,297	34,644	11,859	−15,206	2.05
Completely rural adjacent	11,178	16,315	5,137	3,125	1,070	942	3.44
Completely rural nonadjacent	23,926	32,540	8,614	6,690	2,290	−366	2.80

Source: U.S. Department of Commerce *County Business Patterns* 1985, 1974.

TABLE 7-9

Annual Average Consumer Services Employment Growth Rates by City Size in Six Study States (Percent)

City Size	*Metropolitan/Rural*	*CA*	*KA*	*MD*	*MA*	*NY*	*VA*	*Total*
	MSA	3.28	2.85	3.67	3.39	2.49	2.43	2.79
	Rural	2.41	−1.00	.91	−.39	−1.10	2.18	.51
Above 1,000,000	MSA	.23	—	—	—	2.80	—	1.79
500,000–999,999	MSA	3.43	—	1.77	7.17	—	—	3.94
250,000–499,999	MSA	4.90	2.01	—	—	.41	2.96	3.21
100,000–249,999	MSA	4.19	1.77	—	4.27	2.75	3.48	3.67
50,000–99,999	MSA	2.89	6.71	5.29	−1.29	.47	7.59	2.12
25,000–49,999	MSA	4.09	5.15	3.06	3.71	5.41	1.63	4.00
10,000–24,999	MSA	5.56	−3.92	−3.01	4.74	4.18	5.03	4.47
5,000–9,999	MSA	3.60	3.75	−1.84	1.94	2.13	5.93	2.55
2,500–4,999	MSA	9.75	1.83	1.89	1.02	1.01	5.24	3.13
25,000 and up	Rural	0	−.24	0	7.26	.83	8.63	1.76
10,000–24,999	Rural	1.84	−.34	−.09	2.27	−3.70	3.76	.69
5,000–9,999	Rural	4.21	−3.09	7.77	.52	2.44	2.99	2.04
2,500–4,999	Rural	−3.40	.18	−1.81	−.31	−1.57	1.28	−1.29
2,500 and Below		4.24	−2.70	2.68	NA	−1.17	.19	.16

Source: University of Maryland Analysis of USEEM data, 1980 to 1986. Using 1983 definition of metropolitan/nonmetropolitan counties.

TABLE 7-10

Consumer Employment Growth Rate in Metropolitan and Nonmetropolitan Areas, by State 1980–1986 (Annual Average Percent Change)

	Metropolitan	*Rural Adjacent*	*Rural Non-Adjacent*	*Rural Total*
California	3.8	2.7	1.6	2.6
Kansas	3.1	−1.5	−.8	−1.0
Maryland	4.1	4.4	−.7	.9
Massachusetts	3.8	−.2	−1.2	−.4
New York	2.7	3.2	−1.6	−1.1
Virginia	4.2	3.4	1.4	2.3

Source: University of Maryland analysis of USEEM data 1980 and 1986. Using 1983 definition of metropolitan/nonmetropolitan counties.

TABLE 7-11

Share of Each Region's Consumer Employment in Independent, Headquarters, Subsidiary, and Branch Establishments

	Independent			*Headquarters*			*Subsidiary*			*Branch*			*Total*		
Year	*MSA*	*Rural Adj.*	*Rural Nonadj.*	*MSA*	*Rural Adj.*	*Rural Nonadj.*	*MSA*	*Rural Adj.*	*Rural Nonadj.*	*MSA*	*Rural Adj.*	*Rural Nonadj.*	*MSA*	*Rural Adj.*	*Rural Nonadj.*
							California								
1980	58	78	76	14	3	8	5	5	—	23	13	16	100	100	100
1986	55	69	73	11	4	6	6	7	5	27	20	15	100	100	100
							Kansas								
1980	64	83	80	11	4	8	7	1	1	18	12	12	100	100	100
1986	58	7	79	10	11	9	4	0	1	28	10	12	100	100	100
							Maryland								
1980	69	81	76	11	8	7	4	6	4	15	4	13	100	100	100
1986	64	76	76	11	4	13	6	7	6	20	13	5	100	100	100
							Massachusetts								
1980	66	85	90	10	7	9	3	0	—	21	8	1	100	100	100
1986	57	84	80	12	6	18	7	0	—	25	10	2	100	100	100
							New York								
1980	68	74	74	13	12	4	8	2	0	12	12	22	100	100	100
1986	65	78	73	11	7	3	7	3	0	18	12	24	100	100	100
							Virginia								
1980	59	80	70	12	7	18	3	3	2	25	11	10	100	100	100
1986	55	76	64	14	6	11	3	4	2	29	14	23	100	100	100

Source: University of Maryland analysis of USEEM data, 1980 and 1986. Using the 1983 definition of metropolitan/nonmetropolitan counties.

TABLE 7-12

Sources of Employment Growth, Consumer Services, Annual Average Rate, 1980–1986

	CA	*KS*	*MD*	*MA*	*NY*	*VA*
Branches and Subsidiaries	.9	−.3	−.5	.4	−.7	1.5
Independents and Headquarters	1.7	−.4	2.1	−.5	−.1	.6
Total	2.6	−.7	1.6	−.1	−.8	2.1

Source: University of Maryland Analysis of USEEM data, 1980 and 1986.

primarily the elderly and low-income residents, are diminished, and access to retail and consumer services can become seriously inadequate.

One final and striking finding for retail trade is the displacement of independent retailers with branches of multi-unit firms. In all six states, branches were responsible for nearly all of the growth in retailing employment. Yet, this pattern was not evident in our data on consumer services activities. Although branch outlets may supply a wider range of goods at more competitive prices, the quality of local jobs may be diminished. More part-time work, a loss in profit income, and a weakened downtown are frequent consequences.

8

Conclusions

As we move through the decade of the 1990s, rural America suffers from many of the persistent problems that trouble our central cities: high unemployment, above-average rates of poverty, population losses, and lagging educational attainment. Rural communities are reeling from the triple impacts of falling commodity prices and restructuring in agriculture; the stagnation and cyclical instability of manufacturing; and losses in mining income. It is not surprising that those concerned about the welfare of rural America are looking to service jobs as one promise for the future.

Will service-led growth be the basis for the next phase of development in rural America? Without public intervention to encourage them, will services fill the vacuum of lost farming, manufacturing, and mining jobs and stabilize, if not revitalize, rural communities? Or are deliberate policies and investments necessary to integrate rural economies into the information age and permit the full participation of rural communities in the global service economy? If public and private interventions are mandated, what types of strategies make sense? And where should investments be made? These are the questions that motivated this book. In this final chapter, we summarize our major findings and reflect upon opportunities for public policy action.

The Service Economy in Rural America

The recent stream of rural research admonishes scholars to recognize the diversity of rural economies and warns of the misconceptions that arise when rural America is analyzed as an undifferentiated whole. Although we don't doubt the general validity of this advice, the national growth of services plays out in a remarkably consistent pattern across rural economies of all types. Services are the major job generator in rural America. A disproportionate share of rural service jobs and job growth are in residentiary rather than export-oriented services, and rural service job growth lags behind that of metropolitan centers. With exceptions noted below, the most interesting insights emerged when our analyses cut across categories of services rather than types of rural economies. Therefore, we summarize the results of our analysis by type of service: directly exported services, indirectly exported services, and residentiary services.

Export-Oriented Services

Examples of sophisticated export-oriented firms in rural, or even remote rural, areas exist. However, these firms generally tend to be small and independently owned, and site selection has been based on quality of life considerations rather than on economic rationality or profit maximization criteria. Directly exported services are underrepresented in rural economies, and the growth of rural producer services is not keeping pace with that of cities. Rural counties contain a small proportion of producer services relative to their share of population. And with few exceptions, the service employment to population ratio in rural areas remained constant in the six case study states between 1980 and 1986.

There is only limited evidence that producer services will follow the path of manufacturing and filter down to nonmetropolitan counties. Most producer service industries rely on highly skilled and highly compensated labor. Any tendency for export-based service jobs to decentralize appears to occur on the fringes of metropolitan areas. In the case of producer service industries, urban core counties and remote rural locations clearly lag behind suburban areas. The need for face-to-face contacts and access to new markets and a diverse client base, combined with a high dependence on skilled labor, weds export services to urban agglomerations.

Service industries in which the labor process is divisible demonstrate some potential to filter jobs down the urban hierarchy. Yet this prospect may prove to be ephemeral. Location decisions in the 1990s are occurring in an environment in which there is intense foreign competition for markets; improved communications makes real-time interaction across long distances possible; domestic managers have acquired substantial experience in the operation of off-shore production locations; and governments of less developed nations have grown quite sophisticated in working with investors wishing to establish foreign operations. Service firms that might have previously selected a rural location for a facility site are now shifting operations directly off-shore, by-passing rural America altogether.

This rather grim prognosis does not negate the fact that rural export-oriented services exist and are major employers for a number of rural communities. Without a conscious policy to preserve these jobs in their present locations, the long-run viability of these rural back-office functions and ultimately for the rural communities in which they reside is uncertain. Rural America is increasingly in direct competition with less developed nations for low-skilled jobs in services as well as manufacturing industries.

Indirect Exports

The long-standing rural dependence on branch plant manufacturing, agribusiness, and corporate mining has stunted the structure of the rural service sector. The paucity of rural business support services inhibits future competitiveness for attracting higher skilled, more complex manufacturing activities. As service inputs become a more important component of all manufactured outputs, a complement of supporting services may be increasingly important in firm location decisions. Rural economies are clearly disadvantaged on this front.

Residentiary Services

In general, residentiary services do not act propulsively to create additional rural income growth. Rural residents are increasingly traveling to shop and are spending more of their incomes in larger, more urbanized communities. Small towns in the shadow of urban centers have exhibited the slowest retail employment growth.

Rather than facilitating the filtering of services, telecommunications innovations appear to be costing rural communities traditional residentiary jobs. For example, in the banking industry, for which rural institutions once held a spatial monopoly, telecommunications technology now allows urban-based banks to infiltrate, compete with, and displace rural banks or traditional rural banking functions.

Historically, rural services were organically grown and thus independently owned. Whereas this characterization is still true for consumer services, externally owned businesses are rapidly replacing small rural retailers. Case studies from individual towns and our empirical evidence clearly document the corporate takeover of rural retailing. The ultimate impact on rural downtowns, quality of retailing jobs, and locally owned businesses are issues for further study.

Implications for Development Practice

There are three principal ways in which rural economies can and are experiencing development and change: (1) through carefully crafted federal, state, and local initiatives that encourage investment; (2) through market forces that favor particular rural communities; and (3) through the efforts of local citizens, churches, and nonprofit organizations.

Public Policy and a Services-based Development Policy

Services are not a cure-all for the economic decline experienced in many rural places over the decade of the 1980s. Nonetheless, cultivating a vibrant service base is an important component of any comprehensive development strategy. Rather than abandoning current practices, it is necessary to fine-tune existing programs to better account for global trends in services. A number of approaches to services development are possible. Most importantly, industry and firm recruitment efforts should be balanced with efforts to encourage home-grown activities. In order for any service development strategy to be successful, greater emphasis must be placed on education and training of the labor force. Investment and technical assistance programs should be developed based on making local firms more competitive in, and having better access to, national and international markets. Incentives should also be established that encourage existing firms to diversify into new activities and new lines of business. These programs should extend to procurement assistance with the goal of increasing purchases of local services. Communities with tourism and recreation potential should develop policies and activities designed to market their natural, cultural, and historical amenities. Regional market niches in residentiary services should be exploited by revitalizing downtowns and encouraging local entrepreneurship.

Selecting specific services as targets for rural investment raises much of the criticism associated with chasing manufacturing firms. Problems arise in identifying potential service activities appropriate for rural development programs. In general it is difficult to accurately identify industries with a local future. Data limitations constrain a community's ability to identify potential businesses or industry sectors as appropriate recipients of public assistance. Based on broad industry classification schemes, economic development officials might target service industries because they are growing nationally. But trends at the national level often mask highly variable growth experiences of firms in different communities. Organizational issues are also relevant in considering policies designed to attract back-office functions. Branch activities often exhibit only a tenuous commitment to location. In addition, the arrival of branch facilities may adversely affect existing businesses with longer-run commitments to a local region. For all of these reasons, strategies that aim to build and strengthen existing local service firms and activities hold the most promise.

Strategies for Rural Service Exporters

Rural economies will continue to hold an advantage relative to urban areas in labor-intensive tasks and in activities with weak linkages to suppliers and markets. Compared to less developed countries, rural America offers close proximity to markets and the advantage of a work force capable of performing tasks that require some knowledge of standard American business practices and some ability to make decisions about questionable data. The best alternative for future rural development is to build on the skill base associated with existing industries. This would involve moving the existing labor force up the skills ladder and providing more specialized services for existing and new customers.

Technical Assistance

Limited technical and financial resources and distance from competitors make it difficult for rural firms, particularly the smaller ones, to keep abreast of new markets and technological change in industry. A number of model technical assistance programs are already in place. One is PENNTAP, a Pennsylvania state-funded program, designed to provide technology transfer and technological assistance to Pennsylvania businesses and other organizations. Economic development is the program's explicit objective. Started in 1965, the Pennsylvania State University/State Department of Commerce program was designed to disseminate information on new technologies. The staff includes engineers, scientists, and librarians. In 1987, nearly 80 percent (982 out of 1,200) of requests for assistance originated in small-town and rural Pennsylvania.

Training Assistance

One commonly cited barrier to upgrading the technological base of rural area industries is long-standing deficiencies in the technical education levels of the rural work force. New technologies and evolving markets require upgrades in work force skills as well as changes in production and firm organization. Yet, small rural service firms find it difficult to provide training for workers. Larger branch establishments generally have organized education programs for managers and supervisors, but it is usually left up to these employees to arrange for training of other workers. Because profit margins are modest for most service providers, small- and medium-size firms find it especially difficult to finance training and education programs for workers. And although most published studies examining the impact of education on rural economic development find the relationship tenuous at best, there is widespread agreement that training linked to specific jobs in targeted industries can be a successful development strategy.

Capital Subsidies

Low-interest government loans, such as those offered by the Urban Development Action Grant (UDAG) program in rural areas, are a proven means of assisting firms with the purchase of capital equipment when new adoptions are cost effective. A study of the now-defunct UDAG program found that rural firms mostly used the program to obtain financing not accessible to them in private markets and to take advantage of lower financing costs (Howland 1990). Although the results of this survey of program recipients may be biased (because only surviving firms were available for interviews), new equipment purchased with capital subsidies improved business competitiveness and was often critical to enterprise longevity.

Telecommunications

The value of integrating rural communities into urban and international networks via improved telecommunications technologies is not at issue. Most agree that the quality of rural education, health care, and employment could improve with better telecommunication linkages. The key question is whether the costs of supplying each rural location with fiber optic cables and digital switching are justified by the benefits to be reaped. For many communities the answer is no.

One option is to develop demonstration projects based on the model of Nordic telecottages (where selected rural communities received enhanced telelecommunications linkages). Initial experiments in rural America could be carried out in communities with track records in computer-based industries. Although access to fiber optic cables, digital switching, and satellite links will not ensure that jobs remain in rural areas, nonetheless, rural data entry operations cannot remain competitive without upgrades of antiquated telephone lines and electronic switching.

Implications for Development Theory

Aside from policy issues, our findings have implications for development theory. The spatial division of labor model allocates economic units on the basis of minimizing labor costs for a given skill level. At one end of the continuum, complex manufacturing concentrates in urban centers for proximity to a skilled labor force. At the other end, the lowest skilled tasks are dispersed to regions of the world with the lowest labor costs. In the spatial division of labor model, international labor costs drive location. Firms' management capabilities and industrial structure influence the scope of locations considered. Improvements in telecommunications increase the range of feasible production locations.

The spatial division of labor model was developed with manufacturing in mind; yet it applies, with some caveats associated with the importance of markets, to a range of services. A large share of services are transitory in nature, requiring face-to-face contact and proximity to markets to complete transactions. In this instance the nature of a transaction defines a critical axis in the location decision, and local labor quality is less a determinant, if not irrelevent. For example, when services are internationally or cross-regionally traded, a client will travel to the point of production or a consultant will travel to the point of consumption.

Yet, other services for which the labor process is divisible can be executed or transacted without regard to market location. Location decisions in these types of industries are driven by the search for the lowest wage, literate labor force. Technology and institutional factors are a critical axis constraining the range of locations. For example, there is a limit to the speed with which the hard copy of a document can be shipped off-shore. Rural areas maintain a market niche because they can complete data entry activities and return products to clients in as little as 24 hours. Off-shore data entry generally requires at least 48 hours. Imaging technology such as facsimile is improving with time and will eventually permit the speedy transmission of hard-copy documents. When this can occur instantaneously over telephone lines, rural data entry firms will lose their market niche to off-shore firms with lower labor costs.

Technological change can also move firms beyond the purview of the labor-driven location decision (away from the high-skilled versus low-skilled continuum search). For example, optical scanning displaces labor almost entirely. Firms are then free to locate data entry facilities on the basis of criteria other than labor costs, such as proximity to clients and material inputs.

Nonetheless, for some services, the spatial division of labor model accurately places rural America in the position of being a way-station between urban America and off-shore production. With improvements in telecommunications and transportation technologies and the growing sophistication of American firms operating in international locations, rural areas can no longer count on receiving service jobs that might be capable of decentralizing to lower-cost locations. Those of us concerned about the future of rural America would be wise to look at the experiences and successes of the newly industrializing countries (NICs). Singapore, Taiwan, South Korea, and Hong Kong along with other success stories were once the recipients of low wage, low skilled employment from the core industrialized countries. Rather than passively waiting for externally owned companies to move on to even lower wage regions, the NIC governments adopted conscious and well-conceived policies to upgrade their work force, to install the infrastucture that integrates local business into the global economy, and to develop competitive export sectors. The case study of computer services shows that other low income countries are doing the same. Without a similar strategy for rural America, we risk reducing the rural standard to that approaching the poorest regions of the world.

Appendix I: Geographic System Used to Identify Rural Areas

The urban-rural continuum used in the analysis of County Business Patterned Data was designed by Calvin Beale of the U.S. Department of Agriculture, Economic Research Service, Economic Development Division. The criteria for designating a county as urban or rural are based on population size, commuting patterns of residents in individual counties, and the county's spatial position relative to a metropolitan area. Metropolitan status is that announced by the Office of Management and Budget in June 1983, when the current population criteria were first applied to results of the 1980 Census. Adjacency was determined by physical boundary adjacency and a finding that at least 2 percent of the employed labor force in the nonmetropolitan county commuted to metropolitan central counties. This scheme has subsequently been updated to take into account the 1983 redefinition of metropolitan areas and the incorporation of formerly adjacent rural counties into metropolitan areas.

The classification scheme consists of ten urban-rural categories. Categories 0–3 identify counties that are metropolitan in nature. Metropolitan is defined as counties with populations between 50,000 and 1 million or more. Both central counties and fringe counties of a metropolitan area are separately identified.

Rural counties are classified based on population and adjacency to a metropolitan area. Categories 4–9 classify counties on the basis of population size—20,000 or more, 20,000 or less, and completely rural—and on the basis of whether they are adjacent to a metropolitan area.

Metropolitan Counties

0 Central counties of metropolitan areas of 1 million population or more.
1 Fringe counties of metropolitan areas of 1 million population or more.
2 Counties in metropolitan areas of 250,000 to 1 million population.
3 Counties in metropolitan areas of less than 250,000 population.

Nonmetropolitan Counties

4 Urban population of 20,000 or more, adjacent to a metropolitan area.
5 Urban population of 20,000 or more, not adjacent to a metropolitan area.
6 Urban population of less than 20,000 adjacent to a metropolitan area.
7 Urban population of less than 20,000 not adjacent to a metropolitan area.
8 Completely rural, adjacent to a metropolitan area.
9 Completely rural, not adjacent to a metropolitan area.

Appendix II: Data Sources and Limitations

This study is based on two levels of geographical analysis. Nationwide, our analysis of a detailed 97-sector data set was drawn from *County Business Patterns*. We attempted to accumulate an aggregated perspective of rural services and the extent to which rural counties' experiences reflect those of the nation. Data for 1974 and 1985 were analyzed to determine the spatial structure of service industries in rural areas. In addition to analysis of all service sectors, as defined by the SIC code book of the U.S. Department of Commerce, a subset of industries classified as producer services and manufacturing industries was also examined.

We also picked six states for their economic characteristics and varied rural experiences. These states include California, Kansas, Maryland, Massachusetts, New York, and Virginia. The Small Business Administration's U.S. Establishment and Enterprise Microdata (USEEM) file on wholesaling, trade, finance, insurance and real estate, and personal business and health services was examined. The dataset includes the establishments in SIC codes 40 through 89 in either 1980 or 1986. The USEEM file was developed by the Small Business Administration (SBA) to provide a detailed record of the activities of large and small American firms and establishments with employees. The Duns Market Identifiers (DMI) file, from which it was constructed, focuses particularly on establishments which purchase insurance, intermediate products, or sell to other firms on credit or that borrow in private credit markets. The coverage of the USEEM file is compared to other federal data sources, and finally the results of local data checks and corrections are reported.

In this appendix we describe the characteristics of each of these datasets and outline their advantages and disadvantages for the study of rural economies. An awareness of these datasets' shortcomings are crucial to their proper application and interpretation.

The Organizational Basis of County Business Patterns, Recent Revisions and Classification Changes

County Business Patterns (CBP) data include employment and establishments which are covered under the Federal Insurance Contributions Act (FICA). According to this legislation, employers are required to file quarterly statements of wages and Social Security benefits paid on behalf of workers. Employment that is *not* included under FICA includes government, domestic service, self-employed persons, agricultural production workers, foreign employment, ships at sea, and railroad employment that is jointly covered by Social Security and railroad retirement programs. Thus, this employment is also not included in County Business Patterns employment or establishment counts.

Prior to 1984, nonprofit organizations were not required to file FICA reports, and filing was elective for religious organizations. Only since 1984 have these employees and establishments been included in CBP data.

The implications for these changes in data reporting in CBP may be significant for this study. Large gains in employment in these specific services sectors over the 1974–1985 period may be partly attributable to the fact that these workers were simply not counted in earlier periods.

Gains in other sectors may be due to a combination of factors to which the CBP changes also contribute. For example, anecdotal evidence shows that during the 1970s and 1980s decades, many rural county-owned hospitals were sold to for-profit or nonprofit medical care corporations. Hospitals are also often operated by religious organizations. Thus, large gains in medical services employment may be partly due to shifts in employment from government to services sectors, and partly attributable to the fact that nonprofit and religious organization employment began to be counted for the first time in 1984.

Educational services employment and establishment counts may also be affected by changes in reporting in CBP data since 1984. Although there has been documented proliferation of educational institutions in the last decade, employment gains may also be partly attributable to the fact that nonprofit and religious organizations make up a fairly significant proportion of parochial schools and other primary, secondary, and higher-education institutions. Thus, it would be difficult to separate the effects of changes in data reporting from actual job growth over the study period.

The Use of County Business Patterns for Rural Research

Using CBP data for rural research has a number of limitations. Perhaps the most significant problem is the exclusion of certain industries. Neither agriculture nor government industries (two important rural sectors) are included in CBP. This omission problem can be overcome by substituting information from other (comparable) sources.

A secondary problem associated with using CBP data to study services employment in rural areas is the possibility of underreporting small establishments. Services are volatile sectors. Detailed analysis of other data sources (such as Dun and Bradstreet and Economic Census') identifies a high frequency of sector switching—the movement of establishments among sectors—and a high rate of business failure. Furthermore, many small service establishments are operated out of individuals' homes. Whether these organizations are incorporated into federal data bases fundamentally depends on whether the proprietor reports the business for tax purposes and employs one or more workers in the establishment. While CBP data are considered a census of establishments over 250 employees, the remaining establishments are accounted for by using other data sources such as administrative records (e.g., Internal Revenue files).

An equally intractable problem using any government data source is establishment classification based on the SIC code system. At high levels of disaggregation, comparison of Dun & Bradstreet, Iowa sales tax records, and County Business Patterns data indicates significant differences among the number of reporting units. This variation in establishment classification results in erratic reporting of establishments by SIC code. This is a particular problem given service industries' volatility and the high frequency of sector switching. Readers should be advised that these problems are no-doubt reflected in the data used in this study.

USEEM Dataset

The USEEM file includes information on individual establishments, as opposed to firms, so that branch plant and subsidiary information are recorded separately from that of its headquarters. The variables available for each establishment are listed in Table A-1.[1]

The most important advantage of the USEEM data is that they provide employment and location information on individual establishments. As a result, aggregate growth figures can be examined at fine levels of geographical and industrial detail.

There are other sources of macroeconomic data maintained by the Bureau of Census, the Bureau of Labor Statistics, and the Internal Revenue Service of the U.S. Department of Commerce. Only one source, *Enterprise Statistics*, collected by the Bureau of the Census, contains information that may be broken out by firm or enterprise. *Enterprise Statistics* does not, however, include geographical information, which limits its usefulness for studying regional growth patterns.

Because confidentiality of the establishment is not an issue in the USEEM file, as it is in all federally collected data sources, the USEEM data includes each establishment's exact address and 4-digit SIC code. This is of particular advantage in

TABLE A-1

Variables Included in U.S. Establishment and Enterprise Microdata File

For All Establishments
- Business Name
- Street Address
- Mailing Address
- Zip Code
- City Name
- County Code
- State Code
- Telephone Number
- Number of Employees at that address
- SIC Code at the 4-digit level
- Establishments status as an independent, branch, headquarters, or subsidiary

For Headquarters Only
- Year the firm started

For Branches and Subsidiaries Only
- Name of ultimate owners
- Street address of ultimate owner
- Zip code of ultimate owner
- City name of ultimate owner
- Mailing address of ultimate owner
- Number of employees in firm (all affiliates)
- Ultimate owner's SIC code at the 4-digit level
- Telephone number of ultimate owners

the study of rural economies. Using the USEEM data file, we are able to examine the composition and employment growth of rural economies to the town level (or smaller if desired) and to the 4-digit level of industrial detail.

A second advantage is that the file includes telephone numbers for each establishment. Therefore, we could easily conduct telephone surveys with establishments to crosscheck the data or accuracy and to gather information not available in the data set.

A third advantage of the USEEM file is that data on individual establishments can be linked over time to gain a time-series view of establishment behavior. This permits aggregate employment growth to be subdivided into the sources of growth by start-ups, expansions, migration, or closures. These components of growth can be further divided by size of firm or establishment status as a branch or headquarters. *Enterprise Statistics* (*ES*) does not permit the linking of establishments' employment over time, thus the USEEM data base provides the only data that allow a researcher to determine the sources of economic growth.

Fourth, the SBA has taken on a major effort to tie the data for each establishment to data for each establishment's parent or headquarters. Thus, we can determine whether the growth (or decline) in rural service employment is coming from "home grown" firms or those with headquarters out-of-state.

A fifth advantage is that these data are collected by Dun and Bradstreet (D&B) in the process of conducting credit checks on firms. Thus, establishments in this case have an incentive to cooperate and to give correct information. This is not always the case for government-collected data.

Detection and Correction of Errors

Like all data sets, the USEEM file has its limitations, and these must be understood in order to assess the questions these data can appropriately address. One shortcoming of the data is that DMI may not be complete in its coverage of all establishments affiliated with some firms. Because the data are collected for credit rating purposes and data on specific branches are not important for assessing a firm's credit rating, DMI is less assiduous in collecting data on branches than on headquarters. Therefore, some large firms do not provide D&B with all the detailed information necessary to completely disaggregate their firm-wide employment into separate reports for each and every affiliated location. It is difficult to assess the extent of this problem. The SBA compared the total firm employment as reported in headquarters records with the sum of all employees as reported in all affiliated locations. Using this method, it was estimated by the SBA that nearly half of the branch locations have not been covered in the DMI file, leaving a third of branch employment unaccounted for. However, other researchers claim that most of these unaccounted-for branches are oversees operations. For example, MacDonald (1985) examined the reliability of the USEEM data for the Food and Tobacco industries and found that virtually all of the unaccounted-for affiliate employment was in foreign operations.

In constructing the USEEM file, additional branch records were imputed to account for any part of each firm's reported firm-wide employment which was not already allocated to a particular location and industry. These "proxy" branch records are constructed by assuming the previously unaccounted-for employment is in branch establishments in the same state and industry as their headquarters. This allocation probably over- states the actual employment in those states with a high proportion of headquarters, and understates it for those with a relatively low proportion of headquarters. Comparisons with the Census's *ES* is of little use to assess the allocation of proxy records for branch locations. The published *ES* have no geographic dimension, and, furthermore, show fewer branch locations in total than the unedited USEEM.

We have treated this problem by excluding the proxy branches. These observations have no location, other than a state variable. Therefore, they can not be assigned to a rural or metropolitan location.

A second bias occurs because D&B often does not recognize start-ups until several years after the business's inception. The SBA estimates that about 45 percent of the reported births of firms are firms which are already over two years old. Thus, there is a tendency to understate the number of new firms for sectors or areas with rapidly increasing start-up rates and overstate it during recessionary downturns for the national economy, when actual start-ups are falling. In reference to this study, we suspect there is undercounting of start-ups across the service categories because of this sector's rapid growth. In addition, relative to rural counties, there will be a slight downward bias in the growth rates for urban counties, where employment growth is highest.

Similarly, the dissolution of an establishment may not be picked up promptly by D&B, therefore all closures are probably not fully accounted for within any given file period. A detailed comparison of USEEM data with Unemployment Insurance data for 1980–1982 for Texas, indicated that the lags in reporting births and delays in purging closing tended to offset each other, so that the stock of establishments reported to be in existence was unaffected by these lags in adding establishment start-ups and eliminating establishment closures (Jacobsen 1985).

MacDonald (1985, p. 180) studied the accuracy of the data for the food and tobacco industries and reported that "it appears to be quite accurate and timely in recording changes due to merger, divestiture, plant closure and new plant construction."

Merger of USEEM File and County City Data Book

The USEEM data set was merged with the 1983 County City Data Book, published by the U.S. Bureau of Census. This merger permitted us to identify the characteristics of the county, city, and town where each service establishment was located. These two data sets were combined with a third variable, created in-house, that noted whether each county was metropolitan, rural and adjacent to a metropolitan area, or rural and not adjacent to a metropolitan area.

As with any dataset, the USEEM file has its weaknesses. However, a solid understanding of the data's advantages and shortcomings can ensure that its applications are appropriate for scientific enquiry, assist in the recognition of biased outcomes, and promote the correct interpretation of results. The major advantages of the dataset are that they permit an analysis of changes in local economies and the sources of economic growth at fine levels of industrial and geographical detail.

Selection of States

Initially four states were selected for analysis, including California, Kansas, New York, and Virginia. The selection criteria included regional representation, variation in the percent of state population in metropolitan versus rural counties, and differences in the size of the state's major city or cities. Regional representation was important because decentralization patterns vary by region of the country, with the Northeast experiencing some decentralization of employment and the remaining three regions, including the Midwest, South, and West, all exhibiting faster urban than rural employment growth (Majchrowicz, 1989). The variation in the urban-rural population distribution was important for testing hypotheses about rural growth trends in already-urbanized states versus rural states. Variety in city size of the major cities permitted a test of the hypothesis that corporate services tend to decentralize from the major corporate service centers such as New York City, Los Angeles, and San Francisco into rural areas close to headquarters. In contrast, we expected to find less service decentralization in the states without headquarters cities.

Examination of these four states indicated that population and employment were centralizing in three of the four cases. In the fourth state, California, rural population grew more rapidly in adjacent rural counties than in either urban or nonadjacent rural counties, but the state is highly urbanized with a very small proportion of population in rural counties. To examine patterns in other states where population is decentralizing, two additional states, Maryland and Massachusetts, were added to the sample. In both states population grew faster in both types of rural than in urban counties in the 1980 to 1986 period.

Population decentralization in Kansas, New York, and Virginia are due to migration patterns that favor metropolitan counties. In Kansas, migration was positive in the urban counties and negative in rural counties. In New York, migration was negative in all types of counties, but the losses where greater in the rural counties. In Virginia, growth was positive in all counties, but greater in the metropolitan counties. The decentralization of population of Massachusetts and Maryland is shown with greater rates of inmigration in rural than urban counties in both states. (See authors for detailed tables covering selected states' characteristics.)

Notes

Chapter Two

1. See Nelson (1987) for a perspective on the role of branch offices in the spatial evolution of suburbs.

2. Using detailed data on the revenues of individual firms, Greenfield (1966) found that approximately 50 percent of the revenues in legal services, finance, insurance and real estate are derived from households.

3. Boddewyn et al. (1986) and Enderwick (1987) distinguishes between services in which the commodity can be separated from the production process and, therefore, can be traded across country boundaries, such as computer software; the service is location-bound and therefore necessitates a foreign presence to sell, such as hotel accommodations, and combination services where locational substitution is possible.

4. Although the *Current Population Survey* would permit a cruder occupational version of this approach, again the analyst could extract only limited geographical detail. For example, these data will not illuminate differences in occupational structure between larger and smaller rural jurisdictions, or between rural counties adjacent and nonadjacent to metropolitan counties.

5. Three available sources of rural employment and earnings data are the *County Business Patterns*, the Bureau of Economic Analysis (BEA) data, and the Dun and Bradstreet data. All three sets are industry- rather than occupation-based. The *County Business Patterns* and Dun and Bradstreet data provide information on rural services disaggregated to the 4-digit SIC code level. The BEA data are disaggregated to the 2-digit level. Only the Dun and Bradstreet data will permit an analysis of services by town size. Both *County Business Patterns* and BEA data are available geographically disaggregated to the county level.

A serious shortcoming of either the *County Business Patterns* or the BEA data for rural analysis is that information for low population counties is suppressed when the confidentiality of an individual establishment's identity is in jeopardy. This is a serious problem for rural counties, where low population counts lead to high rates of suppressed data. Researchers have developed algorithms which allocate missing industry/county data based on column and row totals for the states. Such an enhanced version of the *County Business Patterns* circumvents some of the biases that may result from concealed employment totals in rural economies. Because it is not a government data source, confidentiality is not an issue with the Dun and Bradstreet data.

A second problem with both the *County Business Patterns* and BEA data is that establishments designated as sole proprietorships are not included in either establishment or employment totals. This omission is particularly worrisome for analyses of the service sector, which contains a high proportion of sole proprietorships. This bias affects employment and establishment counts for the service sectors of both urban and rural areas. Sole proprietorships are included in the Dun and Bradstreet data.

6. Measured as employment outside of agriculture, construction, and manufacturing.

7. Because data were missing for most SIC codes for non-MSA counties of 50,000 population and below, these results do not hold for the smallest population rural towns.

8. Howells and Green (1986) found that the location quotient ffor producer services decreased in London from 2.04 in 1971 to 1.85 in 1981, while the location quotient for southern rural areas increased from .72 in 1971 to .89 in 1981.

9. Horan and Tolbert II (1984) examined the question of whether these rural and urban differences in occupational structure altered the opportunity structure for males and females and blacks and whites. They found that women and blacks fared better in the range of occupations available in the more industrialized rural and urban labor markets.

10. Fuguitt, Brown, and Beale (1989, p. 273) found that 13.3 percent of metropolitan counties' employment was in producer services, compared to only 7.7 percent of rural counties' employment. The difference was made up by rural economies' greater dependence on extractive industries.

11. For example, Riefler (1976) found that all services, with the exception of government, are closely tied to market size. Moreover, Riefler found that services became more rather than less market-oriented over time. He argues "[S]ervice activity remains market oriented. As such, [services] are likely to respond to but not initiate regional growth" (p. 88). Although Riefler shows that a large and perhaps growing proportion of the service sector is market-oriented, he does not prove that all services are. His model only explains about 50 percent of service sector growth in terms of markets.

12. Porterfield and Pulver (1991) also point out that service firms generally export less than manufacturing firms. They argue that partial compensation may occur because rural services buy more of their inputs from within the state.

13. Beyers (1991) also finds that larger establishments and core regions dominate the interregional trade in services.

14. There are two possible reasons for export service decentralization. One line of reasoning is that many entrepreneurs would rather live in less-congested, more-pastoral environments (Bradshaw and Blakely 1979). A second argument draws upon the spatial division of labor and product cycle models to argue that routine service functions of large corporations may decentralize to rural areas to take advantage of low-wage, non-unionized labor (Hepworth 1990). Both possibilities hinge on innovations in telecommunications technologies, an issue discussed in more detail below.

Pensions, investment returns, and social security checks to rurally based retirees also act as an export base. It is not the geographical base of the resident that is fundamental, but the source of the income. Transfer payments to rural residents contribute to a local economy in the same way as tourism, the export of computer services, or advertising (Gillis 1987). Dependence on passive income is another difference between rural and urban economies. In many rural communities and labor market areas, passive income is more than half of total regional personal income (Hirschl and Summers 1982).

15. For example, estimates are that only 10 to 15 percent of the purchase price of an IBM personal computer reflects the actual cost of manufacturing. The remaining value is comprised of a collection of research, design, engineering, sales, and maintenance services (Reich 1991).

16. Hansen (1990) provides empirical support for this argument, and for the critical role of education services in enhancing the productivity of the work force. He measures the strength of the relationship between per capita income and producer services density and education levels across MSAs and finds that the more dense the producer services and the higher the education levels, the higher a city's per capita income.

17. Prior work has addressed the manufacturing/service linkage. Majchrowicz and Alexander (1991) conducted one of the few recent studies to examine the service/agriculture linkage. Using the *County Business Patterns*, he found that between 1975 and 1987, farming and agriculture services employment declined 16.3 percent in rural counties, but grew slightly in urban counties. Whereas the rural decline may not be surprising in light of the hardships faced by agriculture during this period, the decline is noteworthy in light of employment gains in agricultural service employment in metropolitan counties. One possible interpretation to these findings is that the agricultural sector is turning to metropolitan areas for service inputs.

18. Finally, it is worth noting that new modes of production and organization may strengthen the pull between distributive services and manufacturing (Scott 1988). For example, "just-in-time" (JIT) operations minimize on-site inventories. A smaller stockpile requires wholesalers' and suppliers' proximity in order to ensure quick deliveries and to minimize down-time. Again, these changes cannot be separated from the revolution in telecommunications options.

19. The latter finding is supported by the work of Stabler (1987), Stone (1987), and Deller and Holden (1991).

20. In the South, differences in the demographic composition of employment in services versus manufacturing are even more pronounced. Despite the dramatic growth of service jobs in the South over the last two decades, minorities still occupy the least-desirable jobs in the services sector (Falk and Lyson 1988).

Chapter Three

1. There may be two extenuating explanations for some of this apparent employment growth. Employment data for County Business

Patterns are collected based on reports of social security contributions paid by employers to the federal government. Prior to 1983, employment in nonprofit organizations was largely not included because employers were not required to pay a portion of their workers' social security tax. In 1983, social security laws were amended to require nonprofit employers to make contributions to the system for their workers and to file reports. Additionally, in the 1970s and 1980s, many hospitals (especially rural) that were traditionally county owned and operated were sold to for-profit and nonprofit medical services corporations; thus, employment that would have been designated "government" and not counted now might appear under medical services. See Appendix 1 for detailed description of data.

2. Conversation with Carolyn Brown, Economic Research Service, U.S. Department of Agriculture. During the 1970 to 1980 decade, the rural elderly grew at a slightly faster rate than did the urban elderly. This pattern reversed between 1980 and 1990.

3. Detailed tables are available from the authors.

4. The use of "percentage change" as an indicator of economic trends has always been a matter of controversy. On the surface, rapid rates of change are commonly interpreted as signifying the relative competitiveness of a geographic area for the receipt of highly variable (in this instance growth) sectors. The proverbial problem remains "when does percentage change matter"? In other words, when does the measure accurately reflect long-term economic trends?

Research on rural development is riddled with reports of large percentage changes in various indicators such as population and employment. Too often, however, authors fail to point out the initial base (usually very small). More importantly, little concern is expressed about whether change in employment (or population) reflects short-term adjustments in response to immediate economic events or whether it is an indicator of longer-term and more permanent change. Changes in employment can be due to: employment and the establishment of new facilities; the momentary redeployment of production schedules to contend with short-term demand fluctuations; or the shift of employment—often through consolidation—to a target facility accompanied by the closure of others. Only in the first case are new jobs permanently created. The latter two conditions reflect momentary adjustments in employment resulting from corporate planning. Thus, the importance of percentage change must be tempered by an understanding of historic industry trends.

Publicly available data bases are too coarse to distinguish among these different developments. Most data reflect a single point in time and fail to clarify between short- and long-term trends. The only viable means of determining the importance of percentage change is to incorporate more detailed understanding of individual sectoral developments. To the extent possible, the following discussion incorporates insights about growth experience.

5. The widespread use of temporary personnel may be tapering off. Anecdotal evidence indicates that firms are reducing demand for temporary personnel and up-skilling permanent workers. The benefits of using temporary personnel revolved around the flexibility firms achieved in work force management. The down side, however, was the lack of employee commitment and the expense of training workers only to lose them to other employers. It appears that firms are once again investing in work-place skills and hiring employees in full-time, covered positions. Interestingly, wages are not increasing at rates commensurate with increased job skills (Baran 1986). This new development may have serious long-term consequences for the national economy. It certainly breaks with longstanding trends of rewarding increased education with higher compensation levels.

6. Any typology has flaws. In this case, the designation of agriculture, mining, manufacturing, and government counties is based on income shares that capture only a portion of total income, never exceeding 30 percent. With 70 percent of economic activity not accounted for, there is a potential for great diversity of an economic base with each county type. This problem is less serious than it might appear at first glance, however, because services comprise more than one-half of employment and income in most rural counties. There is, nonetheless, the potential for multiple income sources and allocation of a county to more than one typology grouping. In most cases, however, county classifications are mutually exclusive, and counties are allocated to a single group. The same problem is also true for the three groupings based on population and demographic characteristics. Finally, there are a number of counties that remained unclassified because no activity reaches the threshold proportion.

The danger in creating a typology is that it fails to provide definitions fine-grained enough to distinguish among the multifold and complex experiences of rural areas. At the same time, given similarities in income level, income distribution, extent of transfer payments, and underlying institutional structure of counties with the same economic base, some grouping is appropriate. Thus, although there are no doubt limitations to to the original classification scheme, the intent was laudatory and appropriate given the diverse experiences of rural counties.

7. The classification procedure used to construct the typology is commonly known as Cluster Analysis. The method allows researchers to summarize a rectangular data matrix through statistical procedures that identify groups of cases, in this instance counties, that exhibit some similarity.

8. Nonmetropolitan status, as defined in 1970, was maintained. In other words, a county was considered rural based on its population characteristics in 1970. Therefore,the changes in categories do not reflect the incorporation of formally adjacent rural counties into metropolitan areas.

9. Because agricultural counties were concentrated in the Midwest and Southeast, the effect of the recession in agriculture was regionally concentrated. More than average losses occurred in Iowa, Illinois, Missouri, and Arkansas. Whereas movement from the agricultural group was primarily due to declines in agriculture, shifts to other groups also occurred in instances where other sectors grew faster than agriculture. In other words, while some counties left the agricultural category because of a decline in farming, other counties shifted to new classifications because of higher-than-average increases in other sectors.

10. Losses were regionally concentrated in the Southeast and Midwest. Losses in the Midwest reduced the region's share of rural manufacturing counties. The South now contains 69 percent of all rural manufacturing counties.

11. The dramatic rise in the number of unclassified counties implies that no other sector grew to fill in the gap left by declines in traditional sectors. Overall there has been a weakening of the traditional

rural economic base. While for cities services have been an important antidote to manufacturing decline, rural areas have only partially shared in this transformation.

12. Contact authors for detailed tables for ERS county types.

13. See authors for more detailed tables.

Chapter Four

1. Considerable controversy exists concerning the interpretation of the third (regional) growth effect in shift-share analysis. Some researchers treat this measure as an indicator of regional competitiveness. The assumption is that a region experiencing industrial growth proportionately higher than that at the national level is more competitive relative to other regions. Others argue that shift-share analysis provides no theoretical explanation of the competitive effect and therefore should not be interpreted as normatively suggesting a particular path for future development. The method further suffers from problems of aggregation. In addition, shift-share analysis is static (cross-sectional comparisons of two points in time). In this report, shift-share analysis is employed as a descriptive tool to decompose the individual growth experience of rural areas. No inferences are made regarding why particular results are evident, and we cannot account for the specific changes in industry mix.

2. The ratios in Table 4-5 represent:

$$(EP_r/Pop_r)/EP_{us}/Pop_{us})$$

Where

EP = Employment in producer services
Pop = Population
Subscript r = In the region (i.e., metropolitan, adjacent rural, or nonadjacent rural)
Subscript us = In the nation

A ratio of 1 indicates that the region has the same share of population in producer service employment as does the nation. A value lower than 1 indicates that the region has a smaller share of employment in producer services relative to population than does the nation as a whole.

3. The numbers should be interpreted as follows. For Kansas, in 1980, 50 percent of the metropolitan counties' producer services employment was in independents while 66 and 59 percent of rural adjacent and rural nonadjacent employment was in independent firms (respectively). The share of MSA's employment in independents, headquarters, subsidiaries, and branches (.50 + .22 + .6 + .23) = 101 percent (due to rounding error).

4. Because random data errors may bias small samples, the results are only reported for cases in which the number of establishments is greater than 250.

5. It is important to note at this point that two biases in the data may influence results. First, branch plants are underrepresented due to the failure of some firms to report all of their affiliated locations. Imputed values are recorded in employment totals, but not in specific regional locations. Therefore, we cannot include these imputed values. A second bias occurs because the start-ups among independents may be underrepresented due to the failure to capture a firm at its inception. Fortunately, these biases operate in opposite directions and tend to cancel each other out. Unfortunately, the extent of the biases is unknown. Therefore, conclusions should not be drawn based on small differences between the independents/headquarters and branch/subsidiary categories.

Chapter Five

1. For a detailed discussion of the USEEM data and the selection of the six study states, see Howland, Marie, "Using the USEEM Data for the Study of Rural Economies," unpublished paper, University of Maryland, College Park, October 1990.

2. The Standard Industrial Classifications (SIC) were revised in 1987 to reflect emerging industry trends. There were major changes in SIC 737. SIC 7372, Computer Programming and Software Development; SIC 7374, Data Preparation and Processing Services; and SIC 7379, Computer Related Services, not elsewhere classified were subdivided into three categories, resulting in a total of nine categories of

4-digit computer services. Here we retain the pre-1987 definition. See U.S. Census of Service Industries, 1987, Appendix H for a discussion of these changes.

3. See the list below of the on-site and telephone interviews.

Domestic On-site Interviews

TDEC, headquartered in Washington, D.C., with plants in rural Maryland and West Virginia. Interviews held with J. Timothy Mann, Director, in Washington, D.C. headquarters and with Wanda Dawson, Vice President, in Oakland, Maryland.

Highland Data, headquartered in Blue Grass, Virginia, and a branch office in West Virginia. Interview held with Edward Hevener, Manager, in Blue Grass.

Appalachian Computer Services (ACS) headquartered in London, Kentucky, with branches in Berea, Bateyville, and Montecello, Kentucky and Mount Vernon, Illinois. Interview held in London, Kentucky with Ed Miller, Vice President.

Computer Science Corporation (CSC), headquartered in El Segundo, California, offices in a number of cities in the United States. Interviews held in Falls Church, Virginia with Howard Chambers, Vice President, and Floyd H. Jean, Vice President.

C C and H, headquartered in Los Angeles, branch offices throughout cities in the United States. Interview held in Walnut Creek, California with Hank Klor, Assistant Director.

Automated Data Processing, headquartered in Roseland, New Jersey, with offices in urban centers across the United States. Interview with Tom Ryan, Operations Manager, in Towson, Maryland.

General Electric in Rockville, Maryland. Interview with William McGowen, Manager.

Automated Business Systems and Services, offices in Washington, D.C., and Riverdale, Maryland. Interview with James T. Young, Program Manager in Riverdale, Maryland.

Domestic Telephone Interviews

Mead Data Central, a large data entry user, based in Dayton, Ohio. Interview with Michelle Love, Public Relations.

ILM, headquartered in Fredericksburg, Virginia, an independent firm with a sister operation in Jamaica. Interview with James Griggs, Vice President, in Fredericksburg.

Saztec, headquartered in Kansas City, with branches in the Philippines and Ardrossan, Scotland. Interview with Scott Fancher, Vice President, in Kansas City.

Off-shore On-site Interviews

Donnelly & Sons, headquartered in Chicago, interview held in Barbados branch with Ronald Wolfe, Senior Vice President.

American Demographics, headquartered in Denver, interview held in Barbados branch with Enid Blackman, Division Manager.

Southwest, headquartered in Dallas, interview held in Barbados branch with Cynthia Chandler, Manager.

Data Research LTD, a Barbadian-owned firm, interview with Ms. Sharpe, owner.

Compudata Business Bureau, a Barbadian-owned firm, interview with Jean Alleyne, branch manager.

The Barbados External Telecommunications (BET) Agency, interview with Keith Seale, Manager of Telecommunications Services.

The Barbados Industrial Development Corporation, the agency responsible for economic development. Interview held with Reginald Farley, Business Development Officer, in Barbados, and John Mills, Business Development Officer, in New York, N.Y.

Saztec Europe, Ardrossan, Scotland, interview with Ralph Wassell, Operations Manager.

Producers of Telecommunications, Optical Scanning, and Imaging Technologies

International Business Machines, interview with Mark House, Senior Engineer, and Jeff Hamilton, Advisory Programmer, Arlington, Virginia.

Xerox Imaging Systems, Interview with Haley Collins, Account Representative, Southeastern Region.

4. Credit card receipts that look like traditional cash register receipts are generally examples of point of sale data capture.

5. Literacy rates are not collected in the United States. One proxy is the percent of population with less than five years of schooling. In 1987 the percentage for rural areas was 2.6 (U.S. Department of Commerce, 1988).

6. A point of presence is a privately provided tie-in to the international fiber optic network viaviaviavia satellite, etc., that bypasses local telephone lines.

Chapter Six

1. The designation of a bank as small, medium, or large is based on the institution's asset base. Small banks have total assets of less than $100 million. Medium banks have between $100 million and $1 billion in total assets. And large banks have more than $1 billion in total assets (see Mikesell and Marlor 1991).

2. This chapter uses the terms rural/nonmetropolitan and urban/metropolitan interchangeably. Unlike the data described and analyzed in other chapters of this book, here we do not base the urban/rural designation on the Beale urban-rural county continuum codes. Instead, due to the nature of available data published by the Federal Deposit Insurance Corporation and the U.S. Department of Agriculture, it is possible to distinguish only between institutions within Metropolitan Statistical Areas (urban) and those outside Metropolitan Statistical Areas (rural).

3. Analysis by geography is also problematic. For example, much research is based on the Federal Deposit Insurance Corporation's *Summary of Deposits*, which reports the activities of a bank and its branch facilities on a combined basis. All banks are designated according to the location of their headquarters, and it is impossible to accurately gauge the true geographic distribution of banking activity.

4. De novo branches are new establishments.

5. Except where noted, the information contained in this section was largely derived from Hoover 1991; and *Moody's Bank and Finance Manual* 1991.

6. These states include: Colorado, Hawaii, Indiana, Iowa, Louisiana, Montana, New Mexico, South Dakota, North Dakota, and Wyoming (First Interstate Bancorp. 1991).

7. The factual information in this section is summarized from First Interstate Bancorp. (Disclosure Online Data Base Report); *Moody's Bank and Finance Manual* 1991; and Hoover 1991.

8. The observations contained in this section are the compilation of findings from interviews conducted with First Interstate branch managers in nonmetropolitan communities in California and affiliate bank presidents in Montana and Wyoming.

9. In some instances Business Bankers visit the branch facilities as infrequently as once or twice a month. Although this does not mean that the Business Bankers are not operating in the area, it is an indication of the bifurcation of activities between branch personnel and commercial loan officers.

10. Although it should be noted that numerous state-level regulatory impediments exist to complete homogenization of operating procedures, increasingly regulation poses fewer barriers to the process.

11. Except where noted, the factual information contained in this section was derived from Hoover 1991; *Moody's Bank and Finance Manual* 1991; and NCNB Corporation undated.

12. The factual information in this section was compiled from Hanley et al. 1991.

13. The factual information in this section was compiled from NCNB annual reports and from Hanley et al. 1991.

14. The observations contained in this section are the compilation of findings from interviews conducted with NCNB branch managers in nonmetropolitan communities in North Carolina.

15. According to a recent investment profile prepared by Salomon Brothers, NCNB appears intent on eliminating full-time employees and nonessential operations from branch offices. The authors estimate that one or two intermediate management layers will be removed from the consumer banking hierarchy (Hanley et al. 1991).

16. The factual information in this section is derived, except where noted, from *Moody's Bank and Finance Manual* 1991.

17. Return on total assets is the ratio of income to total assets and is a measure of overall profitability.

18. The observatiations contained in this section are the compilation of findings from interviews conducted with Norwest affiliate presidents in nonmetropolitan communities in Wyoming, Minnesota, and Montana.

19. These transaction thresholds are rough estimates informed by conversations with bankers, among whom was Mary Houghton of the Shorebank Corporation (1991) and Mary Matthews of the Northeast Entrepreneur Fund (1991).

Chapter Seven

1. For a more detailed description of this data set, please see Appendix 2.

Appendix Two

1. In this research project, the County Business Pattern data were generously provided by Dr. William Beyers of the University of Washington, Seattle, Geography Department. Using a biproportional matrix adjustment procedure, Dr. Beyers allocated employment totals to employment size categories using an iterative computer routine. This procedure is widely used and has been shown to produce accurate and efficient estimates. The results constitute a data file with counts of both employment and number of establishments in counties at a 4-digit level of industry detail.

Bibliography

Abler, R. and T. Falk, 1981. "Public Information Services and the Changing Role of Distance in Human Affairs" *Economic Geography* 57:10–22.

Anding, T., J. Adams, W. Casey, S. de Montille, and M. Goldfein, 1990. *Trade Centers of the Upper Midwest: Changes from 1960 to 1989.* Center for Urban and Regional Affairs, University of Minnesota, Minneapolis.

Armbruster, William, 1990. "Japan's NTT Plans NJ Data Center," *Journal of Commerce.* February 22, 383:4a.

Aydalot, P., 1984. Editor, *Crise Economique et Espace.* Economica, Paris.

Bailly, A., 1986. "Le sectuer des services: Une Change Pour Le Development Local," in *The Present and Future Role of Services in Regional Development.* Edited by S. Illeris. OP-74. Commission of the European Communities, Brussels.

Bailly, A., and D. Maillat, 1986. *Le Secteur Tertiaire en Question.* Anthropos, Paris.

Bailly, A., D. Maillat, and W. Coffey, 1987. "Service Activities and Regional Development: Some European Examples," *Environment and Planning A.* May (19):653–668.

Baran, Barbara, 1985. "Office Automation and Women's Work: The Technological Transformation of the Insurance Industry," in *High Technology, Space, and Society.* Edited by Manuel Castells, Sage Press.

———. , 1986. "The Technological Transformation of White Collar Work: A Case Study of the Insurance Industry," dissertation, University of California, Berkeley.

Barkley, David, 1978. Plant Ownership Characteristics and the Locational Stability of Rural Iowa Manufacturers," *Land Economics.* February, 54(1):92–99.

Bates, James, 1991. "Wells Risky Loan Strategy Comes to Light," *Los Angeles Times.* June 27:D2.

Beale, C., 1975. *The Revival of Population Growth in Nonmetropolitan America.* ERS 605, USDA, Economic Research Service, Washington, D.C.

———., 1991. Prepared comments presented at the conference on population change and the future of rural America, Wye Plantation, Maryland, May 30–June 1, 1991.

Beale, C., and G. Fuguitt, 1986. "Metropolitan and Nonmetropolitan Population Growth in the United States Since 1980," *New Dimensions in Rural Policy: Building Upon Our Heritage.* Joint Economic Committee, Government Printing Office, Washington, D.C.

Beers, David, 1987. "Offshore Offices: Corporate Paperwork Sneaks Out of the Country" *Working Woman* (September): 55–57.

Bender, L., B. Green, T. Hady, J. Kuehn, M. Nelson, L. Perkinson, and P. Ross, 1985. *Diverse Social and Economic Strategies of Nonmetropolitan America.* Rural Development Research Report 49, U.S. Department of Agriculture, Economic Research Service, Washington, D.C. (September).

Beyers, W., 1991. "Service Industries, Service Occupations, and the Division of Labor." Paper presented at the North American Regional Science Association Meetings, New Orleans, LA.

Beyers, W., and M. Alvine, 1985. "Export Services in Postindustrial Society," Regional Science Association, Papers of the Thirty-First North American Meetings of the Regional Science Association, 57:33–45.

Beyers, W., M. Alvine, and E. Johnson, 1985. "The Service Sector: A Growing Force in the Regional Export Base," *Economic Development Quarterly.* 2:3–7.

Bloomquist, L., 1987. "Performance of the Rural Manufacturing Sector," in *Rural Economic Development in the 1980s.* Edited by David Brown, Norman Reid, Herman Bluestone, David McGranahan, and Sara Mazie. United States Department of Agriculture, Economic Research Service, Washington, D.C. (July)

Bluestone, B., and B. Harrison, 1988. *The Great U-turn: Corporate Restructuring and the Polarizing of America*. Basic Books.

Bluestone, B., and J. Hession, 1986. *Patterns of Change in the Nonmetro and Metro Labor Force Since 1979*. U.S. Department of Agriculture, Economic Research Service.

Boddewyn, J., M. Halbrich, and A. Perry, 1986. "Service Multinationals: Conceptualization, Measurement and Theory," *Journal of International Business Studies*. 17(3):41–57.

Bradshaw, T., and E. Blakely, 1979. *Rural Communities in Advanced Industrial Society*. Praeger: New York.

Browne, L., 1992. "Why New England Went the Way of Texas Rather Than California," *New England Economic Review*. January/February, 23–42.

Buck, N., 1988. "Service Industries and Local Labor Markets: Towards an Anatomy of Service Job Loss," *Urban Studies*. 25:319–332.

Business Wire Inc., 1990. "C&S/Sovran Reports Loss for Quarter," INVESTEXT. October 15.

Butler, Margaret, 1990. "Rural-Urban Continuum Codes for Metro and Non-Metro Counties," Staff Report 9028, Economic Research Service, U.S. Department of Agriculture, April.

Cappellin, R., 1988. "The Diffusion of Producer Services in the Urban System," Regional Science Association European Summer Institute on Theories and Policies of Technological Development at the Local Level Department of Economics, Universita' L. Bocconi, July, 1–23.

Christaller, W., 1966. *Places in Southern Germany*, translated by C.W. Baskin. Prentice Hall: Englewood Cliffs, N.J.

Christopherson, S., 1989. "Flexibility in the U.S. Service Economy and the Emerging Spatial Division of Labor," *Transactions of the Institute of British Geographers*, N.S. 14:131–143.

Clark, Colin, 1982. *Regional and Urban Location*. St. Martins Press: New York.

Cline, Kenneth, 1991. "NCNB Gambit Big Rewards, Big Risks, Too," *American Banker*. June 28:1–5.

Coffey, W., and A. Bailly, 1990. "Producer Services and the Rise of Flexible Production Systems." Paper presented at the Bilingual Special Session on Services and Regional Development, Western Regional Science Association Meetings, Molokai, Hawaii, February.

Coffey, W., and M. Polese, 1987. "Trade and Location of Producer Services: A Canadian Perspective," *Environment and Planning A*. May (19):597–611.

Cohen, Steven, and John Zysman, 1987. *Manufacturing Matters: The Myth of the Post-Industrial Economy*. Basic Books: New York.

Colclough, Glenna, and Charles M. Tolbert II, 1992. *Work in the Fast Lane: Flexibility, Divisions of Labor, and Inequality in High-Tech Industries*. SUNY Press: Albany, NY.

Corey, K., 1991. "The Role of Information Technology in Singapore's Planning and Development," in *Collapsing Time and Space: Geographical Aspects of Communications and Information*. Edited by Stanley D. Brunn and Thomas R. Leinbach, Unwin Hyman Press, London.

Dallas Morning News, 1991. "Corporation Resurrects Town's Spirit," April 28.

Daniels, P. W., 1982. *Service Industries: Growth and Location*. Cambridge, England: Cambridge University Press.

———. , 1985. *Service Industries: A Geographic Appraisal*. Methuen & Co. Ltd.: London.

———. , 1987. "The Geography of Services," *Progress in Human Geography*. 11:433–447.

Daniels, T., and M. Lapping, 1988. "The Rural Crisis and What to do About It: An Alternative Perspective," *Economic Development Quarterly*. 2(4):339–341.

Danielson, Arnold, 1991. "The Megamerger: What It Means in Northeast States and Elsewhere," *Law and Business*. August 19.

Deans, A., 1991. *Norwest Corporation*. Company report for Smith, Barney, Harris Upham & Company, INVESTEXT. April 10.

Deller, S., and J. Holden, 1991. "Rural Retail Market Development: A Policy for Economic Development," *Proceedings from the Rural Planning and Development: Visions of the 21st Century Conference*. Orlando, FL, February 13–15, 253–264.

Detrick, S., 1991. Unpublished dissertation. Department of City and Regional Planning. University of California, Berkeley, CA.

Dickstein, C., 1991. "Offshore Competition for Back Offices: Policy Implications for Promotion of Back Offices in West Virginia." Report to the Institute for Public Affairs, West Virginia University, October.

Dillman, D., and D. Beck, 1986. "The Past is Not the Future: Urban Quality of Life as We Approach the 21st Century," *Urban Resources*. Spring (3):43–47.

———., 1987. "Information Technologies and Rural Development." Paper presented to Jobs, Education, and Technology Conference, Center for Agriculture and Rural Development, Council of State Governments. Lexington, Kentucky. October 5.

Drennan, M. P., 1989. "Information Intensive Industries in Metropolitan Areas of the United States of America," *Environment and Planning A*. 21:1603–1618.

Drucker, Peter F., 1989. "Information and the Future of the City," *The Wall Street Journal* (April 4):A22.

Duncan, J., 1988. "Service Sector Diversity—A Measurement Challenge," *The Service Economy*. A Publication of the Coalition of Service Industries:1–5.

Dunning, J., and G. Norman, 1987. "The Location Choice of Offices of International Companies," Environment and Planning A. May (19):613–631.

Eckstein, A., and D. Heien, 1985. "The U.S. Experience: Causes and Consequences of Service Sector Growth," *Growth and Change*. April (2):12–17.

Enderwick, P., 1987. "The Strategy and Structure of Service-Sector Multinationals: Implications for Potential Host Regions," *Regional Studies*. June (3):215–223.

Falk, Lawrence H., and Adam Broner, 1980. "Specialization in Service Industry Employment as a State Policy," *Growth and Change*. 11(4):18–23.

Falk, W., and T. Lyson, 1988. *High Tech, Low Tech, No Tech*. SUNY Press: Albany, New York.

Federal Deposit Insurance Corporation, 1990. *FDIC Annual Report 1989*. Washington, D.C.

Fersko-Weiss, Henry, 1987. "The Return of Outside Data Processing," *High Technology Business*. (December) 7:41–46.

First Interstate Bancorp., 1991. *Annual Report*, 1992. Headquartered in Los Angeles, California.

Forester, T., 1988. "The Myth of the Electronic Cottage," *Futures*. June 20(3):227–240.

Fuchs, Victor Robert, 1968. *The Service Economy*. National Bureau of Economic Research: New York.

Fuguitt, G., 1991. "Internal Migration and Population Redistribution." Presented at the conference on Population Change and the Future of Rural America, Wye Plantation, Maryland, May 30–June 1, 1991.

Fuguitt, G., D. Brown, and C. Beale, 1989. *Rural and Small Town America*. Russell Sage Foundation: New York.

Garnick, D., 1983. "Shifting Patterns in the Growth of Migration in Metro and Non-metro Areas," *Survey of Current Business*. 63(5): 39–44.

Gershuny, J., and I. Miles, 1983. *The New Service Economy*, Praeger Publishers: New York.

Ghelfi, Linda M., and Alexander T. Majchrowicz, 1990. "Jobs and Earnings in Nonmetro Industry, 1987," United States Department of Agriculture, Economic Research Service, Bulletin No. 589, February.

Gillespie, A., and A. Green, 1987. "The Changing Geography of Producer Services Employment in Britain," *Regional Studies*. June, 21:397–411.

Gillespie, A., and K. Robbins, 1989. "Geographic Inequalities: The Spatial Bias of the New Communications Technologies," *Journal of Communication*. Summer, 39(3):7–18.

Gillis, W., 1987. "Can Service-Producing Industries Provide a Catalyst for Regional Economic Growth?" *Economic Development Quarterly*. 1(3):249–256.

Ginsberg, B., and M. Shefter, 1990. *Politics by Other Means*. Basic Books: New York.

Glasmeier, A., and G. Borchard, 1989. "From Branch Plants to Back Offices: Prospects for Rural Services Growth," *Environment and Planning A*. 21:1565–1583.

Glasmeier, A., and M. Howland, 1989. "Services in the Rural Economy." A collaborative research proposal to the Ford Foundation, Rural Economic Policy Program, Washington, D.C.

Glasmeier, A. 1991. The *High Tech Potential: Economic Development in Rural America*. New Jersey: Rutgers University Press.

Goe, R., 1990. "Producer Services, Trade and the Social Division of Labor," *Regional Studies*. 24, 4:327–42.

Goode, F., 1990. "Community Service Sector Structure as an Industrial Location Determinant." Unpublished paper, Pennsylvania State University, July.

Gorham, L., 1991. "The Slowdown in Nonmetropolitan Development: The Impact of Economic Forces and the Effect on the Distribution of Wages." Presented at the Conference on Population Change and the Future of Rural America, Wye Plantation, Maryland, May 30–June 1, 1991.

Gottman, Jean, 1983. *The Coming of the Transactional City*. University of Maryland Institute for Urban Studies, College Park.

Green, A. E., 1987. "Spatial Prospects for Service Growth in Britain," *Area*. 19(2):111–122.

Greenfield, H., 1966. *Manpower and the Growth of Producer Services*. Columbia University Press: New York.

Guile, B., 1988. "Introduction to Services Industries Policy Issues," *Technological Forecasting and Social Change*. 34:315–325.

Guile, B., and J. Quinn, 1988. "Editors' Note," *Technological Forecasting and Social Change*. 34:313–314.

Gullo, Karen, 1991. "Determined Banks Still Dominate Processing of Card Receipts," *American Banker*. April 22:17–18.

Hamilton, John Maxwell, 1990. *Entangling Alliances: How the Third World Shapes Our Lives.* Seven Locks Press: Cabin John, Maryland.

Hanley, Thomas, et al., 1991. *NCNB Corporation: The National Bank of Tomorrow.* Stock research report for Salomon Brothers. March.

Hansen, N., 1990. "Do Producer Services Induce Regional Economic Development?" *Journal of Regional Science.* 30(4):465–476.

Harrington, J., 1992. *Information-Intensive Services and Local Economic Development.* Paper presented at the Southern Regional Science Association Meetings, Charleston, South Carolina, April.

Harrington, J., Jr. and J. Lombard, 1989. "Producer-service Firms in a Declining Manufacturing Region," *Environment and Planning A.* 21:65–79.

Harrington, J., A. Macpherson, and J. Lombard, 1991. "Interregional Trade in Producer Services: Review and Synthesis," *Growth and Change.* 22(4):75–94.

Heimstra, Stephen, 1990. *Prospective Rural Effects of Bank Deregulation.* United States Department of Agriculture, Economic Research Service, Washington.

Hemel, E., 1991. *Norwest Corporation.* Company Report for the Managers. *Pensions & Investment Age.* September 16:1–5.

Henderson, Jeffrey, 1990. *The Globalization of High Technology Production.* Routledge: New York.

Hepworth, Mark, 1990. *Geography of the Information Economy.* Guilford Press: New York.

Hepworth, Mark, A. Green, and A. Gillespie, 1987. "The Spatial Division of Information Labor in Great Britain," *Environment and Planning A.* January, 19:793–806.

Hirschl, T., and G. Summers, 1982. "Cash Transfers and the Export Base of Small Communities," *Rural Sociology.* Summer (47): 295–316.

Hoover, Gary et al., 1991. Editor, "First Interstate," *Hoover's Handbook.* The Reference Press: Austin.

Horan, Patrick M., and Charles M. Tolbert II, 1984. *The Organization of Work in Rural and Urban Labor Markets*. Westview Press: Boulder, Co.

Houghton, Mary, Vice President of Shorebank Corporation, 1991. Personal interview conducted by Jeffery Thompson. Telephone interview, December 5.

Howells, J. R. L., 1984. "The Location of Research and Development: Some Observations and Evidence from Britain," *Regional Studies*. 18(1):13–29.

Howells, J., and A. E. Green, 1986. "Location, Technology, and Industrial Organization in U.K. Services," *Progress in Planning*. 26(2): 85–183.

Howland, Marie, 1990. "Measuring the Cost and Accomplishments of Capital Subsidies: The Case of Rural UDAG Grants," *Journal of the American Planning Association*. Winter (1):54–63.

———. , 1990 "Using the USEEM Data for the Study of Rural Economies" Unpublished paper, University of Maryland, College Park, October.

———. , 1993. "Technological Change and the Spatial Restructuring of Data Entry and Processing Services," *Technological Forecasting and Social Change*. 43:185–196.

Howland, Marie, and Ted Miller, 1990. "UDAG Grants to Rural Communities: A Program that Works," *Economic Development Quarterly*. 4(2):128–136.

Illeris, S., 1989. *Services and Regions in Europe*. Aldershot: Avebury, England.

Jaffe, N., 1991. *Norwest Corp*. Company Report for Fox-Pitt, Kelton, Inc., INVESTEXT. August 21.

Jacobson, Louis, 1985. "Analysis of the Accuracy of SBA's Small Business Data Base," Working paper (CNA) 85–1958. Alexandria, Virginia: The Public Research Institute, Center for Naval Analysis, October.

Kahan, S., 1990. "The Service Economy—At Present, Employment Tells the Whole Story," *The Service Economy*. A publication of the Coalition of Service Industries, Washington, D.C., 4(2):1–8.

Keil, Stanley R., and Richard Mack, 1986. "Identifying Export Potential in the Service Sector," *Growth and Change*. 17(2):1–10.

Kellerman, Aharon, 1985. "The Evolution of Service Economies: A Geographical Analysis," *The Professional Geographer*. May, 37 (2):133–143.

Kennedy, Maureen, 1991. Personal conversation with Executive Director, Rural Economic Policy Program, Aspen Institute, Washington, D.C.

Killian, M., and T. Parker, 1991. "Higher Education No Panacea for Weak Rural Economies," *Rural Development Perspectives*. October–January, 7:1.

Kirk, R., 1987. "Are Business Services Immune to the Business Cycle?" *Growth and Change*. 18(2):15–23.

Kirkland, R., Jr., 1985. "Are Service Jobs Good Jobs?" *Fortune*. June 10, III, 2:38–43.

Kirn, Thomas, 1987. "Growth and Change in the Service Sector of the U.S.: A Spatial Perspective," *Annals of the Association of American Geographers*. 77(3):353–372.

Kirn, T., R. Conway, and W. Beyers, 1990. "Producer Services Development and the Role of Telecommunications: A Case Study of Rural Washington," *Growth and Change*, Fall, p. 33.

Kraut, R., 1989. "Telecommuting: The Trade-Offs of Home Work," *Journal of Communication*. Summer, 39(3):19–47.

Kuzela, Lad, 1987. "New Jamaican Teleport to Serve U.S. Business," *Industry Week* (August 10) 234:64–65.

Kuznets, S., 1977. "Notes on the Study of Economic Growth of Nations," *Economic Development and Cultural Change*. 25:300–314.

Langdale, John, 1983. "Competition in the United States' Long-Distance Telecommunications Industry," *Regional Studies*. 17(6): 393–409.

Levy, F., 1988. *Dollars and Dreams: The Changing American Income Distribution*, W. W. Norton: New York.

Lichter, D., 1991. "Demographic Aspects of the Changing Rural Labor Force." Presented at the Conference on Population Change and the Future of Rural America, Wye Plantation, Maryland, May 30–June 1, 1991.

Lipietz, A., 1982. *Towards Global Fordism?*, New Left Review, March/April.

Lohr, S., 1989. "The Growth of the 'Global Office'," *New York Times*. February 2, 27.

Ludlum, David A., 1986. "Off-Shore Data Entry Pays Off," *Computerworld*. (June 9) 20:103, 112.

McCall, Allen, and James McFadyen, 1986. "Banking Antitrust Policy: Keeping Pace with Change," *Issues in Bank Regulation*. 10(1): 13–19.

McDonald, James, 1985. "Dun and Bradstreet Microdata: Research Applications, and the Detection and Correction of Errors," *Journal of Economic and Social Measurement*, 13:173–185.

McGranahan, D., and L. Ghelfi, 1991. "The Educational Crisis and Rural Stagnation in the 1980s," *Education and Rural Development: Rural Strategies for the 1990s*. Edited by R. W. Long, Washington, D.C., Economic Research Service of the Department of Agriculture.

McGranahan, D., J. Hession, F. Hines, and M. Jordan, 1988. *Social and Economic Characteristics of the Population in Metro and Nonmetro Counties, 1970–80*. Rural Development Research Report 58, U.S. Department of Agriculture, Economic Research Service, Washington, D.C.

Majchrowicz, Alexander T., 1989. *Patterns of Change in the Rural Economy, 1969–86*. U.S. Department of Agriculture, Economic Research Service, Rural Development Research Report No. 73, December.

Majchrowicz, Alexander T., 1990. "Regional Economic Performance of Nonmetropolitan Counties, 1969–1987." Paper prepared for the Southern Regional Science Association Meetings, Washington, D.C., March 22–24.

Majchrowicz, T., and R. Alexander, 1991. "Employment Changes in Rural America's Farm and Farm Related Industries, During

1975–1987." *Proceedings of the Rural Planning and Development: Visions of the 21st Century Conference*, Orlando, FL, February 13–15, 562–573.

Markley, Deborah, 1990. *The Impact of Deregulation on Rural Commercial Credit Availability in Four New England States: Empirical Evidence and Policy Im-plications.* Final report to the Ford Foundation and the Rural Economic Policy Program of the Aspen Institute, May.

Marshall, J. N., P. Damesick, and P. Wood, 1987. "Understanding the Location and Role of Producer Services in the United Kingdom," *Environment and Planning A.* 19:575–595.

Marshall, J. N., and C. Jaeger, 1990. "Service Activities and Uneven Development in Britain and its European Partners: Determinist Fallacies and New Options," *Environment and Planning A.* 22, 1337–1354.

Marshall, J. N., P. Wood, P. W. Daniels, A. McKinnon, T. Bachtler, P. Damesick, N. Thrift, A. Gillespie, A. Green, and A. Leyshon, 1988. *Services and Uneven Development.* Oxford University Press: New York.

Martinelli, F., 1986. *Producer Services in a Dependent Economy: Their Role and Potential for Regional Economic Development.* Ph.D. Dissertation, Department of City and Regional Planning, University of California, Berkeley.

———. , 1989. "Business Services, Innovation, and Regional Policy: Consideration of the Case of Southern Italy," *Regional Policy at the Crossroads.* Edited by L. Albrechts, F. Moulaert, P. Roberts, and E. Swyngedouw. Jessica Kingsley Publishers, London.

Matthews, Mary, Director of the Northeast Entrepreneur Fund, 1991. Personal interview conducted by Jeffery Thompson. Telephone interview, November 21.

Mawson, J., 1987. "Services and Regional Policy," *Regional Studies.* June, 21:471–475.

Meehan, John, 1991. "If Mergers Were Simple, Banking's Trouble Might Be Over," *Business Week.* No. 3210, April 22:77–79.

Meehan, John, and Suzanne Woolly, 1991. "Bank Scoreboard: Mediocre Didn't Look Half Bad," *Business Week*. No. 3210, April 22:80–85.

Metzger, R., and M. Glinow, 1988. "Off-site Workers: At Home and Abroad," *California Management Review*. Spring, 30(3):101–111.

Mikesell, James, 1989. *Nonmetro, Metro, and U.S. Bank-Operating Statistics, 1986*. United States Department of Agriculture, Economic Research Service, Washington, D.C.

Mikesell, James, and Felice Marlor, 1991. *Nonmetro, Metro, and U.S. Bank Operating Statistics, 1987–89*. United States Department of Agriculture, Economic Research Service, Washington, D.C.

Miles, I., 1988. "The Electronic Cottage: Myth or Near-Myth?" *Futures*. August, 20(4):355–366.

Milkove, Daniel, and Patrick Sullivan, 1990. *Deregulation and the Structure of Rural Financial Markets*. United States Department of Agriculture, Economic Research Service, Washington, D.C.

Miller, James P., 1987. *Recent Contributions of Small Businesses and Corporations to Rural Job Creation*. U.S. Department of Agriculture, Economic Research Service Staff Report AGSH61212, U.S. Government Printing Office, February.

Miller, J., and H. Bluestone, 1988. "Prospects for Service Sector Employment Growth in Nonmetro America," *Rural Economic Development in the 1980s: Prospects for the Future*. U.S. Department of Agriculture, Economic Research Service, Rural Development Research Report 69, Washington, D.C., 135–157.

Milligan, John, 1991. "Love in a Cold Climate," *Institutional Investor*. February:37–51.

Moody's Bank and Finance Manual, 1991. Moody's Financial Publishers. New York.

Moody's Investor Service, 1991a. "First Interstate Bancorp," *Moody's Bank and Finance Manual*. New York.

———., 1991b. "NCNB Corporation," *Moody's Bank and Finance Manual*. New York.

———. , 1991c. "Norwest Corporation," *Moody's Bank and Finance Manual.* New York.

Moore, G., 1987. "The Service Industries and the Business Cycle," *Business Economics.* April, XXII, 2:12–24.

Morrill, Richard L., 1982. "A Note: Continuing Deconcentration Trends in Trade," *Growth and Change*, January, 13(1):46–48.

Myers, Edith, 1986. "A New Ballgame," *Datamation.* (August 1) 26:26–27.

NCNB Corporation, 1991. Annual Report, 1992. Headquartered in Charlotte, North Carolina.

———. , undated. *NCNB: A Brief History.* Headquartered in Charlotte, North Carolina.

Nelson, C., 1987. "Labor Demand, Labor Supply and the Suburbanization of Low Wage Office Workers," *Production, Work, Territory.* Edited by A. Scott and M. Storper, Allen and Unwin: London.

New York Times, 1988. "American Express Goes High Tech," July 31.

Nilles, Jack, 1985. "Teleworking from Home," in *The Information Technology Revolution.* Edited by T. Forester, Basil-Blackwell Press: Oxford, England.

Nilles, Jack, R. Carlson, P. Grey, and G. Heineman, 1976. *Telecommunications-Transportation Trade-Offs: Options for Tomorrow.* Wiley Press: New York.

North, D., 1955. "Location Theory and Regional Economic Growth," *Journal of Political Economy.* 63:243–258.

Noyelle, T., 1986. "Economic Transformation," *Annals of the American Academy of Political and Social Science.* November, 488:9–17.

———. , 1987. *Beyond Industrial Dualism: Market and Job Segmentation in the New Economy.* Westview Press: Boulder, CO.

Noyelle, T., and T. Stanback Jr., 1983. *The Economic Transformation of American Cities.* Rowman and Allanheld: Totowa, NJ.

O'Connor, K., 1987. "The Location of Services Involved with International Trade," *Environment and Planning A.* May (19):687–700.

O'Farrell, P., and D. Hitchens, 1990. "Producer Services and Regional Development: Key Conceptual Issues of Taxonomy and Quality Measurement," *Regional Studies*. 24(2):163–171.

Padley, Karen, 1991. "NCNB Proposal May Be Only the Beginning," *Investor's Daily*. July 2:1.

Parker, Edwin B., Heather E. Hudson, Don A. Dillman, and Andrew D. Roscoe, 1989. *Rural America in the Information Age: Telecommunications Policy for Rural Development*. University Press of America: Boston.

Parker, E., H. Hudson, D. Dillman, S. Strover, and F. Williams, 1992. *Electronic Byways: State Policies for Rural Development through Telecommunications*. Westview Press: Boulder, Colo.

Pelzman, Joseph, and Gregory K. Schoepfle, 1988. "The Impact of the Caribbean Basin Economic Recovery Act on Caribbean Nations Exports and Development," *Economic Development and Cultural Change*. (July) 36:753–796.

Planque, B., 1982. *Le Development Decentralise*. Litrec: Paris.

Polese, M., 1982. "Regional Demand for Business Services and Interregional Service Flows in a Small Canadian Region," *Regional Science Association*. 50:151–163.

Porat, M., 1977. *The Information Economy: Definition and Measurement*, Special Publication 77–12(1), Office of Telecommunications, U.S. Department of Commerce, Washington, D.C.

Porterfield, Shirley, and Glen C. Pulver, 1991. "Services Producers, Exports and the Generation of Economic Growth," *International Regional Science Review*. 14(1).

Pred, A., 1975. "Diffusion, Organization, Spatial Structure and City-System Development," *Economic Geography*. 51:252–268.

Price, D. G., and A. M. Blair., 1989. *The Changing Geography of the Service Sector*. Belhaven Press: London.

Pulver G., 1987. "The Changing Economic Scene in Rural America." Paper prepared for the Center for Agriculture and Rural Development, Council of State Governments, Lexington, KY.

Quinn, J., 1988. "Technology in Services: Past Myths and Future Challenges," *Technological Forecasting and Social Change*. 34:327–350.

Quinn J., J. Baruch, and A. Paquette, 1987. "Technology in Services," *Scientific American*. December, 257, 6:50–58.

———. , 1988. "Exploiting the Manufacturing Services Interface," *Sloan Management Review*. Summer, 29(4):45–56.

Quinn, J., and T. Doorley, 1988. "Key Policy Issues Posed by Services," *Technological Forecasting and Social Change*. 34:405–423.

Quinn, J., and C. Gagnon, 1986. "Will Services Follow Manufacturing into Decline?" *Harvard Business Review*. November/December (6):95–106.

Redwood, A., 1988. "Job Creation in Nonmetropolitan Communities," *The Journal of State Governments*. 61(1):9–15.

Reich, R., 1988a. "The Rural Crisis, and What to do About It," *Economic Development Quarterly*. 2, 1:3–8.

———. , 1988b. "Response to Letter from Daniels and Lapping," *Economic Development Quarterly*. 2, 4:342.

———. , 1991. "The Real Economy," *The Atlantic Monthly*. February, 267(2):35–52.

Reid, N., and M. Frederick, 1990. *Rural America: Economic Performance, 1989*. Agriculture and Rural Economy Division, Economic Research Service U.S. Department of Agriculture. Agriculture Information Bulletin No. 609.

Richter, K., 1985. "Nonmetropolitan Growth in the Late 1970s: The End of the Turnaround?" *Demography*. 22:245–263.

Riddle, Dorothy, 1986. *Services Led Growth*. Praeger Press: New York.

Riefler, R., 1976. "Implications of Service Industry Growth for Regional Development Strategies," *Annals of Regional Science*. 10:88–103.

Roosevelt, Philip, 1991. "Loan Servicing May Get New Giant, Merger of NCNB, C&S/Sovran Would Form No. 5," *American Banker*. July 8:6.

Rose, Peter, 1987. *The Changing Structure of American Banking*. New York: Columbia University Press.

Sauvant, K., 1986. *International Transactions in Services: The Politics of Transborder Data Flows*. Westview Press: Boulder, CO.

Scholl, S. R., 1991. *Norwest Corporation*. Company report for Oppenheimer & Co., INVESTEXT. June 10.

Schorr, Juliet, 1991. *The Overworked American, The Unexpected Decline of Leisure*. Basic Books: New York.

Scott, A. J., 1988. *New Industrial Spaces*. Pion Press: London.

Scott, A. J., 1988. *Metropolis: From the Division of Labor to Urban Form*. University of California Press: Berkeley.

Singlemann, J., 1979. *From Agriculture to Services*. Sage Press: Beverly Hills, CA.

Smith, S. M., 1984. "Export Orientation of Nonmanufacturing Businesses in Nonmetropolitan Communities," *Journal of Agricultural Economics Association*, 66:145–155.

Smith, S., and G. Pulver, 1981. "Nonmanufacturing Business as a Growth Alternative in Nonmetropolitan Areas," *Journal of the Community Development Society*. 12(1):32–47.

Stabler, Jack C., 1987. "Non-Metropolitan Population Growth and the Evolution of Rural Service Centers in the Canadian Prairie Region," *Regional Studies*. 21(1): 43–53.

Stabler, Jack C., and Eric C. Howe, 1988. "Service Exports and Regional Growth in the Postindustrial Era," *Journal of Regional Science*. 28(3):303–315.

Stanback, T., 1979. *Understanding the Service Economy: Employment, Productivity, Location*. Johns Hopkins University Press: Baltimore, MD.

Stanback, T., and T. Noyelle, 1982. *Cities in Transition*, Allenheld, Osmun: Totowa, N.J.

Stone, K., 1987. "Impact of the Farm Financial Crisis on the Retail and Service Sectors of Rural Communities." Paper presented at AAEA Symposium on Farm Debt Stress, Kansas City, Missouri.

———. , 1989. "The Impact of Wal-Mart Stores on Other Businesses in Iowa." Unpublished paper, Iowa State University, Ames, Iowa.

Storper, Michael, and Richard Walker, 1984. "The Spatial Division of Labor: Labor and the Location of Industries," in *Sunbelt-Snow-*

belt: Urban Development and Regional Restructuring. Edited by Larry Sawers and William K. Tabb, Oxford University Press: New York.

Summers, G., F. Horton, and C. Gringeri, 1990. "Rural Labor Market Change in the U.S.," *National Rural Studies Committee: A Proceedings.* Cedar Falls, IA, May, 61–79.

Swaim, P., 1990. "Rural Displaced Workers Fare Poorly," *Rural Development Perspectives.* June–September, 6:3.

Teixeira, R., 1991. "Demographic Change and the Human Capital Endowment of Rural America." Paper presented at the conference on Population Change and the Future of Rural America, Wye Plantation, Maryland, May 30–June 1, 1991.

Thompson, E. T., 1991. *First Interstate Bancorp.* Company report for Keefe Bankwatch, INVESTEXT. April 8.

Thompson, Wilbur, 1965. *A Preface to Urban Economies.* Johns Hopkins University Press: Baltimore, MD.

Thompson Financial Networks, Inc., 1991. *Norwest Corporation.* Company report, July 24.

Thurow, L., and G. Billard, 1989. "Service Activities and Deindustrialization," *Deindustrialization Experiences of the U.S. and Japan.* Edited by Lloyd Rodwin, Allen and Rowenfeld Press: London.

Thurston, Charles, 1990. "U.S. Company Joins With Jamaicans in Data Processing," *The Journal of Commerce.* (March 23) 383:4a.

Tiebout, C., 1956. "Exports and Regional Growth," *Journal of Political Economy.* 64:160–164 and 169.

———. , 1975. "Exports and Regional Growth: A Reply," reprinted in J. Friedman and W. Alonzo, *Regional Policy: Readings in Theory and Application.* M.I.T. Press: Cambridge, MA.

Tschetter, J., 1987. "Producer Services Industries: Why Are They Growing So Rapidly?" *Monthly Labor Review.* December, 110: 31–39.

United States Congress, 1987. Office of Technology Assessment, *International Competition in Services*, Washington, D.C.: U.S. Government Printing Office, chapter 5.

U.S. Congress Government Accounting Office, 1990. *Facilities Location Policy: GSA Should Propose a More Consistent and Businesslike Approach.* September 28, 1–31.

U.S. Department of Commerce, 1985. Bureau of the Census, *County Business Patterns*, 1985, 1974.

———. , 1987. *U.S. Census of Service Industries, 1987, Geographic Area Series.*

———. , Bureau of the Census, 1988. *Educational Attainment in the U.S.*, March 1986–87, Series P-20, No. 428, Table 10.

van Dinteren, J. H. J., 1987. "The Role of Business Service Offices in the Economy of Medium-sized Cities," *Environment and Planning A*. 19:669–686.

Vernon, Raymond, 1966. "International Investment and International Trade in the Product Cycle," *Quarterly Journal of Economics*. 80(2):190–207.

Walker, R., 1985. "Is There a Service Economy? The Changing Capitalist Division of Labor," *Science and Society*. XVIX, 1:42–83.

Washington Post, 1989. "Global Offices on Rise as Firms Shift Service Jobs Abroad," April 20.

Wheeler, James O., 1986. "Corporate Spatial Links with Financial Institutions: The Role of the Metropolitan Hierarchy," *Annals of the Association of American Geographers*. 76(2):262–274.

Wong, F., et al., 1991. *First Interstate Bancorp.* Company report for Fitch Investors Service, INVESTEXT. March 18.

Worthington, Rogers, 1991. "Telecommunications Companies Tune In to North Dakota," *Wall Street Journal*, January 13:H2.

Zimmerman, J., 1986. *Once Upon a Future.* Pandora Press: London.

INDEX